ROUTLEDGE LIBRARY EDITIONS:
ENERGY ECONOMICS

Volume 5

THE COAL PROBLEM

THE COAL PROBLEM

A Survey: 1910–1936

J. P. DICKIE

Routledge
Taylor & Francis Group
LONDON AND NEW YORK

First published in 1936 by Methuen

This edition first published in 2018
by Routledge
2 Park Square, Milton Park, Abingdon, Oxon OX14 4RN

and by Routledge
711 Third Avenue, New York, NY 10017

Routledge is an imprint of the Taylor & Francis Group, an informa business

British Library Cataloguing in Publication Data
A catalogue record for this book is available from the British Library

ISBN: 978-1-138-10476-1 (Set)
ISBN: 978-1-315-14526-6 (Set) (ebk)
ISBN: 978-1-138-30187-0 (Volume 5) (hbk)
ISBN: 978-0-203-73212-0 (Volume 5) (ebk)

Publisher's Note
The publisher has gone to great lengths to ensure the quality of this reprint but points out that some imperfections in the original copies may be apparent.

Disclaimer
The publisher has made every effort to trace copyright holders and would welcome correspondence from those they have been unable to trace.

THE COAL PROBLEM

A SURVEY: 1910-1936

by

J. P. DICKIE

METHUEN LONDON
36 ESSEX STREET, W.C.2

First published in 1936

PRINTED IN GREAT BRITAIN

FOREWORD

As a Member of Parliament representing a mining constituency in the House of Commons from 1931 to 1935, I found great difficulty during the frequent discussions on coal in obtaining the information which I required in such a form as to be handy at any time when it was needed.

This little volume is an attempt to provide the information necessary for an intelligent understanding of the problems of the industry, and to provide it under one cover, so that it may be readily available to any citizen who desires it.

The coal-mining industry is not the concern of colliery owners and mineworkers alone. It is of vital interest to the nation as a whole.

On March 1, 1933, when I brought forward in the House of Commons a motion calling attention to the state of the industry, I was asked "on whose behalf I was speaking". I replied, "I am speaking here as a Member of Parliament representing a mining division —the owners, the miners, the railwaymen, the postmen, the grocers, and everybody else in the constituency."

It is in that spirit that I submit this volume to the judgement of my fellow citizens of all parties and of no party.

J. P. DICKIE

15 Pollards Hill South,
Norbury,
London, S.W. 16

CONTENTS

INTRODUCTION

For the purpose which this volume is intended to fulfil, the history of the Mining Industry in this country may be said to be contemporaneous with the reign of H.M. King George V.

Those twenty-five years have seen remarkable changes in almost every sphere of human activity. The coal-mining industry is no exception, for the character, the technique and relative position of the industry in the structure of our economic life, have undergone very considerable changes in that period.

Without some knowledge of the coal trade, its recent history, production, and distribution, the wages paid and other relevant factors in the conduct of the industry, it is exceedingly difficult for the average citizen to understand where the truth lies in the disputes between the owners and the men, or to judge for himself of the merits of the claims advanced by either side.

This volume is an endeavour to set out impartially the economic facts of the industry and the happenings of the last twenty-five years as briefly and concisely as possible, in the hope that it will prove a useful guide to "the man in the street" and help him to understand the meaning of the controversies which from time to time stop the pits working, inflict grave injury on the State, and result in bringing untold misery and suffering into a million homes.

Nature has been very kind to these little islands, but in no direction kinder than in the gift bestowed on the country by the wonderful deposits of high-grade coal to be found in so many parts of Great Britain and so near to our seaports. Our industrial supremacy was built on a foundation of coal; coal has contributed in a very large measure to the commanding position obtained by our Mercantile Marine in the carrying trade of the world, and it is safe to predict that whatever may be the achievements of applied science in the utilization of other sources of power, coal will remain for many, many years the bedrock foundation of British industrial prosperity. It should be understood that no attempt is being made here to deal with the growth and development of coal mining in its early stages. We are here concerned only with the immediate past, with the present, and with the immediate future.

In considering the industrial history of the last quarter of a century, two developments stand out above all others as of paramount importance, directly affecting all industry and largely governing the conditions of labour and the wages paid in almost every sphere of industrial productivity. These are the growth of the combinations of employers on the one hand, and employed on the other, and the extension of Government intervention in the industrial field.

The present century has seen the former growing larger and larger, each move by either side to that greater unity which brings strength being followed by a similar move by the other, in most cases the simple fact that their interests are identical and not opposed being lost sight of by both parties. This is what has happened in the mining industry, the colliery owners and the workers each being organized in District Associations with certain autonomous powers. The local owners' associations are all linked up with the Mining Association and the workers' local organizations are nearly all linked up with the Mineworkers' Federation. An explanatory note as to their respective strength and powers will be found in later pages.

The second was inevitable. With the spread of education there came a new social consciousness which would not stand for either sweated labour or degraded conditions of employment or life for the worker engaged in any industry. The great constitutional questions which had so divided our forefathers were settled and done with; industrial and economic questions were occupying the legislature to an ever-increasing extent, to the exclusion of purely political questions, whilst the powerful trade unions were calling more and more insistently for legislative action for the protection of the workers and the improvement of their standard of life and conditions of labour.

The combined effect of all these forces has led to Parliament intervening more and more in industrial affairs, regulating largely the conditions under which industry shall be carried on and holding the balance as evenly as possible between all the sectional interests involved.

Under modern conditions it is impossible to separate politics completely from industry, but if an industry is to thrive there can be no doubt whatsoever that the economics of that industry should be regarded as being both the primary and the paramount consideration, and the political side held firmly to be of secondary importance. Some regulation, some control, some protection even (for both capital and labour), is undoubtedly essential in these times, and so long as these do not strangle enterprise or handicap efficiency may be to the advantage of the State and to the benefit of all engaged in the industry.

The mining industry affords by far the most striking illustration of the extent to which politics and industry have become interwoven, for in almost every session of Parliament during the last twenty-five years, and particularly in the post-war period, the legislature has been called upon to consider and discuss some aspect of the problems arising from the conduct of the industry.

Here, then, are the two outstanding features of the situation: the combined forces of the coal-owners arrayed against the combined forces of the workers, with the latter threatening to stop the pits unless their demand for higher wages is conceded, and Parliament, bound, in the national interest, to use every effort to avoid a stoppage, to hold the scales evenly between the two sides to the dispute, and to secure, if possible, an agreement satisfactory to both with the minimum of legislative action.

On pages 1 and 2 will be found a chronological record of the most important Acts of Parliament, etc., relating to the industry in the period under review. In the following pages a brief summary of the more important is given, and later, full particulars are given of the number of men engaged, the wages now being paid, method of calculating wages, output distribution, export and other relevant data.

A study of the history and facts, although presented here only in brief outline, should enable the reader to appreciate the difficulty and complexity of the problem, and help him to weigh for himself the merits of the claims advanced by the miners for higher wages and an ever-increasing measure of State control, as well as the soundness or otherwise of the arguments advanced by the owners and the Government in refusing to concede them in full.

THE COAL PROBLEM

CHAPTER I

Parliament and the Mining Industry—The Minimum Wage Act, 1912—"The Miner's Next Step"

PARLIAMENT AND THE MINING INDUSTRY

THE extent to which the coal-mining industry has been dominated by politics and the amount of time the House of Commons has devoted to the consideration of matters relating to it, may be gauged by the number of Acts of Parliament placed on the Statute Book. Here is a list of them for the period we are reviewing. It is by no means complete, for it includes only the principal measures.

(1) Coal Mines Regulation Act, 1908.
(2) Coal Mines Act, 1911.
(3) Coal Mines (Minimum Wage) Act, 1912.
(4) Coal Mines Act, 1914.
(5) Coal Mines Act, 1919.
(6) Mining Industry Act, 1920.
(7) Mines (Working Facilities and Support) Act, 1923.
(8) Mines (Working Facilities and Support) Act, 1925.
(9) Mining Industry (Welfare Fund) Act, 1925.
(10) Mining Industry Act, 1926.
(11) Coal Mines Act, 1926.
(12) Coal Mines Act, 1930.
(13) Coal Mines Act, 1931.
(14) Mining Industry (Welfare Fund) Act, 1931.
(15) Coal Mines Act, 1932.
(16) Mines (Working Facilities) Act, 1934.
(17) Mining Industry (Welfare Fund) Act, 1934.

In addition to these and other Acts, Parliament has, from time to time, appointed Royal Commissions or other Courts of Enquiry to investigate either the condition of the industry as a whole or some particular aspect of it. The most important of these are:

Royal Commission on Mines, 1907.
Royal Commission on Coal Industry, 1919 (The Sankey Commission).
Court of Enquiry into the Wages Position (The Buckmaster Enquiry).
Court of Enquiry into Coal Dispute, 1925 (The Macmillan Enquiry).
Royal Commission on Coal Industry, 1925 (The Samuel Commission).
Departmental Committee Enquiry into Co-operative Selling in the Mining Industry, 1926 (The Lewis Enquiry).
Royal Commission on Mining Subsidence, 1926.

The industry has a department of the Board of Trade to itself (established in 1920) with a Minister responsible to Parliament. The department issues its own statutory rules and orders, and conducts its own inquiries, makes its own reports to Parliament, and is endowed with very extensive powers under the various Acts of Parliament already quoted. It provides at regular intervals official reports on the working of the industry and the various schemes for regulation of production and marketing of coal, inspection of mines, safety, research, disease, accidents, etc., and is charged by Parliament with the duty and responsibility of supervising the conduct of the industry in all its numerous activities.

Among the more important of these reports is the Statistical Summary, issued quarterly, which gives particulars of output, costs of production, proceeds, number of workpeople, profits or losses, wages and number of shifts worked, and the Annual Report of the department.

A brief account of the provisions of the more important of these Acts of Parliament and of the reports of the Commissions will be given in subsequent pages.

THE MINIMUM WAGE ACT, 1912

In the early years of the present century there became evident a greater appreciation of the evil effects of low wages.

The activities of the Press, the efforts of the trade unions and the increasing extent to which Parliament was being compelled to devote its attention to economic, social, and industrial questions, to the exclusion of the purely political, shed a fierce light on the shocking conditions which prevailed in some secondary industries, and compelled the legislature to take steps to put an end to a condition of things which was a disgrace to our national life.

The first Act of Parliament to deal with low wages was the Trade Boards Act of 1909. It was first applied to such industries as chain-making, cardboard box making and tailoring. These Trade Boards established minimum rates of payment and the benefits to the workers may be gauged by the substantial increases in the wages now paid in these formerly "sweated" industries.

These industries, however, are minor ones. The first Act of Parliament to enforce the principle of a minimum wage in a great industry was the Coal Mines Minimum Wage Act of 1912. This set up Joint District Boards in each of the districts with power to fix the minimum wage rates for the district under its authority. During the debate, the figures generally mentioned as a mimimum daily rate were 5s. for adult workers and 2s. for boys. A very strong effort was made during the passage of the Bill to have these figures inserted, but the Government of the day resisted this, on the grounds that it was an unsound principle to include actual wages figures in an Act of Parliament, and also because, in their belief, a minimum so fixed would tend to become a maximum, and thus operate to the disadvantage of the workers. At the time the general level of miners' wages was rising and compared favourably with that of other industries.

The Government view is now generally held to have been sound so far as the insertion of actual figures in the Act was concerned, but the principle of a minimum wage in the industry was thus definitely established.

"THE MINER'S NEXT STEP"

Some time before the passing of the Minimum Wage Act of 1912, a movement began in South Wales which was destined to influence very considerably the politics of the mining industry, and to affect seriously the relations between the coal-owners and the miners.

It was a definitely revolutionary movement, directed against the leaders and the policy of the Miners' Federation as much as against the coal-owners. It was sponsored by an unofficial committee, and the keynote of its policy was open and avowed hostility to conciliation with the owners, to fight rather than negotiate, and to destroy completely any conception of identity of interest between the employer and the workers.

The method, objective, and policy of this committee were set out fully in a small pamphlet issued in 1912 and entitled *The Miner's Next Step*. They may be summarized as: Industrial action for political ends, the complete elimination of the employer and the carrying on of the mines in the interest of the workers. Nationalization was condemned and a policy of the "Mines for the Miners" advocated instead. No name appears as author of the pamphlet, and it is explained that it was not the work of any one individual. It is generally believed, however, to have been the work of Mr. A. J. Cook,[1] later Secretary of the Miners' Federation, and Mr. Noah Ablett.

The following extracts from the chapter on Policy (Chapter V, page 25) will give the reader a clear idea of the aims and objects of the "Unofficial Reform Committee."

(1) "The old policy of identity of interest between employers and ourselves be abolished and a policy of open hostility installed."

(10) "Lodges should, as far as possible, discard the old method of coming out on strike for any little minor grievance. And adopt the more scientific weapon of the irritation strike by simply remaining at work, reducing their output, and so contrive by their general conduct to make the colliery unremunerative."

(13) "That a continual agitation be carried on in favour of increasing the minimum wage and shortening the hours of work until we have extracted the whole of the employers' profits."

(14) "That our objective be, to build up an organization, that will ultimately take over the mining industry and carry it on in the interests of the workers."

[1] In *Labour's Who's Who,* published by the Labour Publishing Co., Ltd., the authorship of this pamphlet is definitely ascribed to Mr. Cook. Mr. Ablett was later a member of the Executive of the Miners' Federation.

It will be observed that in this policy there is no mention of the interests of the coal-consuming industries, of the interest of the individual citizen, or of the interest of the nation as a whole. It is a policy not even of Socialism, but one of pure Syndicalism.

During 1913 and 1914 a violent agitation was carried on not only in South Wales but also in the other coalfields with a view to popularizing this policy. In 1914, however, the war intervened. The nation and the miners who played such an important part in the successful prosecution of the war were concerned with graver and more pressing issues. Sowing the seeds of disaffection became a serious offence, and propaganda on behalf of these methods of securing higher wages and a better standard of life for the miners was temporarily abandoned, only to be resumed with greater vigour and more distressing results on the termination of the war.

CHAPTER II

THE WAR YEARS, 1914–1918

THE four years of the war provided in themselves ample material for a separate volume on the history of the mining industry. It was a hectic and troublous period, so packed with incident as to make it one of the most interesting and most important in the history of coal mining. I am mainly concerned, however, with the years 1918–1936, and must, therefore, pass over it lightly, asking my readers to regard this brief chapter as one intended merely to link up the pre-war with the post-war period.

As one who was living in the heart of a mining community in 1914, my most vivid recollection of the early days of the war was the amazing rush to the colours of the young men from the pits. They flocked to the recruiting depots in such numbers that the authorities found it almost impossible to deal with them. So nobly did they respond to their country's call that in a few short months after the outbreak of war, nearly half the miners of military age were in the army, the pick and shovel abandoned for the rifle and bayonet.

They were accepted for military service in unlimited numbers before it was fully realized that the coal which they were producing was to prove the nation's most valuable material asset in the struggle, or that any substantial reduction in the output would seriously affect the efficient conduct of the war.

The results of the economic and financial confusion

which are the inevitable accompaniment of modern warfare were speedily evident in the coalfields. Production began to fall as the younger and stronger men joined the ranks; prices began to rise, and as they rose brought a perfectly natural demand for higher wages; increases in varying amounts were granted in all the districts, but the steady rise in prices (particularly foodstuffs) led to continual friction over wages. Strikes and threats of strikes interfered with output as the demand for more and more coal became intensified; while the miners who had "joined up" in the first few months of the war were "doing their bit" in the field thousands of other men found employment in the pits, with exemption from military service, the latter dating from early in 1916; the whole industry came under complete Government control in March 1917; a Coal Control Department was established; exports of coal were prohibited except under licence, home supplies were rationed, and the miners voluntarily curtailed the customary holidays in order to maintain the output. Profits were limited by statute, wages regulated by a Government Department, neither of them having any economic basis, and for the first time in the industry, increased wages were granted on a national flat-rate basis irrespective of any district variations in output or basis rates. The military age was raised to fifty-five towards the end, and more men were withdrawn from the mines, necessitating more drastic restrictions on the use of coal, particularly for household purposes.

When the end came in November 1918, there was a serious shortage of coal both at home and in the allied countries, particularly in France where many mines had been destroyed. Priority in demobilization was given to miners, and those serving in France and

Belgium were specially thanked by the Commander-in-Chief for their valuable work in the famous Tunnelling Companies.

At home the Miners' Federation had been busy preparing for a militant campaign in all the coalfields as soon as hostilities ceased, with a view to enforcing, in the industry, those far-reaching changes which had been under continuous discussion during the war. The Federation officials lost no time in formulating their programme, and less than three months after the armistice they demanded a 30 per cent increase in wages, a six-hour day, and nationalization of the mines. A delegate conference held early in February 1919 rejected the Government offer of a Committee of Enquiry and a flat-rate increase of 1s. per day in wages, and submitted the programme to a ballot vote of all members with a recommendation to vote for a national strike unless their demands were conceded in full. An overwhelming majority having voted for a strike in these circumstances, the demands were presented to the Prime Minister on February 21st. He made an offer to set up a Royal Commission to inquire into the state of the industry, undertaking that an interim report on the two important questions of hours and wages would be available not later than March 20th. The strike notices had been due to expire on the 15th, but on the Federation accepting the offer of the Prime Minister, they were suspended until March 22nd. The Commission was appointed under the chairmanship of Lord Justice Sankey, and got to work immediately. The terms of reference were exceptionally wide, and in redemption of the promise given by the Prime Minister the interim reports were presented on March 20th.

CHAPTER III

THE MINING INDUSTRY IN 1913 AND 1935

THE statistical summary here given with the comparative table on the next two pages give all the relevant data for enabling a comparison to be drawn between the conditions prevailing in 1913 and those of 1935. The reader should beware of drawing any conclusion from the figures without examining carefully all the factors relating to the aspect of the problem he is considering and which have influenced the relative positions in the intervening period.

MINES DEPARTMENT STATISTICAL SUMMARY FOR THE YEAR 1935

GREAT BRITAIN—96 PER CENT OF OUTPUT

	Tons	
Output of Coal:		
1. Tonnage of saleable coal raised ..	214,944,239	
2. Mine consumption	11,235,938	
3. Miners' coal	4,078,003	
4. Tonnage disposable commercially	199,630,298	
	Amount	Per ton disposable commercially
Costs of Production:	£	s. d.
5. Wages	85,284,004	8 6·53
6. Stores and timber	15,128,515	1 6·19
7. Other costs (management, salaries, insurances, repairs, office and general expenses, depreciation, etc.)	24,658,483	2 5·64
8. Miners' Welfare Fund contributions	356,417	0 0·43
9. Royalties (including the rental value of freehold minerals where worked by the proprietor) ..	4,806,139	0 5·78
10. Total costs	130,233,558	13 0·57
11. Deduct proceeds of miners' coal ..	739,812	0 0·89
12. Net costs	129,493,746	12 11·68
Proceeds:		
13. Commercial disposals	134,697,326	13 5·94
Balance:		
14. Debits	—	—
15. Credits	5,203,580	0 6·26
16. Number of workpeople employed	720,267	
17. Number of man-shifts worked (including week-end and overtime shifts):		
(*a*) At the coal face	71,191,901	
(*b*) Elsewhere below ground ..	70,977,667	
(*c*) On the surface	41,974,313	
(*d*) Total above and below ground	184,143,881	
18. Number of man-shifts lost which could have been worked (including absences due to sickness or accident)	11,857,436	
19. Output per man-shift worked ...	23·35 cwt.	
20. Earnings per man-shift worked (exclusive of allowances in kind)	s. d. 9 3·15	
21. Value of allowances in kind per man-shift worked	0 4·51	

	1913	1935
	million tons	million tons
Tonnage of saleable coal raised	287·35	222·25
Tonnage of coal commercially disposable	Not available	206·4
Tonnage of coal retained for home use	183·85	164·47
Tonnage of coal exported (total)	98·34	55·54
Tonnage of coal exported (exports)	73·4	38·7
Tonnage of coal exported (bunkers)	21·03	12·5
Coal equivalent of coke and manufactured fuel exported	3·91	4·34
Average number of persons employed (total)	1,104,406	769,474
Average number of wage earners employed	Not available	754,300
Average number of clerks and salaried persons	Not available	15,174
Average number of persons under sixteen	73,069	31,041
Average number of wage earners under twenty	Not available	107,223
Average number of adult wage earners	Not available	647,077
Average output per wage earner per shift worked	20·32 cwt. (1914)	23·35 cwt.
Average output per person employed per annum	260 tons	289 tons
Average wage per wage earner per shift worked	6s. 5¾d.	9s. 3¼d.
Average wage per annum per wage earner employed	£82	£118 8s. 1d.
Ministry of Labour cost of living index figure	100 (July 1914)	143 (July 1935)
Ministry of Labour average earnings index figure	100 (year 1913)	144·4 (year 1935)
Average wages cost per ton of output (commercially disposable)	6s. 10½d.	8s. 6½d.
Average "other costs" per ton of output (commercially disposable)	2s. 7d.	4s. 5¼d.

Average cost per ton excluded from the ascertainments (interest, bank charges, etc.)	Nil	3d.
Average total net cost per ton commercially disposable	9s. 5½d.	12s. 11¾d.
Average proceeds per ton commercially disposable	11s.	13s. 6d.
Average credit balance per ton commercially disposable	1s. 6½d.	6¼d.
Average royalty per ton commercially disposable	6d.	5·78d.
Average number of shifts worked per week	See Note below	4·92
Average number of shifts worked per annum	See Note below	256
Average number of hours worked per week	See Note below	36·9
Average number of mines working under Coal Mines Act	3,267	2,075
Average consumption per head of population	89 cwt.	72 cwt.
Average fatal accident rate per 1,000 employed	1·55	1·10
Number of persons killed	1,753	861
Number of persons seriously injured	5,675	3,257
Number of persons employed per million tons output	3,846	3,460

NOTES.—In cases where meticulous accuracy is desired, it should be noted that the 1913 figures refer to all persons ordinarily employed and the calculations are based on that figure.

With regard to the number of shifts and hours worked in 1913, no strictly accurate data is available. The year, however, was the "peak" year of production. There was practically no short-time working; the hours were eight per shift, so that the hours worked probably averaged about 45 or 46 with shifts varying from 5½ to 6 per week. The comparison is on the basis of the nominal shift and does not include in either case the "one-winding time", averaging half an hour per shift, which should be added to give the full time spent underground.

The accident rate in 1913 was swollen by the terrible explosion at Senghenydd, the greatest disaster in the history of the industry, in which 439 lives were lost.

CHAPTER IV

THE SANKEY COMMISSION

THE reports and recommendations of this Commission have excited more discussion and caused a greater amount of controversy than those of any other body of enquiry set up in connection with the industry. It is well, therefore, to review briefly its findings and its recommendations.

In the early days of 1919, in the aftermath of war, industrial unrest began to become acute. It manifested itself most strongly in the mining industry, and led, at the end of February, to the appointment of this Royal Commission on February 25th.

The Commission was set up by a special Act of Parliament and its terms of reference were remarkably wide—so wide in fact as to cover practically every phase of the industry and every aspect of its problems. Its members were:

Lord Justice Sankey (*Chairman*)

Mr. Arthur Balfour, J.P.	Mr. Frank Hodges
Mr. R. W. Cooper	Mr. Robert Smillie
Sir A. Duckham	Mr. Herbert Smith
Sir T. Royden	Sir Leo Chiozza Money
Mr. J. T. Forgie	Mr. R. H. Tawney
Mr. (now Sir) Evan Williams	Mr. Sidney Webb (now Lord Passfield)

The assessors were Sir Richard Redmayne, Sir A. L. Dickinson, Mr. S. J. Chapman, and Mr. H. J. Wilson.

It began its sittings on March 5th.

In its personnel, it was the most extraordinary Commission ever appointed to enquire into any industry, and in its conduct of the enquiry there were one or two features quite alien to British judicial methods.

It was composed originally of three members directly representing the miners, three directly representing the coal-owners, three representing the workers in other industries,[1] and three representing the employers in other industries, with a Judge as Chairman. The personnel changed during the inquiry, for two members dropped out after the presentation of the interim reports, and their successors repudiated any responsibility for these. Whilst taking evidence, some of the "judges" left the bench and went into the witness-box to give evidence in the case they were sitting to try. With such a tribunal, composed, in the main, of interested parties and of men whose interests were diametrically opposed, it is difficult to understand how anyone could have expected it to agree on anything. In any case, it was soon made clear that anything even approaching unanimity was impossible. The Commission had one rare virtue. It got to work most expeditiously. The Prime Minister had promised that it would give an immediate report on the two vexed questions of hours and wages, and on March 18th the interim reports appeared. There were three of them, all differing, and two of them went far beyond the two issues on which the Commission had been urged to report without delay. All, however, were agreed that *some* increase in wages and *some* reduction in hours were essential. The Government acted at once, and the mines being still under State control, the Act of 1919 was passed by Parliament reducing the hours to seven and increasing the wages by 2s. per shift (flat rate basis).

[1] Nominated by the Miners' Federation.

The Commission continued its sittings and on June 20, 1919, issued its final reports. There were four of them. The first was an individual report by the Chairman, Lord Justice Sankey. The second was signed by the three miners' representatives and the three representatives of the workers in other industries. The third was by the three coal-owners' representatives and two of the three independent business men representing other industries. The fourth was an individual report by the third independent member.

The Chairman's report recommended both the nationalization of the minerals and of the industry itself with fair and just compensation to the royalty owners.

The miners' and workers' representatives, while in substantial agreement with the Chairman, refused to sign his report and issued their own. Their chief objection to the scheme of nationalization which he propounded was that, in effect, it deprived the miners of the right to strike, once the mines came under State management, and, in addition, the three miners' representatives objected to any payment of any kind being made to the mineral or royalty owners as compensation or purchase price for the ungotten coal.

The third report declared against nationalization of the industry but in favour of the nationalization of the minerals, as did also the fourth or individual report. Both these reports made certain recommendations as to the organization of the industry.

Having considered all the reports, the Government announced in the House of Commons on August 18th that it had decided to accept the unanimous recommendations of the reports and to purchase the mineral rights in coal for the State. The Prime Minister, however, announced at the same time that the Government had decided also against the nationalization of the industry itself. He then outlined the Government's proposals, which included a levy on the purchase price of the royalties for the amelioration of social conditions in the mining villages, and the adoption of other recommendations of the Commission.

A few days afterwards the Executive of the Miners' Federation met and summarily rejected the Government scheme. Early in September the Trades Union Congress passed a resolution condemning the Government scheme and pledging itself to co-operate with the miners to the fullest extent with a view to "compelling the Government" to accept nationalization.

On October 10th the Prime Minister received at 10 Downing Street a deputation composed of the Executive of the Miners' Federation and the officials of the Trades Union Congress. He then informed them officially of the Government decision with regard to nationalization and offered them, instead, an Act of Parliament which would:

(1) Nationalize the royalties.
(2) Devote part of the purchase price to improving social conditions. The levy would yield from £5,000,000 to £10,000,000.
(3) Give the miners a voice in the executive control of the industry by virtue of a seat on the Area Boards.
(4) Give the miners a share in the daily management of the pits through the medium of a joint committee to be established at every colliery.

Whilst these proposals went a long way to meet the miners' demands, the refusal to concede their full demand (the complete nationalization of the industry) proved an insurmountable obstacle. The spokesman of the deputation contended that the Government had pledged itself in advance to nationalize the mines if the Commission reported favourably on this course of action. This claim was based on a statement made by Mr. Bonar Law in the House of Commons on March 20, 1919, when he announced that the Cabinet had considered the three interim reports and were prepared to adopt that of the Chairman and the independent members "*in the spirit as well as in the letter*". But, he added: "Nationalization must be decided by Parliament which represents the country."

It is obvious that he could not have been referring to the final reports, for these were not issued until June 20th, and at this (October 10th) interview, he expressly repudiated this interpretation as well as having given any such pledge in the discussions before the Commission was set up.

Mr. Lloyd George was both definite and vigorous in his denial of having given any such pledge. He said he knew of no Government in this country or any other country which would abdicate its own judgement, invite Parliament to abdicate its functions, and pledge itself in advance to adopt and put through the recommendations of any Commission "on a great question of policy even it it were only by a majority of one or two".

The Prime Minister having announced the decision of the Government against nationalization asked the President of the Miners' Federation a direct question: "Would the miners prefer the existing conditions of things or would they prefer unification on some such lines as had been indicated, with a voice given to the miners in the executive control of the areas?"

He got an equally direct answer. Mr. Smillie said that the miners would prefer going on as at the present time, or at least as they were prior to the war. He said: "We are strongly against your taking over the mining industry and unifying it in districts and leaving it with the present owners or any owners, even with the miners on the Board."

There need be little wonder that the Prime Minister said, in replying later, that he "deeply regretted" this answer, and added: "I think Labour is throwing away a great opportunity of having an effective voice in the control of its own industry."

In the light of subsequent events every impartial observer is bound to admit that the Prime Minister was right and the miners' leaders wrong. In a mistaken belief in their own strength and the power to use it in order to force the Government to yield to their full demands, they not only lost sight of the interests of their own followers, but showed themselves devoid of the first attribute of real leadership, i.e. to take a step forward whenever the opportunity offers, to consolidate the position, and to make ready to take another step forward immediately another opportunity presents itself.

The refusal to accept this wonderful offer is the more remarkable when it is realized that its acceptance would not in any way have prejudiced the case for nationalization, unless, indeed, in practice, the scheme should prove so successful that the mineworkers would no longer demand State ownership and control of the mines.

However, the offer was rejected, and in the stormy period which followed, the Prime Minister who had made it was denounced in all the mining areas as the man who had "betrayed the miners". One illustration will serve not only to show how unjustified was this charge, but also how shortsighted the miners' leaders were in refusing the offer.

The Miners' Federation have for many years demanded nationalization of mining royalties, complained bitterly of the heavy royalty charge, averaging 6d. per ton, and made great play on political platforms by contrasting the payments made to royalty owners with the wages paid to the miners.

It is now 1936. Had this offer been accepted, and a sinking fund set up for redemption in 1919, the royalty charge on the industry would have become progressively less, and in four years' time (1940) it would have disappeared altogether, leaving approximately £5,000,000 to be added to the fund available for wages and profits.

The reader should remember that the mines were still under State control. The South Wales mines were brought under State control on December 1, 1916, and the rest on April 1, 1917. Some particulars of the effect of State control will be found in another chapter.

CHAPTER V

After the Sankey Reports—The 1920 Stoppage—The Comparison with 1920—The 1921 Stoppage—The Mining Industry Act, 1920 (Part 2)

AFTER THE SANKEY REPORTS

THE year 1920 proved to be a very difficult one for the industry. The chaos and confusion due to the war made a reversion to normal conditions an extremely difficult task. Under State control production had fallen heavily and in this year was not keeping pace with the demand. Output per person employed had decreased substantially, whilst wages costs had increased enormously. With a return to peace-time conditions, the demand for coal had increased, not only at home, but abroad. Export was permitted only under licence and so great was the demand that the average price obtained abroad was £4 per ton. Twenty-five million tons were sold abroad, bringing in £100,000,000, and out of this the home trade was being subsidized and surplus profits diverted to the National Exchequer.

The demand of the Miners' Federation for nationalization became more insistent, and coupled with it there now came a claim to regulate home prices in conjunction with the claim to higher wages. The Government refused the former and firmly rejected the latter as being a claim on the part of an outside body to usurp the functions of Parliament, the action of the

Government in fixing prices having been sanctioned and approved by the House of Commons.

Late in 1919, following upon the dislocation caused by the Railway Strike of October and a long stoppage in the Yorkshire coalfield, the Government took the first preliminary steps towards decontrolling the industry and placing it once more on a self-supporting basis. Gas and electricity were freed from control, rationing was ended, and special provision made for transport to ensure adequate supplies for railway companies, public utility concerns, and domestic consumers.

In March 1920 this process was carried a stage farther by the passing of the Coal Mines (Emergency) Bill, the chief feature of which was that, in addition to making provision for dealing with profits, it definitely fixed the date for the ending of State control at August 31, 1921.

Following on this, the Government proceeded to implement the undertaking given by the Prime Minister on October 10, 1919, and on several subsequent occasions, and introduced the Mining Industry Act, 1920. This is one of the most important Acts ever placed on the Statute Book in connection with the industry. Given a little more vision before its introduction on the part of its opponents, a little more courage on the part of its sponsors during the passage, and a little more of the spirit of compromise on the part of both, it could have been made an even more valuable measure and probably averted a good deal of the subsequent trouble in the industry.

Neither Mr. Lloyd George nor the Government can be blamed for the inadequacy of the measure. Deeply involved in the effort to find a solution for each and all of the industrial and economic problems arising out of the transition from war to peace, torn with anxiety over the increasing gravity of the Irish problem, and faced with the prospect of Labour troubles in the mining and other industries, the Cabinet was forced to compromise. On the vital question of the Nationalization of the Royalties, it was faced with the unreasoning hostility of the Miners' Federation and the determined opposition of a powerful section of the House of Commons, and was compelled to drop the proposal.

The remaining proposals, however, were embodied in a Bill which became an Act of Parliament on August 15, 1920.

This measure (The Mining Industry Act, 1920) was in two main parts. Part 1, the principal part, set up a Department of State under the Board of Trade to deal with everything connected with the industry. This was the origin of the Mines Department of the Board of Trade.

The Act provided also for a levy of a penny per ton on all coal for the purpose of improving the social conditions of the mining villages. This was the origin of the Miners' Welfare Fund.

Part 2 made provision for the setting up of a National Board, Area Boards, District and Pit Committees, and defines their powers and functions, which include regulation of prices and wages. A clause was inserted in the Act providing that Part 2 should only become operative if accepted by both owners and men and the representatives on the various boards and committees appointed by both sides within one year of the passing of the Act. The mine-owners accepted the Act and the conditions laid down in it and agreed to work Part 2. The Miners' Federation passed a resolution declining to operate the Act at all and refused to nominate representatives for the boards or committees. Before the expiry of the stipulated year a voluntary agreement between owners and men regarding wages was entered into and when the year was up the owners exercised their right, as the Federation had done previously, refused to operate Part 2, and that part of the Act automatically lapsed. This interesting story is told in another place.[1]

THE 1920 STOPPAGE

During and after the passage of the Mining Industry Act (1920), the miners continued their agitation for an increase of wages and a reduction in the price of domestic coal. The latter had been advanced in May by 14s. 2d. per ton, and in July the Miners' Federation demanded the removal of the increase. As already indicated, the Government firmly declined to permit the Federation to dictate Government policy on prices, and in September the miners dropped the proposal, and asked instead for the appointment of a representative tribunal to investigate prices.

The demand for increased wages was for a flat rate increase of 2s. per day for adults, 1s. per day for youths, and 9d. per day for boys. The claim was based mainly on the increased cost of living, and the miners had a very good case. The rise in wages had just kept pace with the increase in the cost of living, and that was all, so that the workers in the industry were really no better off than in 1914.

The problem of higher wages was complicated by the fact that output was declining, production costs

[1] See page 33.

very high, that the Government still controlled home prices at the pithead, and that there was a very big demand for coal for export. The Government, in September, offered an increase of wages based on an increased output of coal. This was refused by the Federation, and a ballot taken in August declared by a very large majority for a strike to enforce the wages demand irrespective of any increase in output, the strike notices to expire on September 27th. Negotiations continued, and on September 24th the miners agreed to suspend the strike notices for a week to allow of further discussion. On October 1st a deadlock was reached, the miners insisting on the 2s. increase on the then output, and the owners offering an increase on a rising scale only when the output reached 240 million tons (the datum line). The 1920 output for the full year (including ten days' stoppage) was 229 million tons. The miners' representatives agreed to again suspend the strike notices, this time for a fortnight, and to take a ballot on the owners' proposals. The men rejected the owners' offer and the strike began on October 18th.

It was of brief duration. On October 21st the conversations were resumed and on October 28th a settlement was arrived at. The settlement was a compromise. The miners obtained their 2s. per shift increase at once, until the end of the year. After that, wages were governed by a sliding scale based on the output and price of export coal. Home prices being controlled, the only free market was in export coal. All coal produced in excess of 219 million tons was regarded as export coal. The agreement provided a great inducement to both owners and men to increase the output and work was resumed on a basis which seemed likely to give a fair share in the increased prosperity of the industry to all concerned.

THE COMPARISON WITH 1920

Anyone desirous of understanding the real position of the workers in the industry or the course of events which has led to the present situation should beware of any comparison between 1920 and any recent year. Such a comparison can give no guidance as to the difficulties of the industry to-day.

The industry was under State control, output was low, wages high, profits guaranteed, exports restricted, the country in the confused aftermath of war, and the cost of living still far above the peace-time level.

The accounts already given of the conditions existing in 1919 and at the stoppage of 1920 afford convincing proof that such a comparison is of no use whatsoever, and why the Miners' Federation should have selected 1920 as a basis of comparison is a mystery to anyone in any way familiar with the facts of the case. The very fact that the output per person employed had fallen so badly compared with pre-war days, renders any such comparison utterly valueless. As shown elsewhere, that fall was from 20·32 cwt. to 14·54 cwt. per man shift, and from 260 tons to 187 tons per annum per person employed, a decline in output sufficient to ruin the industry in any coal-producing country where the slightest consideration is given to the ordinary economic factors governing its operation.

THE 1921 STOPPAGE

The hopes founded on the settlement arrived at after the stoppage in the autumn of 1920 turned out to be entirely illusory. Output failed to rise, production costs showed no signs of falling, export prices slumped badly, completely falsifying the inflated estimates on which the miners had based their claim for higher wages, so that with a greatly reduced revenue, wages costs stood at a level which the industry was quite unable to bear. The industry was drifting to bankruptcy and under the existing conditions there was no indication of any return to a sound economic basis. The mines being still under Government control, the burden of the loss fell on the general taxpayer. In March, the drain on the Exchequer became so heavy that the Cabinet decided it could no longer ask the country to meet the deficiency. They came to the conclusion that the only remedy was immediate decontrol, and accordingly the Coal Mines (Decontrol) Bill was introduced early in March. The measure curtailed the duration of the Coal Mines (Emergency) Act, 1920 (which had provided for State control until August 31st), by enacting that such control should continue until March 31st and no longer. The Bill passed its third reading on March 17th and the industry suddenly found itself faced with the responsibility of "putting its own house in order". It was a tremendous task, for under State control, which was to all intents and purposes a form of nationalization, the loss had grown until in this last month of March it exceeded the sum of £5,000,000 for that month alone.

This hasty decision, whether justified or not, had immediate and very serious consequences. Owners and men were engaged in negotiating terms for the new situation which would arise on August 31st, when Government control would cease. The miners, recognizing the economic situation of the industry, were apparently reconciled to some reduction in wages, but the suddenness of the decontrol gave them a real grievance. They had counted on the existing agreemeut on wages being maintained until August 31st, and in addition they desired a continuance of State control in some form or other. The owners, on the other hand, convinced that the industry could not be placed on a sound economic basis while paying inflated wages based on war-time conditions, proposed a reversion to pre-war rates with an added percentage in those districts which could afford to pay it. The miners objected to going back to pre-war rates, on the ground that they would not give them sufficient to meet the increased cost of living, and also because they did not wish to see district settlements re-established.

They asked for a standard rate of pay, equal throughout the whole of the coalfields of the country, and proposed that a national "pool" of profits should be set up, on which the less prosperous districts could draw to make up any deficiencies in wages. This thoroughly unsound proposal was resisted by the owners, and also by the Government, the Prime Minister declaring it to be a bastard form of nationalization, and nationalization was a political issue to be determined by the nation as a whole and not by any section.

The chaotic state of the industry and the temper of the contending parties rendered an amicable adjustment of their differences quite impossible in the time at their disposal. The miners decided to withdraw their labour, and as State control ended (March 31st) a national strike began (April 1st).

This strike had one ugly feature hitherto absent from stoppages in the coalfields. Orders were given for the withdrawal of the "safety" men, the miners being in some cases prepared to destroy their own means of livelihood in the struggle for better conditions, and a number of the mines were flooded or otherwise damaged.

Almost as soon as the strike began, the railwaymen and the transport workers decided to join them, and arrangements were made for these two powerful bodies to call out their members on April 12th.

To this threat the Government replied by calling up the Navy and Army Reserve and enrolling a new Defence Force of 70,000 volunteers to aid the civil authorities in maintaining law and order.

The two other unions had agreed to assist the Miners' Federation, even to the extent of striking in sympathy with their fellow members of Labour's Triple Alliance in order to strengthen the hands of the former on negotiations regarding wages. A hitch occurred, however, when the miners refused to continue the negotiations on wages unless the Government and the owners *first* conceded the national pool. This method of "negotiation" was too much even for the railwaymen and the transport workers, and almost at the last minute they cancelled their strike order, the short-sightedness of the miners' leaders having alienated the sympathy of their fellow workers as well as that of a considerable section of responsible public opinion.

Whilst entitled to every credit for the prompt and efficient measures taken for the public safety in face of the Triple Alliance threats, the Government could hardly be congratulated on its handling of the dispute itself. The Cabinet had apparently failed to realize the very serious effect on wages of the sudden decontrol of an industry which had for several years been spoon-fed by the Government. It was not until nearly a month after the strike started (on April 27th) that they grasped the fact that, even after the mines got going again, it would be some time before they could be placed on a sound economic productive basis, and that during the transition period some financial assistance would be necessary to ease the inevitable drop in wages. On that date the Government offered a grant of £10,000,000 to tide the industry over this period, with a guarantee that the reduction in wages should not exceed 3s. per shift in May and 3s. 6d. per shift in June. This offer the Miners' Federation promptly rejected, standing firm for the national pool as the best means of meeting the wages difficulty. On submitting the offer to the mineworkers, the action of the Executive in refusing the offer was confirmed by a substantial majority, although a very significant feature of the ballot was that one-third of the members of the Federation did not trouble to vote at all. Had this offer been made in March before the strike the whole trouble might have been avoided.

The Cabinet took a very serious view of this refusal and the Prime Minister at once intimated to the Secretary of the Federation that unless a more accommodating spirit were shown, the offer of £10,000,000 to ease the wages fall would be withdrawn. This letter was in the nature of an ultimatum and it had the desired effect. On June 24th, negotiations were resumed and on the 27th it was announced that a settlement had been arrived at. The Government renewed its offer of £10,000,000 to ease the wages reductions, while the Federation obtained the establishment of a National Wages Board, but definitely abandoned the demand for a national pool.

Summarized, the chief features of this very important

settlement, which in some respects marked an entirely new departure in the relationships between owners and men, were:

(1) The establishment of a National Board and District Boards, each with an independent chairman.
(2) The districts to be grouped for wages purposes.
(3) A "standard" wage, to be the district base rate of March 31, 1921, plus the district percentages payable in July 1914, with adjustments for piece workers to compensate for the reduction of hours from eight to seven. In no district were the wages paid to be less than standard wages plus 20 per cent thereof.
(4) The sum to be applied in each district to the payment of wages above the "standard" to be 83 per cent of the surplus after deducting costs. Owners' proportion of surplus to be 17 per cent.
(5) A three months' "temporary period", during which special mutually agreed arrangements in regard to wages were applicable, after which the general agreement to extend to September 30, 1922, terminable after that date on three months' notice from either side.
(6) The Government subsidy to be used to prevent wages falling below the March rates by:

2s. od. per shift in July,
2s. 6d. per shift in August,
3s. od. per shift in September,

with proportionate reductions for persons under 16 years of age.

These were the main provisions of the 1921 Agreement which established for the first time in any of our great industries the principle of sharing its proceeds on a mutually agreed basis.

On this occasion the Executive of the Miners' Federation took upon their shoulders the mantle of real leadership. They took upon themselves the full responsibility of negotiating a wages settlement in face of an adverse ballot vote, and, in a letter to the members presenting them with a *fait accompli*, told them bluntly that in the existing economic and political situation the National Wages Board with a national profits pool was unobtainable, that a more just method of fixing wages had been agreed upon than they had ever had before in the industry, that the maximum reductions were now known, that the terms were the best that could be secured, and that there was therefore nothing to be gained by continuing the struggle. Firm leadership reaped its reward, for the settlement was not challenged. The men returned to work and the three months' strike with all its inevitable loss and suffering and hardship was at an end.

At the Annual Conference of the Miners' Federation of that year (Llandudno, August 17th) the President made a frank confession that the strike had been utterly futile and the method of conducting it marked by a series of tragic blunders.

He reminded the members of their folly in refusing at first to operate Part 2 of the Act of 1920 and then within a year of that refusal unanimously agreeing to work it.

He then made a staggering confession of timid and spineless leadership, acknowledging that the Executive had swallowed their convictions and better judgement out of loyalty to majority rule, and admitting that "their loyalty was purchased at too big a price—the price of poverty and starvation of their members, and the misery of millions of their fellow countrymen".

As for the Annual Report itself, this consisted of a series of excuses, explanations, and apologies, showing the leaders sitting on the stool of repentance, and revealing clearly that by the exercise of a little common sense and more resolute leadership the whole regrettable business could have been avoided.

The lesson was a hard one for the leaders and the experience a bitter one for the rank and file. Yet subsequent events were to prove only too soon that in neither case was any wisdom derived from them nor did they lead to any genuine effort to stamp out the disruptive elements in their own ranks whose activities were so strongly condemned by the President, and which lost them alike the support of their fellow workers and the sympathy of the public.

THE MINING INDUSTRY ACT, 1920 (PART 2)

Part 2 of the Mining Industry Act (1920) represented an entirely new departure in the organization of the industry, and if it had been accepted by both sides and worked by both sides in a spirit of mutual confidence and good will, would undoubtedly have had far-reaching effects on the future of the industry. The atmosphere, however, was not then propitious, and although the Government played its part by redeeming the promise of October 10, 1919, and actually placed the Act on the Statute Book, Part 2 never came into operation. This part of the Act contained provision for the setting up of the machinery for regulating wages by reference to profits.

It made provision also for establishing by law a system of closer co-operation for carrying on the coal-mining industry between the coal-owners and the workpeople engaged in it, and it is with this that we are here more intimately concerned. The machinery proposed for this purpose was the setting up of joint pit committees and district committees, area boards, and a national board. The Act did not confer compulsory powers on the Government, enabling the latter to intervene with an over-riding authority on any matter concerning the efficient conduct of the industry, but provided that legislative sanction and authority should be given to recommendations made by the industry itself, i.e. by the joint partners working through the machinery set up by Part 2 of the Act.

The coal-owners were tired of Government control and were not at all anxious for the establishment of new machinery containing anything likely to either extend it or perpetuate it. In view, however, of the chaotic state of the industry at the time, and the anxiety of the Government to see it return to a more stable and prosperous condition, they gave a reluctant consent and agreed to co-operate in working this part of the Act.

As already indicated (page 24) the miners at their Annual Conference in July 1920 refused to have anything to do with the Act at all in any of its parts, and passed a resolution pledging the Federation to refuse to co-operate in working it, if it became law. They opposed the measure in its passage through the House, and were not at all reconciled to its provisions when it finally reached the Statute Book. The Act received the Royal Assent on August 16, 1920.

In view of the disagreement on Part 2, the Government inserted a clause in the Act (Section 17) providing that if, at the expiration of one year from the passing of the Act, the scheme had been "rendered abortive" by reason of the failure of those entitled to appoint representatives to do so, this part of the Act should cease to have effect, unless in the meantime a resolution to the contrary was passed by both Houses of Parliament.

One other important point should be noted here. Under the Act, the duty of issuing the regulations providing for the constitution of the various boards and committees and defining their functions devolved upon the Secretary for Mines. He found it necessary to delay doing so, firstly because of the national stoppage of October 1920, secondly because of the negotiations begun on a voluntary basis between owners and men after the settlement of that dispute, and thirdly because of the second and longer stoppage of 1921 (April to July).

The negotiations finally culminated in the settlement of June 28, 1921, which ended the latter dispute. The mines being now decontrolled, owners and men arrived at an agreement governing both procedure and terms on which wages and profits were to be calculated, leaving only certain points in dispute to be settled by the independent Chairman of the National Board, Sir William (now Lord) Plender. Work was resumed, and on August 12th Sir William made his award on the outstanding points. The two parties had thus succeeded in doing voluntarily, and without Government intervention, exactly what that part of Part 2 relating to wages was designed to achieve, and although at the time the Act was actually on the Statute Book, its provisions were scarcely ever referred to during the discussions.

Following on the voluntary settlement of the points relating to wages embodied in Part 2 of the Act, the miners suddenly awoke to the value of the provisions for setting up the various boards and committees, and on the same day as Sir William Plender issued his award (August 12th) they addressed a letter to the Secretary for Mines, notifying him that they were now prepared to co-operate in giving effect to Part 2. *They were too late.* They forgot that if they were entitled to change their minds, the owners were equally entitled to do so as well. Only two days remained before the expiry of the year stipulated in the Act for the appointment of their representatives, and on the day of expiry the Mining Association addressed a letter to the Secretary for Mines, intimating that having regard to the course of events, they had decided not to take any part in the establishment of the boards and committees provided for under Part 2 of the Act. Despite the efforts of the Government to convince the owners that Part 2 of the Act had not been "rendered abortive", they held firmly to their decision and Part 2 thus automatically lapsed.

Then Parliament and the country were treated to the extraordinary spectacle of the miners' spokesmen in both Houses (Lord Haldane in the Lords and Mr. S. Walsh in the Commons) appealing pathetically to the Government not to allow to lapse an Act which only a year before they had spurned and scorned and rejected and refused to operate.

Once again the miners' leaders had "missed the 'bus". Now, whenever there is a dispute or a debate in the House of Commons, they complain bitterly of the fact that they have no voice in either the executive control or routine management of the industry to which they contribute so much.

At the end of 1921 the Mines Department issued a White Paper giving copies of the correspondence and report of a meeting between the Secretary for Mines and the Mining Association (Cmd. 1551 of 1921), and early in 1922 a report under Section 17 of the Act (Cmd. 1583 of 1922), and in these two official publications the whole of this sorry tale of missed opportunities may be read by all who are interested.

CHAPTER VI

A Period of Calm—The March of Events, 1924—The Buckmaster Enquiry—Another Brief Truce—The Macmillan Enquiry—The 1925 Subsidy

A PERIOD OF CALM

As though to compensate for the three hectic years which preceded it, 1922 proved to be a year of comparative calm. The miners had got their national agreement and both sides appeared anxious to give it a fair trial. Only two ripples disturbed the surface, neither of them of any account. At the Miners' Annual Conference in July, Wales proposed a resolution for affiliation with the Third International, which was opposed by every other district. At the same Conference, Lancashire proposed that notice be given to terminate the wages agreement, but the proposal was rejected by an overwhelming majority.

The mining industry, however, is like the Balkans. There's always trouble brewing, and if there is any likelihood of a protracted peace, there are always people waiting to stir the cauldron.

At the end of the year, the Coalition Government fell, and in the ensuing election the Socialist Party almost doubled its strength, returning 142 members, amongst whom the miners were strongly represented. Unlike the railwaymen's leaders, the miners' leaders have always believed they could obtain higher wages and better conditions of labour for their followers by political action than by negotiation through the normal channels of collective bargaining in industry. The results do not justify the belief, but it held the field in 1923, and indeed, still persists. The first fruits of the accession of strength in the Parliament of 1923 was forthcoming early in the year in the introduction of a Nationalization of Mines Bill. This measure, which was debated later, is described and analysed on page 312.

The movement for higher wages now received a fresh impetus from the improved economic position of the industry. In January 1923 the French occupation of the Ruhr gave a great stimulus to the export trade. It was purely artificial, and therefore bound to be temporary, but while it lasted it brought a considerable measure of prosperity to the industry. With the expansion of the export trade the output rose steadily, and in the week ending April 21st all records were broken by an output of 5,824,900 tons, the previous best being 5,776,600 tons. By the end of the year production had reached 276 million tons, the highest since 1913. The output per person employed, however, which is the real test of the economic position, showed no great improvement. The number employed increased, so that at the end of the year the output per person employed had risen only from 217 tons in 1922 to 229 in 1923, compared with 260 tons in 1913. Wages costs were thus still very high, being 12s. 4¼d. per ton, commercially disposable, compared with 6s. 10½d. per ton in 1913. These figures, while indicating that the return to a sound economic basis was not so rapid as could have been desired, were much better than in 1920, when the output per person employed had fallen to 187 tons, and the wages costs were 25s. 9½d. per ton.

As the year advanced the demand for an increase in wages grew stronger and led to suggestions that notice should be given to terminate the National Agreement. A proposal to this effect was discussed at great length at the Annual Conference of the Miners' Federation in July 1923. The Executive Committee, however, were not then desirous of forcing the issue. They succeeded in avoiding a vote on the direct question, and obtained from the Conference instead, a resolution authorizing them to enter into negotiations with the owners with a view to securing improvements in the agreements.

The workers' demands, when framed by their Executive and presented to the owners, took the form of a request for an increase in the minimum wage and for an alteration in the ratio of wages to profits; they asked, also, for fuller information regarding the working costs which entered into the ascertainments. The owners refused the two former, and so far as the latter was concerned said they were prepared to consider any practical proposals to secure the desired end. Another committee of enquiry composed of owners and men met and on December 13th concluded its sittings, the owners indicating the possibility of their making concessions in certain directions.

In November the Prime Minister (Mr. Baldwin) announced the dissolution, and in the election which followed, the Socialist Party strengthened its position in the House still further, returning with 191 members.

The electoral result, however, was a stalemate, and as no party obtained a majority, the Socialists were given their opportunity and the first Labour Government was formed, entering into office in the early days of 1924. With a very powerful section in the Party representing the miners, more attention was concentrated on the coal industry; the agitation for higher wages and better conditions of labour was renewed with greater vigour, the avowed objective was quite frankly declared to be nationalization of the mines, and there were many indications that a renewal of strife within the industry was almost inevitable.

THE MARCH OF EVENTS (1924)

In January of 1924 the Executive of the Miners' Federation decided to take a ballot of their members on the question of the termination of the National Agreement. On the 17th the Secretary (Mr. F. Hodges) announced that 81 per cent of the members had voted for the ending of the agreement, and notice was accordingly given to terminate it on April 17th.

The Mining Association, having consulted its members, a meeting took place on March 6th between owners and men, at which the owners indicated their willingness to make concessions on both the minimum wage and the ratio of profits to wages, but made no definite offer. The men's representatives demanded a Minimum Wage Bill with wages based on the 1914 level and supplemented to meet the increased cost of living, a proposal to which the owners were utterly opposed. A committee of seven from each side continued the negotiations, and on March 12th the owners made an offer which was rejected by a Delegate Conference of the miners on March 14th.

The Secretary for Mines intervened and the discussions were continued, with the result that on March 27th a further conference was held, at which the owners offered further concessions which were summarized in *The Times* of March 29th as follows:

(1) Increase in the general minimum rate of wages from 20 per cent to 32½ per cent.
(2) Standard profits to consist of 15 per cent of standard wages, instead of 17 per cent as existing.
(3) 87 per cent to wages and 13 per cent to profits of any surplus instead of 83 per cent to wages and 17 per cent to profits.

The Miners' Delegate Conference met on the following day and decided to submit the terms to the members; the ballot to take place on April 8th. The ballot resulted in the rejection of the owners' offer, the figures being: for acceptance 322,392, and against acceptance 338,650.

THE BUCKMASTER ENQUIRY

This narrow and indecisive majority created a new and difficult situation. The Ministry of Labour intervened and under the Industrial Courts Act, 1919, appointed a Court of Enquiry to enquire into and report on the wages question and the matters in issue between owners and men. The Court was appointed, with Lord Buckmaster as Chairman, on April 15th, and held its first sitting on April 24th.

On April 16th a joint meeting of representatives of the Mining Association and the Miners' Federation was held, at which it was agreed that pending the findings of the Court of Enquiry wage rates based on the January and February ascertainments should come into operation on May 1st, which meant an increase for all workers on the minimum of 12 per cent.

The report of the Court of Enquiry was issued on May 9th. It consisted mainly of an exhaustive analysis of the wages position, and set out certain conclusions at which it had arrived on the evidence before it.

Chief among these were that the wages paid to all the day workers, and to the piece workers in *some* collieries, were substantially less than the equivalent of their pre-war earnings. That in dealing with claims for higher wages, illustrations given by averages are of little service. That the provision of a minimum wage should have precedence over distribution of profits. And, lastly, that the profits from coking and by-product plants could not be legitimately included in the profits of the coal-mining industry.

The Court strongly recommended an immediate resumption of negotiations between the parties as the most hopeful course for securing a modification of the terms of the agreement of 1921 and of effecting a new wages agreement.

On May 14th the sub-committees resumed their negotiations, and on May 15th a provisional agreement was reached which the Miners' Federation undertook to recommend to their members for acceptance. On May 29th a Delegate Conference accepted the agreement by 473,000 votes to 311,000, the agreement to be for a period of one year, and to be retrospective from May 1st.

The three chief differences between this agreement and that of 1921 were:

(1) Minimum percentage to be added to "standard" wages 33⅓ instead of 20.
(2) Proportion of standard profits to standard wages 15 per cent instead of 17 per cent.
(3) Percentage of surplus proceeds to be allocated to wages 88 instead of 83 and to profits 12 instead of 17.

The agreement was signed on June 18, 1924, and under the new terms, which the economic position of the industry did not justify, work was continued and a stoppage averted.

Two points of general interest, and both of great importance to the industry, should be here noted. Mr. Frank Hodges, on election to Parliament and appointment as Civil Lord of the Admiralty in the Socialist Government, resigned his position as Secretary of the Miners' Federation. and was succeeded by Mr. A. J. Cook, already referred to as joint author of the pamphlet *The Miner's Next Step*. It is interesting to note that one of his first public declarations was: "There is no identity of interests between Capital and Labour, and as long as the present system continues there will be strikes. . . . There has been many a time when the miners have been compelled to adopt the method of reducing output at the pits in order to bring the employers to their senses." (September 12, 1924.)

The other was the defeat of the Government on the Campbell case on October 8th, and the resignation of the Socialist Ministry. In the General Election which followed on the dissolution, a Conservative Government was returned with a clear majority of 215 over all other parties.

ANOTHER BRIEF TRUCE

The 1924 terms of settlement were agreed upon at a time when, as subsequent events proved, the industry was unfortunately entering upon another difficult and trying period in its chequered post-war history.

Throughout the summer and autumn of 1924 there was comparative peace, the only signs of trouble being the possible effects of the payment of reparations in coal by Germany on the British coal-mining industry. Towards the end of the year, however, the general position began to cause the owners very great concern, and on November 28th they addressed a letter to the Miners' Federation proposing a joint meeting to consider the position of the industry and possible remedies. This meeting was held on January 29, 1925, but the miners' leaders then refused to take part in a joint enquiry. A further meeting was held on February 19th, when the owners again pressed the miners' leaders to agree to such an enquiry. The matter was deferred until after the meeting of the Miners' Federation in March, when the Federation agreed to the course suggested, and the Joint Sub-Committee was duly constituted.

In the meantime the Mining Association had published a programme indicating, under two headings, the lines suggested for investigation. These were: "The Coal Market" in two parts, "Export and Inland", and "Production", with terms of reference wide enough to cover practically the whole field (February 20, 1925).

The Miners' Federation published a series of far-reaching proposals ranging over the whole field of the industry, including capital expenditure, organization, administration, wages, and prices (February 20, 1925).

Having agreed to come together, the Joint Sub-Committee decided that its procedure should take the form of an enquiry, in three stages, devoted respectively to:

(1) The Facts.
(2) The Causes.
(3) The Remedies.

The situation which the Joint Sub-Committee had to face was a grave one. The aftermath of war was slowly dissolving, the world was getting gradually back to more normal trading conditions, the country generally was steadily getting back to a sounder economic basis, but the recovery in the mining industry was not keeping pace with the general advance. Compared with 1923, production fell by 9 million tons. The stimulus to the export trade due to the French occupation of the Ruhr disappeared, so that exports fell by 18 million tons of a value of £28,000,000. Production per person employed, which had been steadily increasing from the phenomenally low figure of 187 tons per annum in 1920 to 229 in 1923, fell back to 220 tons, while the wages costs rose from 12s. 4¼d. in 1923 to 13s. 3d. in 1924, and the number of workpeople engaged in the industry had increased by 10,500. Short time was being worked in some collieries, with the result that the weekly cash earnings were insufficient to afford a reasonable standard of life to the miner or his family.

For the first quarter of 1925, six of the thirteen mining districts showed a loss. In most of the others the profit was trifling. On sales of £52,500,000 the profit was £1,400,000 or 2½ per cent on turnover.

The Joint Sub-Committee duly met and after a series of meetings lasting until May 14th, drew up a statement embodying the results of their investigations into the facts of the case, and then, in subsequent meetings, proceeded with their enquiry into the causes and remedies. These, very naturally, speedily merged into one, and as the discussions proceeded, the divergence of opinion on both became wider and more acute. By June 23, 1925, a complete deadlock was reached, and the Joint Sub-Committee broke up without coming to any agreement.

The owners quite definitely attributed the cause of

the grave state of affairs revealed by the enquiry to the cost of production, due mainly in their submission to two causes: the reduction of the working day from eight hours to seven under the Coal Mines Act of 1919, and the wages being paid under the existing wages agreement (the 1924 agreement). In the discussions they proposed the repeal of the seven hours statutory enactment, and a revision of the wages agreement, making it clear that in their judgement, if there were to be a continuation of the seven hours day, the downward revision of wages must inevitably be less favourable to the workers in the industry.

The representatives of the Miners' Federation met the first of these suggestions with a blank negative. They were utterly and absolutely opposed to any extension of the working hours, and flatly refused to consider it.

So far as the wages agreement was concerned, they were strongly opposed to any revision of the agreement which would give the workers less than their 1914 wages, plus an addition corresponding to the increased cost of living.

All the exchanges of views having failed in their object, the owners on June 30th gave formal notice to the Federation terminating the existing wages agreement as from July 31st. This was immediately followed (on July 1st) by the owners presenting their proposals for a new wages agreement. A curious feature of the new proposals was that despite the insistence of the owners on the need for a longer working day, there was no mention of any extension of working hours. On July 3rd the Miners' Federation held a conference, at which the proposals were considered and a resolution was passed unanimously declaring them to be unacceptable. They based their objections to the proposals on four grounds. These were that the proposals involved the abolition of the minimum wage, the guaranteeing of profits irrespective of the rate of wages, and immediate reductions in wages ranging from 13 per cent to 48 per cent. The fourth ground of objection was the continued exclusion of the by-product industries, a very controversial and highly complicated issue, which, whilst indirectly connected with wages, raised questions of vital principle for the coal mining and other industries.

On July 7th the President of the Mining Association proposed a further meeting, but the Miners' Federation replied saying that such a meeting would serve no useful purpose, as there was no room for negotiations on these proposals. On this the Government and the First Lord of the Admiralty, with the Minister of Labour and the Secretary for Mines, interviewed representatives of both sides with a view to bringing them together. The effort failed. Both were on their dignity. The miners said they were quite willing to meet the owners as soon as the latter had withdrawn their proposals. The owners refused to do this, but were quite willing to meet the miners to discuss any proposals they might wish to make.

THE MACMILLAN ENQUIRY

Confronted with this impasse, the Government decided on another enquiry under the Industrial Courts Act. This was set up on July 13th under the Chairmanship of the Rt. Hon. H. P. Macmillan, K.C., the terms of reference being: "To inquire into the causes and circumstances of the dispute in the Coal-Mining Industry and to report thereon."

The Court held its first public sitting on July 17th, and the first document it had to consider was a letter from the Federation refusing to take any part whatsoever in the proceedings, which they said were obviously designed to justify the attack on the miners' standard of living, but expressed their willingness to meet the owners in open conference if the proposals of the latter were withdrawn. The Court decided to adjourn in order to give the Federation an opportunity to reconsider the matter, but on resuming on July 20th letters were read from both the President and the Secretary of the Federation declining to attend.

Despite this rebuff, the Court decided that it was its duty to carry on with the enquiry. Before doing so, another effort was made to get the parties together, and this having failed the enquiry proceeded, the Mining Association giving evidence and the Miners' Federation refusing to do so, a copy of each day's proceedings being, however, sent to the latter.

In the circumstances a week proved sufficient for the purpose for which the Court was set up, and on July 28th the report was completed.

On the attitude of the parties to the dispute the Court made a comment which sheds an interesting light on the relationships existing at the time between the owners and the men. This was: "There has, in our view, been an insistence by both parties on formalities, the necessity for which in a situation so desperate we find it difficult to appreciate."

The report itself, in the first part, gave a very lucid analysis of the causes of the dispute and their effect on the general economic position of the industry. The former were mainly the trade disturbance, due to the war, the use of oil instead of coal in maritime transport, the growth of hydro-electric power, and increased production of coal by other countries. In an addendum Sir Josiah Stamp, one of the members of the Court, expressed the view that an additional cause for the decline in the industry was the reversion to the gold standard by this country in April 1925.

The major part of the report was naturally devoted to the wages question, and on this the Court reached certain conclusions, chief among which were:

(1) That the effect on wages (and output) of a reversion to the eight hours working day could not be predicted with assurance.

(2) That under the existing agreement the wages were, on the average, less than pre-war rates plus an addition representing the official figure for the increased cost of living.

(3) That any agreement should provide for a minimum wage.

(4) That the payment of such a minimum wage should be a charge on the industry before profits.

(5) That the deadlock arose over what was called a "living wage", which the Court did not feel called upon to define. The "economic" wage, however, presented no such difficulty. It was the wage an industry could afford to pay. In the mining industry, that wage varied from district to district, and from colliery to colliery. (The Court might have added from seam to seam.) The industry was not one single concern, and theoretically the appropriate solution for the problem of the uneconomic pit was to close it down.

The reactions of such a step, however, would extend far beyond the industry itself. This led the Court to ask whether the mining industry was one which ought to be left entirely to the free play of purely economic forces, and having asked this question, they left it unanswered on the ground that it was outside their terms of reference.

(6) That the owners' proposals for a new wages agreement involved departures from the existing system which could only be viewed by the miners with anxiety. They would entail an immediate reduction in wages, varying with the district, and as 13 per cent of the net proceeds was to go to profits, there was no protection against a progressive diminution in the actual wages paid. The statutory minimum was payable only to a limited number of the workers, and although there were proposals for subsistence allowances for the lower-paid men, these had not been fixed, and as the new wages lists were in process of preparation they could not pursue it farther.

(7) That there was considerable room for improving the efficiency of the industry as a whole, and so affording some aid to the economic position.

(8) That this particular crisis, unlike others, was to a large extent due mainly to causes outside the control of either party to the dispute, but the calamity was a common one, and they ought to take counsel together in order to avert its worst consequences.

It will thus be seen that whilst this enquiry shed some additional light on the merits of the dispute, it did little to assist in the finding of a solution for the problem the Court had to consider, or in the way of reconciling the conflicting views of the disputants.

The Miners' Federation, before it started, refused to be associated with it in any way, and when it was over the Mining Association announced that they did not regard the report as judicial, and refused to accept it.

THE 1925 SUBSIDY

Events began to move now with dramatic swiftness. The sands were running out. On July 23rd the Miners' Federation had decided to regard the mine-owners notice to terminate the 1924 wages agreement as notice to terminate the miners' contract of service, and the districts were notified accordingly. The object of this was to ensure that in the event of a stoppage, it should be regarded by the public as a lock-out, and not a strike. Apart from the psychological effect, the point is not one of any great importance. Except in the case of the "lightning" strike, when workers "down tools" without notice to obtain the immediate redress of a grievance, or the owners shut down the pit on account of some breach of agreement, all disputes are referred to the properly constituted bodies, where they are fully considered on their merits. If, under the machinery set up for dealing with disputes, the two parties fail to agree, one of them gives notice to terminate their contract and work ceases. In this case, a disagreement on wages was the cause of the dispute. The owners were offering certain rates of wages which the miners refused to accept. Rather than accept them, they said they would withdraw their labour. The owners said: "Very well; if you do so, the pits will be automatically closed." So that, whether the stoppage might be called a strike or a lock-out, it really made no difference at all in the actual position.

On the same day (July 23rd) the special committee set up by the Trades Union Council to deal with the coal crisis communicated with the Prime Minister, asking for an opportunity to discuss the situation. On the 24th the owners and men had a brief meeting. On the 28th the Miners' International met in Paris, under the Chairmanship of Mr. Herbert Smith, and unanimously agreed to support the British miners in the event of a stoppage. On the 29th and 30th the Prime Minister was continually engaged in negotiations with owners and men separately, and finally, late on the night of the 30th, the Prime Minister, after a special Cabinet meeting, announced that in order to avoid a stoppage in the coalfields, the Government had decided to grant a subsidy to the industry for the maintenance of wages at the level prescribed by the 1924 agreement, for the period August 1, 1925, to May 1, 1926.

On the following day, the 31st, the day on which the notices were due to expire, the offer of a subsidy was accepted, and the crisis was over for the time being. The Government had bought a period of peace at the expense of the taxpayer, and the calamity of a national stoppage was temporarily averted. The owners, convinced of the necessity for a speedy return to a sound economic basis, were still opposed to the subsidy but accepted under protest.

On August 5th a White Paper was issued giving the terms of settlement and the basis on which the Government had agreed to grant the subsidy.

This explained that the subsidy was given to bridge the gap between the level of wages under the 1924 agreement and the lower level which would have resulted from the owners' proposals of July 1st in each district. In no case was the minimum to be less than under the 1924 agreement.

The 87 per cent to wages and the 13 per cent to capital

formula[1] was made subject to one qualification, i.e. that in the event of the 13 per cent representing in any district more than 1s. 3d. per ton, the excess was to be transferred to the Government in relief of the subsidy. No subvention was payable in any district if, under the 87 : 13 formula, the minimum level of wages was raised by improved trade above the minimum level of the 1924 agreement.

The White Paper pointed out that the safeguard against any undue lowering of prices lay in the self-interest of the coal-owners. Under the scheme an individual colliery which cut prices unduly suffered the loss itself; a district which did so, could only do it at the expense of the profits of that district.

As a safeguard against expenditure on capital account being charged against revenue, the Government relied on the 1924 agreement, which regulated what costs were admissible as production costs for arriving at a result in each district under the 87 : 13 formula. In addition, the Government reserved for itself a power of audit.

The cost to the Exchequer, the White Paper explained, could not be stated with any degree of certainty, owing to the depressed state of the industry and the doubtful outlook for the future.

A very clear indication, however, of the deplorable state of the industry was given in the estimate of the cost. This showed that if the proposed arrangement had been in operation during the same period the year before—from August 1, 1924, to May 1, 1925—the cost

[1] Standard wages and profits, and also the division of the surplus, were abolished and a sharing of the net proceeds substituted. The 87:13 formula gave the same result but simplified the working of the terms of the 1924 Agreement.

would have been about £7,500,000. If the conditions were the same as in the first quarter of 1925, the cost would be about the same. But if the month of June were taken as the basis for the calculation (and this is the significant feature), the cost to the Exchequer for the nine months would be about £24,000,000.

On the basis of these figures the Government asked Parliament to authorize the expenditure of £10,000,000, indicating that if the amount proved insufficient for the purpose, Parliament would be asked to sanction a further grant-in-aid.

The terms of settlement were received in the country with very mixed feelings. The Prime Minister himself was not too happy about them, while the granting of a subsidy to a particular industry, at the expense of the taxpayer in order to avoid a stoppage of work, was regarded by many responsible people with grave misgiving as a serious departure from principle, and one which was almost certain to lead to further trouble.

On the other hand, the terms of settlement were hailed by the miners' leaders and the extremists of the Socialist Party as a great victory, and led to the use of very strong language by the Secretary of the Miners' Federation and others.

The following extracts from some of the speeches made at the time in the House of Commons will show how the news of the settlement was received in different quarters.

In presenting the motion for the subsidy to the House of Commons on August 6th,

Mr. Baldwin said: "I was unable to get the miners to recede from the position that they would not consider the question of either hours or wages, and so it became quite impossible to say what ultimately the owners might have given had there been a real genuine attempt at negotiations. It was quite obvious that we had reached a deadlock, and it seemed very difficult to find any way round at all" (H. of C., August 6, 1925).

Mr. Lloyd George said: "The danger of this is that it is nationalization in its worst form. It is a guarantee of wages and profits, without any control, without any limit, and without any restriction" (H. of C., August 6, 1925).

Mr. Ramsay MacDonald said: "The situation could have been met only in one way, and that was by a subsidy. You may reject it in principle, as I do, but the cost of the coal stoppage in 1921 had amounted to £287,000,000, and therefore, to secure a truce now, for ten or fifteen millions, was not extravagant or wasteful expenditure. There would never be permanent peace, however, until there is a living wage paid as a minimum, and until the trade is organized nationally" (H. of C., August 6, 1925).

Mr. R. Smillie, one of the miners' leaders, said: "It may be taken that the mining question will never be settled until the nation owns the mines and works the mines for public service and not in order to make a profit" (H. of C., August 6, 1925).

Sir Robert Horne said: "We have only to look at comparative figures to see that a subsidy is not really going to touch the difficulty" (H. of C., August 6, 1925).

In the course of his speech Mr. Baldwin referred to the wild language and the threats which had come from some quarters in these terms:

"I am convinced that if the time should come when the community had to protect itself, with the full strength of the Government behind it, the community will do so, and the response of the community will astonish the forces of anarchy throughout the world" (H. of C., August 6, 1925).

Extracts from other speeches were:

Mr. Ramsay MacDonald: "The Prime Minister has handed over the appearance, at any rate, of victory, to the very forces that sane, well considered, thoroughly well-examined Socialism feels to be probably its greatest enemy" (at Dunmow, August 3, 1925).

Mr. J. H. Thomas: "What has been accomplished is a truce, but not a permanent peace, brought about by a subsidy. In my considered judgement not only is it wrong, but in the end will lead to inevitable disaster in the country" (at Chester, August 16, 1925).

Lord Oxford: "It is time that the country faced the problem as a whole once and for all" (at Caxton Hall, July 31, 1925).

Mr. A. J. Cook: "An armistice has been declared, but, make no mistake about it, the issues during the next nine months are far greater than a mere wage issue. We have got to concentrate our interest on the whole industry, because it is going to be ours" (at Renishaw Park, August 2, 1925).

Sir John Simon: "I object to nationalization not only because it is impracticable for such an industry, but because it would mean the sacrifice of individual freedom" (at Caxton Hall, August 1, 1925).

Mr. A. J. Cook: "What we did last week we can and will do again. They have got a commission. Let them sit and see what they can hatch. These enquiries are only held to sidetrack our objective. . . . Before long there will be a political crisis, the greatest in the history of crises, and Labour is going to sweep in in that crisis" (at Meadowfield, August 9, 1925).

The subsidy came into operation at once, but although it imposed a heavy burden on the taxpayer, it did nothing to help the industry towards a state of greater prosperity.

However good the intentions of the Government in granting it, the method of applying it was singularly defective and open to abuse. It was given indiscriminately to all collieries, those showing a profit as well as those showing a loss, although the former were producing nearly half the output. Spread over the whole country the average loss prior to the subsidy was only 3d. per ton.

The subsidy did nothing to stimulate demand either at home or abroad. Competition became keener, with the result that prices fell to such an extent that by the end of the December quarter (1925), 73 per cent of the coal was being produced at a loss, apart from the subsidy, and the benefit of the latter was being very largely passed on to the consumer. The worst effects were felt in the exporting districts. The number of coal-producing concerns which could show a credit balance grew steadily less and by the end of the March quarter (1926) only one district showed any profit at all.

The year 1925 had ended with an output of 243 million tons against 267 in 1924. The value of the output as estimated by the Mines Department had fallen from £251,500,000 to £199,000,000, or more than 2s. 6d. per ton. Exports fell from 62 million tons in 1924 to 51 millions in 1925, and the value from £72,000,000 to £50,500,000, or a reduction of 3s. 5d. per ton. In practically every district coal was being sold below the cost of production, apart from the subsidy.

The number of workpeople engaged in the industry decreased in the same year by 110,000. The revenue accruing to the industry was insufficient to maintain wages at the level agreed upon under the 1924 settlement and these were only paid by the aid of the subsidy.

When it ended on April 30, 1926, the subsidy had cost the taxpayer £23,000,000, or 2s. 6d. per ton on every ton of coal produced during the nine months of its operation. The average loss per ton had increased from 3d. to 1s. 6d., apart from the subsidy (see p. 363).

For his £23,000,000 the taxpayer got nothing except a brief respite from a complete stoppage of one of the nation's vital industries.

There need be little wonder that the Royal Commission, which held its sittings during the subsidy period, should have recommended that it should be ended at the earliest possible moment and never be repeated.

The lesson is one which the country ought not to forget, particularly at this moment, when demands are again being made by the miners for a further resort to this artificial, unsound, and uneconomic method of obtaining public money for the increase of their wages.

CHAPTER VII

THE SAMUEL COMMISSION

In addition to granting the subsidy, the Government announced that it had been decided to appoint a Royal Commission, composed of impartial persons unconnected with coal mining, to conduct a thorough investigation into the industry, and on August 19th the terms of reference were published. These were: "To enquire into and report upon the economic position of the coal industry and the conditions affecting it, and to make any recommendations for the improvement thereof."

The Government was particularly anxious that the services of men whose names would inspire public confidence should be secured for this Royal Commission, and consequently some delay occurred before its personnel was completed. On September 3rd, however, the Mines Department announced that His Majesty had been pleased to approve the appointment of the following gentlemen:

Chairman: The Rt. Hon. Sir Herbert L. Samuel, K.C.B.
Members: Sir William Henry Beveridge, K.C.B.
General The Hon. Sir Herbert Alex Lawrence, K.C.B.
Mr. Kenneth Lee, LL.D.

The names of the members were received with almost universal approval. Except that the miners protested against the absence of any practical miner from the Commission, the appointments met with very little criticism in any quarter.

As expert assessors the Commission had the assistance of the Chief Labour Adviser to the Mines Department, one of H.M. Inspectors of Mines, the Director of Fuel Research, and an expert from the Geological Survey Department.

The Commission got to work on September 14, 1925. It held thirty-three public sessions, the final sitting taking place on January 14, 1926. During this period the Commission took evidence from a large number of witnesses, and the members also visited a number of the districts in order to acquaint themselves at first hand with the prevailing conditions.

Its report was signed on March 6, 1926, and was made public on March 11th.

The report was a unanimous one. The terms of reference were wide, and the enquiry was an exhaustive and comprehensive one into every phase of the problems confronting the industry. In its examination of those problems, the enquiry was one of the most thorough investigations ever undertaken by any Royal Commission, whilst the report itself, in the impartiality of its conclusions, and the far-reaching nature of its recommendations, is probably one of the most valuable documents ever presented to the nation in connection with any of our great industries.

Naturally the report is a lengthy one, and in a brief review it is only possible to summarize its conclusions and recommendations. Among the most important of these were the following:

The 1925 Subsidy: "The principle is wrong. . . . The resort to subsidy in one crisis or in one trade will inevitably lead to pressure to resort to it in another crisis or in another trade, with destructive results to the national finances.

"A temporary subsidy to collieries on the margin of profitability, which is sometimes advocated, would constitute in many cases a dole to the inefficient, to the disadvantage of the efficient. It is better that these collieries should close or amalgamate with their neighbours, according to circumstances."

A subsidy to the export trade could not be recommended, as by lowering the price of coal to the foreigner it would be, in effect, a bounty to foreign producers of iron and steel, assisting them in their competition with the British iron and steel trade in the markets of the world.

It (the subsidy) "SHOULD STOP AT THE END OF ITS AUTHORIZED TIME, AND SHOULD NEVER BE REPEATED."

Amalgamation of Mines: "The amalgamation of many mines is desirable and practicable, but any measure of compulsory amalgamation on arbitrary lines would be mischievous."

Costs of Production: "We come reluctantly, but unhesitatingly, to the conclusion that the costs of production, with the present hours and wages, are greater than the industry can bear."

Closing of Collieries: The Commission regarded it as inevitable that a certain number of collieries must close down in the near future, and said the same thing would occur under nationalization. The industry was too large for the requirements it had to fulfil.

Efficiency: "It is not sufficient that the best of our mines should be, as we think they are, unsurpassed in efficiency by those of any other country in the world. It is necessary that *all our mines* should be brought as nearly as possible to the level of the best. . . . If all the undertakings could come up to the level of efficiency of the larger ones, the problem of restoring prosperity to the industry would be a long way nearer to a solution."

Research: The methods of utilizing coal are unscientific.

Four-fifths of the coal consumed in the country is burnt in a raw state; oil and valuable by-products are wasted, and the atmosphere is polluted. Research into the methods both of winning and using coal are inadequate. . . . It is essential that the industry as a whole should become imbued with the spirit of science in order that it may utilize to the fullest extent the results of modern scientific developments. Much greater attention should be given to these matters by the State.

National Agreements: The Commission defined the minimum percentage as "the wage to be paid irrespective of the economic ability for the time being of the industry or the district."

The report proceeds: "We do not see how such a wage, in a community so small and so closely united as Great Britain, can ultimately be fixed by other than national authorities. To give a free hand to each district to settle its own standard of living without consultation and without regard to any other, is to expose the standards of the more efficient and prosperous areas, on which the future of the country rests, to undermining by the weaker areas; it opens the door to 'cut-throat competition between different districts at the expense of wages.' We conclude, accordingly, that the minimum percentage for each district should be settled or at least approved by agreement between bodies representing all the employers and all the workpeople in the industry. This does not mean that the minimum percentage for each district may not with advantage be discussed in the first instance by district associations, if they think fit, provided that the minima thus provisionally agreed are afterwards submitted for approval by some national authority."

After adding that such an arrangement need not exclude all flexibility in the district, such for example as a district agreeing to apply part of the proceeds accruing to labour to family allowances, the report goes on: "There remains only the question of the precise form of the national authority for prescribing wage principles. We have already indicated our view that this must be primarily a body representing the two parties in the industry, the mine-owners and the miners. . . . We do, however, suggest for the earliest consideration of mine-owners and miners that the presence of a third impartial element, such as is found in the National Wages Board for the railway service, may prove of great value. . . . The decisions of such a Board could not as such be binding, but we hope and believe that in practice they would be accepted by both sides."

Although the Miners' Federation in their propaganda invoke this recommendation of the Commission in support of their case, it is extremely doubtful whether the constitution or powers of the body envisaged in the report are the same as those they would desire in the body which they wish to set up.

In particular, the vagueness as to whether the minimum percentage should be "settled" or "approved" by the National Board is not at all conclusive, whilst the last sentence in the quotation above (dealing with the decisions of the Board), seems to deprive it of any real authority at all.

Nationalization: The Commission declared against nationalization. It examined the scheme presented by the Miners' Federation, ignoring others, such as that submitted to Parliament in the Nationalisation of Mines Bill (1924) which they regarded as being superseded by that now presented. After declaring that no consideration would have prevented a recommendation for the nationalization of the mines if the case for it had been proved, the Commission's report says: "We have seen, however, no scheme that will withstand criticism. . . . We are not satisfied that the scheme proposed to us is workable, or that it offers a clear social gain. We perceive in it grave economic dangers, and we find no advantages that cannot be obtained as readily, or more readily, in other ways."

Royalties: The Commission recommended that mining

royalties should be acquired by the State. Recalling that the Sankey Commission was unanimous on this point, the report says: "We concur in the general conclusion that the system of private ownership of this great natural resource is open to grave objection." The report recommends, therefore, that the mineral rights in all ungotten coal should be taken over by the State, by purchase in the case of existing royalties, and by a declaration of State ownership in the cases of yet unproved coal deposits, or deposits at such deep levels as to be at present unworkable and therefore with no market value.

Transfer Prices: The Commission reported that without casting any reflection on the "fair dealing of the mine-owners or the impartiality and efficiency of the joint accountants", it was impossible to give the miners a complete assurance that prices might not be depressed in cases where coal was transferred to an undertaking from which profits might be derived independently.

They suggested that from time to time an impartial authority should declare officially and publicly what should be regarded as the market price of every kind of coal sold in the district.

On the decision of Sir Wm. Plender (now Lord Plender) in 1921, as independent Chairman appointed under the agreement of that year, which excluded coke ovens, by-product plants, selling agencies, etc., from the scope of the wages ascertainments, the Commission said: "This appears to us to be a right decision."

Hours: The Commission report against any lengthening of the working day (fixed at seven hours plus one winding time by the Act of 1919). "If a reduction of wages is necessary to enable the industry to surmount its immediate difficulties, this reduction should be made directly, and not indirectly, by a lengthening of working hours for the same remuneration."

The Commission, however, did not rule out an extension of hours by agreement as an alternative to a reduction of wages, or "the unemployment that would be imposed on the industry if it had to continue with the existing hours".

Wages: On this issue the report said: "If the present hours are to be retained, we think a revision of the 'minimum percentage to standard rates of wages' fixed in 1924 at a time of temporary prosperity is indispensable. A disaster is impending over the industry and the immediate reduction of working costs that can be effected in this way, and in this way alone, is essential to save it. . . . Should the miners freely prefer some extension of hours with a less reduction of wages, Parliament would no doubt be prepared to authorize it. . . . We consider that it is essential that there should be, as there always has been hitherto, considerable variation in the rates of wages in the various districts. . . . Revision of the minimum percentage should depend upon acceptance by all parties of such measures of reorganization as will secure to the industry a new lease of prosperity leading to higher wages. . . . The mineowners should not refuse to engage in discussions on a national footing with the Miners' Federation. . . . At the same time, the conditions imperatively require that there should be a large degree of flexibility in the wage rates of the different districts. The Miners' Federation should recognize this, without detriment to the broad policy that the broad principles should be laid down nationally. It appears to us a reasonable course for the national conference to refer the question of minimum percentage and such other matters as they think appropriate to district associations to frame proposals. Those proposals would be submitted to the national conference for approval." (See page 81 on national agreements.)

Output: The Commission point out that the yearly output per person employed has fallen from 319 tons in the period 1879–83, to 257 tons in 1909–13, to 220 tons in 1924 and 217 tons in 1925.[1] The fall was due to a variety

[1] This has now substantially increased, as will be seen from the figures of output given on another page.

of causes, and the report rejects the suggestion that it was due to any general deliberate restriction of output. This must vary from district to district and from mine to mine. In the smallest mines the output per person in 1924 was only 177 tons per annum, whilst in the largest it was 280 tons. Another important factor, the report adds, is the growth of the number of persons employed away from the coal face. Thus, for every hundred workers at the coal face in 1905, there were in 1905 one hundred and fourteen other workers, but in 1924 there were one hundred and forty-five. In 1905 the production of 100 face workers had to be divided by 214, but in 1924 it had to be divided by 245 to give the output per person employed.

Organization of Distribution: "The information collected is sufficient to show that there do exist between producer and consumer substantial margins of profit or expenses, which might be narrowed to the advantage of one or other or both of them. It ought to be possible, either to reduce the price of coal to the consumer, or to raise it to the colliery. . . . The industry as a whole has so far failed to realize the benefits to be obtained by a readiness to co-operate. Large financial advantages might be gained by the formation, in particular, of co-operative selling agencies. . . . Selling associations of this nature would play a useful part in organizing the pools of railway wagons . . . and reducing the waste now caused by the excessive shunting of mineral wagons. In the exporting districts the associations are especially needed. Their function would be to maintain prices at a remunerative level in those foreign markets where the competition is not so much between British and foreign exporters as among the British exporters themselves."

The Commission recommended that power should be given to municipalities to engage in the retail distribution of coal subject to adequate safeguards against any charges being allowed to fall on the rates.

Relations of Employers and Employed: On this important

point the report says: "We have reason to think that such mutual hostility as there is between the central bodies is not a true reflection of the spirit that prevails in the country at large."

The Commission made a number of other recommendations on profit sharing, transport, housing, family allowances, holidays, association with other industries, which there is not space to refer to here.

The Commission's final conclusion was: "The way to prosperity for the mining industry lies along three chief lines of advance: through greater application of science to the winning and using of coal, through larger units for production and distribution, through fuller partnership between employers and employed. In all three respects progress must come mainly from within the industry. The State can help materially—by substantial payments in aid of research; by removing obstacles to amalgamation under existing leases; as owner of the minerals by determining the conditions of new leases; by legislation for the establishment of pit committees and of profit sharing and in other ways. The future depends primarily upon the leadership and the general level of opinion among the mineowners and the miners of Great Britain."[1]

The report was signed on March 6th, and on March 11, 1926, the Prime Minister invited the representatives of the owners and the men to meet him at 10 Downing Street, when he informed them that the Government was giving it immediate consideration and asked them both to refrain from hasty judgement.

On the following day (March 12th) a Delegate Conference of the Miners' Federation decided to refer the question to the districts and to hold another meeting later.

[1] Report of the Royal Commission on the Coal Industry (1925), H.M. Stationery Office (Cmd. 2600, price 3d.).

On March 24th the Prime Minister called the two sides to a further conference and informed them that the Cabinet had discussed the report and that although there were some of the recommendations to which the Government was opposed, they were prepared to undertake such measures as might be required of the State to give effect to it, provided that those engaged in the industry agreed to accept it. Mr. Baldwin said: "If I may put the whole of that into one sentence, it is that we accept the report provided that the other parties do."

On the question of further financial assistance the Prime Minister said that although it would be against the recommendation of the Commission, the Government would be willing, if agreement could be reached by May 1st, to consider extending the period of assistance from the National Exchequer for a further three months, if that were likely to save the situation.

CHAPTER VIII

The 1926 Stoppage—The General Strike

THE 1926 STOPPAGE

FOLLOWING on this (on March 25th) the owners and men met in joint conference, and after a short discussion adjourned until March 31st.

On that date and April 1st joint consultations were held between the two parties to the dispute, but no progress was made towards a settlement. On the latter date (April 1st) the miners' leaders issued a statement declaring that the refusal of the owners to consider the fixation of a national minimum percentage and their insistence on all wages questions being decided in the districts constituted "an almost insurmountable obstacle to an amicable settlement". They added that the Federation could not agree to any further reduction in wages, to any limiting of the functions of the National Board, or the abolition of the national minimum percentage.

A Delegate Conference confirmed the action of the Miners' Executive by passing the following resolution on April 9th:

(*a*) That no assent be given to any proposal for increasing the length of the working day.

(*b*) That the principle of a national wage agreement with a national minimum percentage be firmly adhered to.

(*c*) That inasmuch as wages are already too low we cannot assent to any proposals for reducing wages.

A further joint conference was held on April 13th at which this resolution was considered. The result was a complete breakdown, for the owners took their stand on the recommendations of the Royal Commission on hours and wages as a basis for negotiation, and intimated that they were already inviting the workmen's organization in the districts to confer with them on the basis on which work could be continued when the subsidy ended on April 30th.

The miners had invoked the aid of the Trades Union Congress, a meeting having been held between the Executive of the Miners' Federation and the Industrial Committee of the T.U.C. on April 8th, at which a resolution had been passed calling for a continuance of negotiations and a reduction of the differences between the owners and the miners to a minimum, and the terms of this resolution had been communicated to the miners' Delegate Conference on the 9th.

Following on the breakdown on the 13th, another meeting was held between the Executive of the Miners' Federation and the Industrial Committee of the T.U.C., as a result of which a deputation from the latter waited on the Prime Minister on April 14th. Their chief purpose was to protest against the owners' action in abandoning national negotiations and endeavouring to open negotiations separately with the different districts.

On the same day the owners met the Minister of Labour, following on which it was officially announced that the owners were engaged on "the preparation of a national wages agreement to embody the principles which, in the owners' view, can appropriately be settled nationally". On the 22nd the owners submitted their proposals, but as they contained a clause abolishing the national minimum percentage, they were not acceptable to the miners.

Only a few days now remained before the subsidy must cease and bring about a crisis. The Prime Minister again intervened and negotiations were resumed in a joint conference which he attended, but which proved abortive, neither side being prepared to give way and merely restating its position.

A deadlock seemed imminent and the Prime Minister made one last effort at mediation. He got the parties together in an open conference to discuss the whole situation, and over which he presided. This lasted for two days, but was adjourned on the night of the 29th without any agreement having been arrived at.

On the 30th the Prime Minister communicated the owners' final terms to the miners, the chief features of which were a reversion to the minimum percentage of 1921 (this was 20 per cent above the 1914 standard wage), and a temporary increase of the working day from seven hours to eight. The Government undertook to hold another enquiry before December 31, 1929, to determine whether wages and hours could be improved.

The miners' reply was that they were not prepared to accept a reduction of wages as a preliminary to reorganization, but would give full consideration to all the difficulties when such reorganization had been initiated by the Government.

The Government was not satisfied with this reply, and in view of the refusal of the miners to accept any immediate reduction of wages, the only way, the Royal Commission had declared, to get over the immediate difficulties of the industry, they broke off negotiations. The subsidy period expired on April 30th, and the national stoppage commenced on May 1st.

THE GENERAL STRIKE

On May 1st the delegates of the unions comprising the Trades Union Congress met in London and decided to place the mining industry negotiations in the hands of the General Council of the T.U.C. Then, after consultation with the miners' representatives, it was announced that the General Council had decided to call a strike of all vital services and staple industries in support of the miners, to begin at midnight on May 3rd, unless a settlement was arrived at before then. On the invitation of the President, this decision was unanimously endorsed by the delegates.

We are not concerned here with the wider aspects of this wicked, wanton, and illegal challenge to the constitution, but only with its relation to the dispute which had arisen between employers and employed in one of our vital industries. For an account of how it was defeated by the firmness of the Government, the courage, loyalty, and common sense of the people, the Astbury judgment and the famous speech of Sir John Simon, the reader must look elsewhere. So far as the miners were concerned, however, one thing was clear. As Sir John Simon said in the speech already referred to, it was a "tragic blunder", both in its effect on the miners' case and the future of the trade union movement, and resulted in the loss of a great deal of the public sympathy felt for the miners in the struggle.

The General Strike ended on May 12th, having lasted nine days and being voluntarily terminated by the General Council of the T.U.C. on that day, their decision being communicated to the Prime Minister by a deputation which waited on him at 10 Downing

Street on that morning and announced in the House of Commons in the afternoon.

During the upheaval the efforts to end the mining industry dispute were continued in several directions. On May 8th the Archbishop of Canterbury, with the concurrence of the leaders of all the Christian Churches, made certain tentative proposals for the ending of the General Strike and the settlement of the coal dispute. The latter were elaborated subsequently and are dealt with here on the following pages.

The T.U.C. having taken control of the negotiations for the settlement of the coal dispute, got into touch with Sir Herbert Samuel, the Chairman of the Royal Commission, with the result that the latter submitted to them a memorandum setting out proposals which, after his discussions with them, he considered likely to promote a settlement. Sir Herbert made it perfectly clear that he was acting entirely on his own initiative, and not on behalf of the Government, but undertook to recommend the Government to accept them.

On May 12th the T.U.C. acknowledged this memorandum in a letter signifying their agreement with Sir Herbert that the proposals offered a basis upon which negotiations could be continued. The Executive of the Miners' Federation, however, rejected the proposals, protesting against the action of the T.U.C. in endorsing them without consultation with the miners' representatives, and intimating at the same time in the resolution rejecting the proposals, that if these were to be submitted as a means to call off the General Strike, such a step must be taken on the sole responsibility of the General Council of the T.U.C.

On May 14th the Prime Minister communicated to

the Miners' Federation proposals which the Government considered should provide a reasonable basis for the settlement of the dispute.

On the 20th these proposals were rejected by a Delegate Conference of the miners, and on the 21st they were rejected by the owners also. In his reply the Prime Minister said to the miners that so long as they refused to consider any alteration of wages or hours, and failed to produce themselves any practical proposals, no useful purpose could be served by his meeting them again. He would, however, be ready to meet them if they had any suggestions of the kind to make.

To the owners the Prime Minister said he regretted their uncompromising attitude, and could not agree that the troubles of the industry were due to "political interference". In pointing out that the Government could not have stood aside in a dispute so closely affecting the national well-being, he added that what was called "political interference" was due to the incapacity of the industry to settle its disputes for itself.

On May 28th Mr. Frank Varley, M.P., one of the miners' leaders, put forward proposals on his own initiative and responsibility. They included a reduced national minimum percentage till the end of the year, and a continuance of the subsidy to cover losses only. The proposals were immediately repudiated and rejected by the Miners' Federation.

On the 29th Mr. Frank Hodges, the Secretary of the Miners' International, proposed an extension of the working day to seven and a half hours, as an alternative to the proposed wages reduction. This also was rejected by the Federation.

On May 31st the offer of a further subsidy of

£3,000,000 expired, but on June 1st the Prime Minister announced that while the Government had, as a result of the rejection of their proposals, regained their complete freedom, they recognized that some form of assistance might be needed when a settlement was arrived at.

On June 8th another joint conference was held without result. The official statement issued by the owners said that as the miners refused to move from the position they had taken up all along, there appeared to be no immediate hope of making any progress.

The miners' statement reasserted their view that the only basis for a settlement was that they had consistently advanced—no reduction of wages, no increase in hours, national basis for national wages agreement, and the immediate reorganization of the industry. The two main points in the policy of the Miners' Federation had been summed up in the slogan coined by their Secretary:

"Not a minute on the day,
Not a penny off the pay."

And on these two points they remained adamant.

On June 13th in a debate on the Mines Department vote, Mr. Baldwin made a statement on the Government proposals for dealing with the situation in the industry, foreshadowing two Acts of Parliament to embody them, a speech which led the Secretary to the Miners' Federation to describe the Prime Minister as "the coal-owners' advocate".

It was just about this time (mid-June) that there appeared the first signs of a break in the hitherto solid ranks of the miners, several pits having reopened and started working on local agreements.

On June 23rd the text of the two Government Bills was issued. The first was the Coal Mines Bill (dealing with the hours worked) and the other, the more important, the Mining Industry Bill, dealing with reorganization.

The Coal Mines Bill was a temporary and permissive measure allowing for the extension of the working day from seven hours to eight for a period of five years. The Government view was that if wages were maintained at their existing level without any alteration in hours, large numbers of men must be thrown out of employment. The industry was passing through a period of transition. This was the Government's plan to meet the difficulties of the immediate situation, and no alternative had been suggested by the miners or their supporters in the House. The Bill met with strenuous opposition in its passage through the House, disorder arising on several occasions during the debates. It eventually passed its third reading on July 1st. The Prime Minister spoke and ended his speech by declaring: "If the Miners' Federation even now can accept the report, with all that that report implies, which is what we were struggling for in April, and I believe which was urged on them by many of their best friends, I believe that, even now, a settlement satisfactory to both sides can be arranged." The Bill received the Royal Assent on the 8th amid some disorder created in the House of Lords by the members of the House of Commons who were opposed to the measure.

The second measure, the Mining Industry Bill, is explained on another page (page 90).

On July 8th there was a further indication of the dissension in the ranks of the miners' leaders, when Mr. Frank Hodges said that their refusal to accept the

Royal Commission Report in the initial stages, with all that it implied, would be recorded as one of the great errors of judgement in trade union history.

On the 14th a meeting between the Miners' Executive and the leaders of the T.U.C. afforded further evidence of the differences which had arisen between the two bodies at the time of the General Strike. Coal was being imported for the maintenance of the essential services, and the miners asked that the T.U.C. should, through their respective unions, place an embargo on the handling or transport of all such coal. The request was refused.

In the meantime the Churches had elaborated their proposals, set them forth in a memorandum, and submitted them to separate private meetings of owners and men. On the 16th the memorandum was forwarded to the Prime Minister with an intimation that the proposals had been accepted by the Miners' Executive, and asking him to grant an interview to representatives of the Churches to discuss them. Mr. Baldwin agreed to receive them, but pointed out that "the terms and conditions on which work can be resumed in the coal-mining industry are not within the power of the Government to determine. They can only be settled by agreement between owners and miners". He called attention also to the statement in the report of the Royal Commission, that "an immediate reduction of labour costs, either in wages or hours, was indispensable".

The meeting took place on the 19th, but was altogether without result. The Government and the owners rejected the proposals, and the Miners' Executive, having accepted them, submitted them to a Delegate Conference for approval on July 31st. The Conference decided to refer them to the districts with a recommendation for acceptance. The ballot was taken and on its completion on August 10th it was found that the rank and file had rejected the proposals by a small majority. The Churches' plans for a settlement were thus rejected by all three parties to the dispute.

The dispute dragged along its weary way until August 19th, when a further joint meeting was held between owners and men. Like others it was quite fruitless, and the statements issued afterwards by each side were merely a restatement of their respective positions. The deadlock seemed complete.

On August 26th, however, at the request of the Federation, a meeting was held between their representatives and the Secretary for Mines who was accompanied by the Minister of Labour and the Chancellor of the Exchequer. The miners had no new suggestions to make, but merely re-stated their case again so that this parley was also a barren one, no real step being taken towards a settlement. One important pronouncement, however, was made at this gathering when the Chancellor declared that "the question of giving any financial help to the industry has long passed out of the sphere of practical politics".

In the meantime Britain had been turned from a coal-exporting country into an importing one. Imports of coal were coming in freely and in quantities sufficient to maintain the essential services, a significant indication of the extent to which the miners had lost the sympathy of their fellow trade unionists being the fact that there was very little trouble experienced in unloading or transporting it. At the same time foreign producers were taking full advantage of the stoppage to secure a foothold in markets previously monopolized by the British coal exporter. They expanded their production and by insisting on long-term contracts consolidated their position in many of these markets and dealt a blow to the export trade of this country from which it has not even yet recovered (1936).

After four months' stoppage the opening of September saw no progress towards peace. On September 2nd, however, a step forward was taken at a Delegate Conference of the miners held in London. The Conference empowered the Executive to take "the necessary steps to submit proposals for the setting up of a national agreement" and report to a further Conference.

The Executive thereupon asked the Government to convene and to attend a joint conference of owners and men, saying: "We are prepared to enter into negotiations for a new national agreement with a view to a reduction in labour costs to meet the immediate necessities of the industry."

The Government considered this recognition of the need for "a reduction in labour costs", now acknowledged by the miners for the first time, as a basis sufficient for a resumption of negotiations and asked the owners and men to meet them again. The Government's invitation was promptly declined by the owners. They said: "The Mining Association has no authority to enter into any discussions or negotiations on behalf of the district colliery owners' associations on questions of terms of employment of workmen." The Government then invited the owners to meet them to discuss the situation thus created, and a meeting took place on September 6th at 10 Downing Street between the representatives of the Mining Association and the Cabinet Coal Committee. The Government, at this interview, contended that the owners had given them to understand that they were willing to conclude a national agreement, and had it not been for that understanding, they would not have passed the Coal Mines Bill (extending the hours) without imposing conditions of some kind.

To this the owners replied that they had never had any intention of consenting to a national agreement, that all the discussions had taken place on the basis of district agreements, including those which took place prior to the passing of the Coal Mines Bill. Their spokesman (Mr.—now Sir—Evan Williams) re-affirmed "definitely and emphatically" that the owners would not, under any circumstances, enter on negotiations for a national agreement (see pages 133–4).

On the Government pressing the owners to reconsider their attitude on this point, the latter agreed to refer the question to the district owners. These, with one exception, confirmed and endorsed the attitude of the deputation and the Government was so informed in a letter of the 13th, with an intimation that in view of this decision any further meeting for discussing national negotiations could serve no useful purpose.

On September 17th the Prime Minister again met with the representatives of the owners and later the representatives of the men. The discussions continued all day, and on their conclusion new proposals were formulated by the Government for a settlement. These provided for district settlements, and the establishment, by Act of Parliament, of a National Arbitration Tribunal for reviewing all such matters as, prior to July 1925, had been customarily dealt with by national agreements.

The Government had found the owners firmly resolved not to enter into any national agreement, for reasons summarized on pages 133 and 134, and could not even induce them to meet the miners to discuss such an agreement.

The miners' leaders still adhered to their demand for a national agreement, and again said no to the new offer. They put forward fresh proposals, slightly modified, but on a national basis, and, therefore, not acceptable to the owners.

The Government was not prepared to compel the owners, by legislative action, to enter on national negotiations, and intimated to the miners that they were not prepared to go beyond their offer of the 17th, of which they were free to avail themselves by ordering district negotiations to be opened, these to be subject to revision by the National Tribunal, adding that the offer could not remain open indefinitely.

The signs of unrest and dissatisfaction with the policy of the Federation which had been manifesting themselves for some time in the districts now became intensified. More pits were being reopened, and larger numbers of men were drifting back to work on local terms.

The Federation Executive thereupon called another National Conference for September 29th, and at this it was decided to refer the Government proposals to the districts. This ballot resulted in an almost unanimous vote for rejection, and when the Conference resumed on October 7th it was faced with this and a demand from the Government for an immediate decision if the offer was not to be withdrawn. At this Conference the Nottinghamshire delegates, who had arranged for work to be resumed at certain collieries in their district, were expelled from the Conference. At the same time the Leicestershire delegates decided to abandon the struggle, and advised their members to return to work. The breakaway extended. The safety men re-affirmed their resolve to remain at their posts. The T.U.C. refused the request for an embargo on imported coal. The number of men at work by mid-October had increased to over 200,000.

The need for compromise was now apparent to the Miners' Executive, and after consultation with the General Council of the T.U.C. and their own districts they called at 10 Downing Street on November 5th and informed the Cabinet Coal Committee that they were now prepared, on certain conditions, to concede the principle of district negotiations. The Government obtained from the owners the extent to which they would be prepared to allow national principles to govern district settlements, and then formulated a statement of the national principles which the Cabinet considered should be observed in all district agreements, and submitted it to both sides.

Discussions on these continued for several days. Another Delegate Conference was held on November 13th, and decided to recommend all districts to accept the Government's terms. Voting in the districts commenced at once. On this date the Mines Department reported that 318,000 miners had returned to work.

When the Conference reassembled on November 19th, the voting showed a majority of 100,000 against acceptance of the Government proposals. Faced with this, the Conference carried a resolution recommending "all districts immediately to open negotiations with the coal-owners in their respective districts, with a view to arriving at agreements".

A memorandum was drawn up by the Executive for

the guidance of the districts setting out the principles which were to govern them in their negotiations with the owners and this was unanimously endorsed by the Conference.

Negotiations were at once commenced in the districts. The first agreement to be signed was on the Notts coalfield, where there had been the strongest opposition to the policy of the Federation. This was signed on November 21st, was not submitted to the Federation, and the Notts miners formed a new miners' union for purely industrial purposes in their own district. This is still in existence, but efforts to establish similar unions in other districts were not successful, the miners, if not now as enthusiastic in their support of the Federation, either remaining loyal to the latter or simply dropping out entirely from membership of any union.

The other districts speedily followed and by the end of November agreements had been completed in nearly all the districts and work resumed on district terms.

So ended the most disastrous stoppage in the history of the industry. The financial loss to the nation as a result is incalculable, but must have amounted to hundreds of millions. Neither can the suffering, poverty, and hardship so patiently borne by the miners and their wives and families out of loyalty to their leaders be estimated in any tangible terms. These are imponderable. In both cases, however, the price which had to be paid was a heavy one. At home the industry could and did recover. Abroad it was quite different. The stoppage gave our foreign competitors a golden opportunity of which they availed themselves to the full. Buyers in countries hitherto purchasing only British coal were forced to obtain supplies elsewhere.

Some of those markets have never been regained, and it is very doubtful if they ever will be.

The responsibility for the injury inflicted on the industry must be shared by all three parties to the dispute. The Government was gravely at fault in granting a subsidy from national funds without any stipulations as to how it was to be used (except to maintain wages somehow), for making the grant an unlimited one, for not making provision for some form of Treasury control, for allowing it to grow to such large proportions, and for not taking some action during its operation to prevent its misuse when it was common knowledge that it was not fulfilling its intended purpose. The owners utilized the subsidy for the purpose for which it was provided, that of maintaining wages at the 1924 level. The period was one of diminishing demand and keen competition both at home and abroad and the owners believed that the best way to get the industry back on to a sound economic basis as quickly as possible was to face up boldly to the new and difficult situation, to lower prices and thus, it was hoped, to increase sales.

A situation thus developed in which a struggle between producer and consumer for the benefit of the subsidy became the chief feature both at home and abroad. In such a contest, the odds were on the purchaser. He won handsomely, with the result that prices were forced down, the subsidy did little more than maintain wages at their pre-subsidy level, and when it ended left the industry in worse plight than ever.

For the maladministration of the subsidy and the situation it created, the miners' representatives had no responsibility. They had no share in deciding its method of application, for they had no voice in the executive control of the industry. This was, in part, their own fault. They would have had an effective voice had they accepted the offer made by the Government in 1920. That "great opportunity" was lost, and the power which it would have conferred on them had it been grasped was not available.

For the stoppage itself and its continuance for so long, however, the chief responsibility lies with the miners' leaders. Arrogant, bellicose, stubborn to the verge of stupidity, they would consider no compromise. They rejected every proposal for a settlement, and having led their followers to defeat, they refused, until the end, to face either the facts of the situation or the consequences of their own folly, finally throwing on the districts the odium of accepting terms much less favourable than could have been secured at the beginning without the loss of a day's work, or at any time during the seven months of the stoppage.

The end of the subsidy created a difficult position for all three parties. The dispute was an industrial one. The Government was simply a mediator. The Cabinet had given generously in order that the owners and men might have time to compose their differences, and the Prime Minister had emphatically declared that he was not going to be forced into taking political control of this one industry. The Government, whilst willing to assist in any way, regarded the question of a settlement as being primarily and principally a matter for employers and employed, as in any other industry.

The owners wanted to manage their own affairs in their own way. They were tired of Government intervention, sick of the continual political activity which interfered with the running of their industry, and the tendency of the Miners' Federation to fly to Downing

Street on the slightest pretext. They were convinced that the agitation was really against the existing system of private ownership, and that it was all part of a policy directed towards nationalization of the mines. They did not want a subsidy from public funds. Taking their stand on the report of the Royal Commission, they firmly believed the only hope for the industry was to boldly face the economic facts and reduce production costs so as to meet competition both at home and abroad. This, they averred, could only be achieved by a reduction in wages or an extension of hours, as the Royal Commission said, and there was no other way of meeting the immediate situation. It had to be done sometime, and it was better done at once, and done in districts where owners and men knew each other and knew each other's problems. On this they were adamant. The constitution of their association provided only for district settlements, and they would not alter it so as to enable them to meet the miners on a national basis.

The miners regarded the deplorable economic situation of the industry as being entirely due to the failure of the owners to organize the industry on such lines as would stop the reckless competition which they blamed for its plight, and so obtain higher prices for their product.

They looked upon the proposal to reduce wages or increase hours as being a backward step, one they must fight to the end. They attached great importance to the finding of the Royal Commission that there should be no lengthening of hours, but refused to accept the alternative suggested by the Commission, i.e. a temporary reduction of wages. They were badly led. In fact, the leadership of the miners in the ten years following the end of the war was probably the worst in the history of the Trade Union Movement, and the loyalty of the rank and file the most remarkable.

The Executive of the Federation stubbornly refused, until near the end, to compromise in any way on the two points which the Government, the Commission, and the owners all considered the crux of the problem. In turn, they rejected the proposals of the Government, the owners, the Samuel Memorandum, and their own colleagues. Throughout, they preferred to fight rather than negotiate, unless their demands were conceded in advance.

As the spokesmen of nearly a million trade unionists, they exercised great power both in the national assembly and in the councils of the Trade Union Movement. In both cases they over-estimated it, and in both cases failed to realize its limitations. Their arrogant and unyielding attitude alienated the sympathy of their fellow trade unionists, and in the attempt to coerce the Government into compelling the owners to accept their point of view they found, as others have found, and will find again, that no Government worthy of the name will permit its policy to be dictated by an outside body, and if it did, the British House of Commons would not tolerate it. They could have secured better terms for the men by accepting the Samuel Memorandum as a basis for negotiation early in the struggle (in May). Instead, they fought on a useless slogan and on "the women and children's stomachs", as their own President afterwards expressed it. They taxed the amazing loyalty of their followers until even that broke, weakened the Federation so that it emerged from the struggle with but a shadow of its former power and authority, deprived their own members of the protection they formerly were able to afford them and eventually placed on the shoulders of the district organizations the onus of obtaining the best terms they could in their respective districts.

The lesson of this experience was not lost on the miners' representatives. They have greatly modified their collective outlook; the personnel of the Executive has changed considerably; the Federation has regained something of its power and authority; they realize that if they have a good case they are more likely to triumph by reason and argument than by striking, while still holding the strike weapon in reserve.

That case has aroused great public sympathy and resulted in a better public understanding of the hazardous nature of their occupation and the inadequate reward received by the lower-paid workers for the service they render.

There is evident also a new spirit in the minds of the owners and a desire to lift the wages level in any way compatible with the prosperity of the industry and the general interest of the nation.

The Government can help in the directions indicated by the Samuel Commission, but there are limits to what it can or ought to do. It can no more impose a national agreement policy on the owners than it can impose compulsory arbitration on the men.

It can, however, through its Department of State, the Mines Department, do much to preserve amicable and friendly relationships between the owners and men, and if the new spirit is given full play and fair play, we should see fewer strikes or lock-outs in the future, and never again another stoppage with such appalling consequences as that of 1926.

CHAPTER IX

The Mining Industry Act, 1926—The Lewis Committee

THE MINING INDUSTRY ACT, 1926

THIS measure, placed on the Statute Book during the the period of the 1926 stoppage, deals with the reorganization of the industry.

Part 1 of the Act deals with amalgamation, and provides that where the owners of two or more undertakings agree to amalgamate, either totally or in part, they may prepare and submit a scheme for the purpose to the Board of Trade. It embodies regulations for the drafting of such schemes, and provides that the Board of Trade shall consider any such scheme submitted to it, and if satisfied that a prima facie case is made out that it makes for economy and efficiency, shall refer it to the Railway and Canal Commission. The Board of Trade is empowered to assist in formulating such schemes, if the owners desire it, and any scheme confirmed by the Railway and Canal Commission is binding on all parties. Except that one clause provides that two or more owners who are willing to amalgamate may include in such a scheme a proposal to absorb the collieries of any other undertaking which is unwilling to amalgamate, and submit it for approval, there is nothing of a compulsory nature in the Act dealing with reorganization or amalgamation.

Part 2 deals with "Working Facilities". Its principal object was to extend the facilities embodied in the Act of 1923 for the searching for or the working of minerals.

This part of the Act contained a very important provision empowering the Railway and Canal Commission to free the working of minerals from irksome restrictions or conditions imposed in a mining lease if they considered it in the national interest to do so. This admirable provision broke down in practice, being rendered nugatory by a decision of the Appeal Court in March 1935. See the note on Wayleaves on pages 215–16.

Part 3 deals with the Welfare Fund and provides for a 5 per cent duty on royalties, the proceeds to be paid over to the Welfare Fund Committee and utilized mainly for the provision of pithead baths. Its allocation is in the discretion of the Committee and no part is earmarked for use in any particular district.

Part 4 deals with recruitment for the industry and secures that in engaging persons over eighteen years of age for employment in the industry preference shall be given to those who were regularly employed in the industry prior to April 1926.

Parts 5 and 6 relate to Excess Payments, etc., under previous Acts of Parliament and also with the setting up of profit-sharing schemes in the industry.

THE LEWIS COMMITTEE

This Committee was appointed during the 1926 stoppage. Its official title was the "Departmenal Committee on Co-operative Selling in the Coal-Mining Industry". It was appointed on July 26th, the Chairman being Sir Frederick William Lewis, and the terms of reference "To enquire into and report upon the desirability and practicability of developing co-operative selling in the coal-mining industry and to make recommendations". In addition to the Chairman, there were ten members, all able and experienced public men.

The Committee issued its reports at the end of November, a majority report, and one by a minority of three of the eleven members. A memorandum was attached to the majority report in the name of the two Labour members, in which they express their agreement with the principle of organized marketing but dissent from their colleagues' conclusion against anything in the nature of general compulsion. They advocated a two years' trial on a voluntary basis, and then, if no substantial progress had been made, a scheme should be imposed on the whole of the industry.

The majority report itself expressed the view that organized marketing was desirable, but that it could only be carried out in districts where the owners showed a general desire for it, and then only if the industry could be consolidated into a smaller number of units by amalgamation. It should be developed voluntarily, firstly among neighbouring collieries, then by districts. In the latter case where 75 per cent of the owners supported such a scheme powers should be vested in a tribunal to make it compulsory. Co-ordination of the district schemes would be the ultimate objective.

In the export trade local selling pools and closer co-operation between the exporters and the coal-owners should, the Committee reported, be developed.

The minority report was against co-operative selling on the ground that free and open competition was the system best suited to the needs of the industry. It pointed out that the main object was to compel the consumer to pay higher prices, that control of output was essential for this object, that limitation of output was opposed to the best interests of the industry and the country, which was high production at low cost. Such a policy, in the view of the signatories, must "sterilize the development of the coal industry, hamper the expansion of individual activity, and depress the standard of living all round".

The Committee had confined its enquiry to those within the industry itself, and the reports reveal the wide divergence of opinion on the principle and methods of organized marketing.

The report contains some useful information, but naturally lost some of its value by reason of the failure of its members to agree.

CHAPTER X

THE YEARS 1926–1936

THE end of the 1926 stoppage marked the close of an epoch in the history of coal mining. It was a period of exceptional difficulty, as well as being one of almost continual strife, and the events of those seven remarkable years have left their impress on every phase of the industry.

By December 1926 work had been resumed on district terms in all the coalfields. The miners had been defeated, not by the Government or by the owners, but by the hard economic facts of the situation. Had these been recognized and acknowledged by their leaders at the beginning and a temporary adjustment made in hours or wages, all the loss and suffering entailed by the struggle could have been avoided.

With the return to work, importation of coal ceased (20 million tons had come in during the stoppage) and the industry gradually got back to something like normal conditions. The strength of the Federation was greatly impaired, and for a time there were serious complaints of alleged victimization and lack of tolerance on the part of some of the owners and managers. For a while, this and the general dissatisfaction caused by the terms of settlement led to considerable unrest and the threat of further militant action by the miners. From time to time there were isolated disputes in the districts, but they were all local and settled locally. The industry made a good recovery. The need for replenishing stocks stimulated demand, and by the end of 1927 production had exceeded that of 1925, while exports also reached the 1925 figure. The year 1928 saw exports maintained, but the home demand declined and production decreased by 14 million tons; 1929 saw a partial world recovery and another stroke of luck for the export trade in the freezing over of the Baltic. Both at home and abroad demand increased and production exceeded that of 1927. The stimulus, however, was only a temporary one, and in 1930 there began the decline which continued until arrested by an increase in the home demand in 1934.

In 1929 a General Election had taken place and for the second time a Socialist Government took office. The Act of 1930 regulating output and prices was placed on the Statute Book (see page 97). Its effect has always caused controversy, but whatever the causes the first year of its operation (1931) saw a big reduction in demand both at home and abroad. Exports fell by 12 millions in one year and production dropped heavily. The decline in the home demand persisted in 1932 and 1933, but exports fell only slightly, being already very low indeed. Production in 1933 decreased to 207 millions, the lowest for many years.

In 1934 there was an increase in production of 14 millions due to an increase in the demand at home, and this has been maintained in 1935. Exports appear to have become stabilized at somewhere round about 39 millions. The export position is dealt with on another page.

During the ten years that have elapsed since this disastrous stoppage, there have been many local and some district stoppages, but none on a national scale. Wages have become almost stabilized, but earnings have been low on account of short time, and the miners, by the end of 1935, were in almost exactly the same position as in 1914, allowing for the difference in the value of money wages in purchasing power.

In 1932 the Federation, strongly dissatisfied with the low wages received by a proportion of its members, launched a campaign for an all-round increase, and in October 1935 tabled their demand for a flat-rate increase of 2s. per shift for men and 1s. per shift for boys. Their case, this time calmly and reasonably presented, aroused a great deal of public sympathy. By cleverly synchronizing the ballot vote on the question of whether they should strike for the rise in wages with the General Election of 1935, the Executive, in addition, created a psychology in the coalfields which resulted in their regaining in the House of Commons almost all the mining seats they had lost in 1931, largely by means of the promise of the 2s. increase in wages.

The owners recognized the justice of the miners' claim to some increase and undertook to set up selling agencies for the purpose of obtaining better prices to enable them to grant the increase. Some of the large consumers were persuaded to agree to an increase in price, even on existing contracts, if assured that the addition would be passed on to the workers. On this, the owners offered immediate increases in all the districts, varying in amount from a few pence to a shilling, with a promise to review the position after the results of the new selling agencies were known. The offer being unacceptable to the miners, an improved one was submitted by the owners, and accepted by a miners' Delegate Conference on January 24, 1936.

The dispute is dealt with on p. 132 et seq.

CHAPTER XI

THE 1930 ACT

THIS Act was placed on the Statute Book in 1930 during the lifetime of the second Socialist Government (1929–1931). It provides for "regulating and facilitating the production, supply, and sale of coal", and for the "constitution and functions of a Coal Mines National Industrial Board".

Under the Act the country is divided for administrative purposes into twenty-one districts. In each of these districts there is an "Executive Board" composed of colliery owners elected by a vote of all owners in that district. The "Executive Board" is charged, under the Act, with the duty of regulating the production, supply, and sale of coal in its district.

There is a Central Council composed of representatives of the owners from all the districts, and the Act defines the powers and functions of both the Executive Boards and the Central Council. Both these bodies have statutory authority, while the Mining Association is a purely voluntary association with no statutory powers.

The main object of the Act is to ensure that coal production is distributed as evenly as possible, having regard to their very great differences, over all the districts. For this purpose the Act empowered the Central Council to allocate to each district, after consultation with the Executive Board, a maximum output for the district. For this purpose, the Central

Council, when the Act first came into operation, set up a standard period and on this the first "district allocations" were based.

Every district was required to submit to the Board of Trade a "scheme" for the production, supply, and sale of coal in that district. Each district having received its allocation from the Central Council, it is the duty of the Executive Board in the district to allocate to each coal mine in the district its "quota" of the allocation for the period for which the latter is granted.

Powers are vested in the Central Council for the periodical review of the allocations to the districts and for amending the allocations at any time, if satisfied, on the representations of the Executive Board, that it is necessary to do so in order to meet an increased demand for coal. Penalties may be imposed by the Central Council on any Executive Board which without authority exceeds its allocation or for contravening or failing to comply with the provisions of the central scheme. The Executive Boards are required to make regular returns of output, accounts, etc., to the Central Council as the latter may consider necessary for the operation of the central scheme.

The Executive Boards in the districts are empowered to fix the "quota" for every coal mine and for every class of coal produced in that district and to fix for every class of coal a minimum price below which it shall not be sold. Penalties may be imposed on the owner of any coal mine who exceeds his "quota" or who contravenes or fails to comply with the provisions of the district scheme. The Board may require the owner of any coal mine to furnish such information as it may consider necessary for the operation of the scheme, or call for the production and inspection of the books and accounts relating to any coal mine by an independent accountant on behalf of the Executive Board. The Board is charged with the duty of fairly distributing not only the regular "quota" but also any additional allocation received from the Central Council during the "quota" period, and may make arrangements for the sale or transfer or pooling of any unused "quota" so that it may be available for the use of those coal mines requiring it towards the end of the "quota" period, when the demand for some particular class of coal may have been heavy and some mines may have exhausted their "quota".

Provision must be made in each district scheme for an appeal to arbitration by any owner in any district who may feel aggrieved by any act or omission of the Executive Board in his district.

The Act provides also for the setting up of a National Committee of Investigation for the purpose of enquiring into any complaint made against the operation of the central scheme and for the establishment of District Committees of investigation in every district to enquire into any complaint against the operation of the district schemes.

Very extensive powers are given to the Executive Boards for dealing with all the matters relating to the industry in their district, powers which it is not possible to describe here in detail. All the schemes in which they are embodied, however, are subject to the approval of the Board of Trade and before the schemes can be altered or amended the modifications must be approved by the Board of Trade, and a draft order giving that approval laid before both Houses of Parliament.

The two chief features of Part I of the Act are that

the Central Council has power to regulate production in every coalfield and the Executive Boards have the power to do the same in their districts, and in addition the power to fix the minimum prices at which every class of coal produced shall be sold, both in the home and export market.

Part 2 of the Act deals with the reorganization of the industry. Under this part of the Act there is a Coal Mines Reorganization Commission composed of five members, all debarred from having any financial interest in any coal-mining undertaking or any business supplying or selling coal or the manufacture or sale of by-products or machinery or plant for coal mining.

The worst feature of the Act was that it embodied two contradictory principles. Part 1 provided for spreading employment over as wide an area as possible by giving to each district and to each coal mine a tonnage quota beyond which it was not allowed to produce.

On the other hand Part 2 aimed at obtaining increased efficiency through amalgamations, the direct result of which must inevitably be concentration on the most efficient units, the closing of redundant mines, and an increase in the number of unemployed miners.

The chief task of the Reorganization Commission is to promote amalgamations between any two or more undertakings in any district.

For this purpose the Commission is empowered, if it considers that an amalgamation scheme should be prepared under Part 1 of the Mining Industry Act of 1926, to require the owners of the coal mines concerned to prepare such a scheme for submission to the Board of Trade, and in the event of the owners failing to do so the Commission shall themselves prepare and submit such a scheme, which, if confirmed by the Railway and Canal Commission, shall be deemed to comply with the Act of 1926 and carry the full force of law.

The Act sets forth the grounds on which the Railway and Canal Commission may confirm such schemes, and directs particularly that they shall not confirm such a scheme unless satisfied that it is in the national interest and that "the terms of the scheme are fair and equitable to all persons affected thereby". Section 13, Subsection 2(*b*) lays down that the Railway and Canal Commission shall not confirm a scheme unless satisfied that it "will not be financially injurious to any of the undertakings proposed to be amalgamated unless the scheme contains provisions for the purchase, at a price to be fixed in default of agreement, by arbitration of any such undertakings". The Board of Trade is given power, under certain conditions, to confirm *voluntary* amalgamations without reference to the Railway and Canal Commission (see chapter on Amalgamations, page 147).

Part 2 of the Act is really an amplification of the Act of 1926, and it is expressly stipulated that "this section shall be construed as one with Part 1 of the Act of 1926".

Part 3 deals with the hours of work and provides for the making of agreements between the owners and the workmen, regulating these subject to confirmation by the Board of Trade.

Part 4 provides for the setting up of a Coal Mines National Industrial Board of seventeen members to be appointed by the Board of Trade after consultation with the Mining Association, the Miners' Federation, the Trades Union Congress, the Federation of British

Industries, the Co-operative Union, and the Confederation of Employers' Organizations.

The functions of the proposed National Board are to supervise the regulation of wages, to confirm any agreements entered into between owners and men, and to deal with any disputes arising in the districts which the districts themselves have not been able to settle. This part of the Act has never come into operation.

The Board of Trade is required to report every year to Parliament on the schemes in operation under the Act.

The duration of the Act was originally for two years only, but in 1931 its main provisions were extended for one year with a guarantee that wages would be maintained at the existing rates for that period by the Coal Mines Act of 1931. In 1932 the duration of the original Act was extended by a further period of five years and it is now due to expire in 1937.

Just as the settlement of the 1926 dispute marked the close of an epoch in the history of the industry, so the passing of the 1930 Act ushered in a new one. The principle of the regulation of hours by the State was established by the passing of the Eight Hours Act in 1908, and since 1909 the hours of labour in the mines have been regulated by law.

The principle of the minimum standard of wages in the industry was established by the Minimum Wages Act of 1912, and since then the wages paid have been regulated by law in accordance with the principle of a minimum wage.

The Act of 1930 extended the principle of State regulation to the production and sale of coal and, by giving statutory authority to the owners of coal mines to regulate output and prices, put an end to the system of free and unfettered enterprise under which the industry had been conducted for hundreds of years, except between 1917 and 1921.

After the 1926 stoppage, and particularly in 1928, when output fell to a figure 50 million tons below that of 1913, the colliery owners, alarmed by this heavy fall, were engaged in the framing of a voluntary scheme for regulating and controlling production. In 1929, when the Socialist Government came into office, the colliery owners had already worked out a system of tonnage allocation by means of a "quota" which was supported by a majority. The debates in the House of Commons revealed clearly that the difficulties in the way of regulating output and prices by statute were certainly no less formidable than those in the way of voluntary agreement. The provisions of the Bill were fiercely criticized, particularly those which had the effect of keeping alive the inefficient pits and the fixation of minimum prices. Some of the most trenchant criticism came from Sir Herbert Samuel, the Chairman of the Royal Commission of 1925. Amongst other hard things he said: "Efficiency? This is the endowment and entrenchment of inefficiency. Rationalization? This is the irrationalization of the coal mines." (Official Report, House of Commons, December 17, 1929.)

The very imperfect measure had a narrow escape on second reading on December 19, 1929, when the Liberal Party voted against it, and owing to the absence of a number of Conservative members it scraped through by only eight votes, 281 to 273.

Between the second and third readings political considerations once again had a powerful influence on the future of the industry. The Government was a minority Government. Defeat on a measure of first-class importance would have created a first-class political crisis, involving the resignation of the Government. Although maintained in office by Liberal votes, the Government was not on particularly friendly terms with the Liberals in the House, and the latter themselves were not at all happy about this Bill. They demanded certain concessions, and, obtaining these, undertook in return not to oppose the passage of the measure. On the third reading on April 3, 1930, they abstained from voting and the Bill passed with a majority of 43. The Act was, therefore, in its final form, a sort of political compromise which satisfied no one and antagonized many, embodying a milk-and-water Socialism which established a vague and indirect measure of State control without any real State authority or any definite State responsibility.

Having thus passed safely through the stormy waters of political controversy and the more dangerous shoals of political compromise, the Act became law and came into operation on January 1, 1931.

The Act was no sooner on the Statute Book than the difficulty of applying it became apparent. The rivalry between the districts created some trouble with regard to the allocation of tonnages to each area, whilst in the districts themselves, the fixing of the quota for each coal producer or colliery on a basis satisfactory to all proved more difficult than had been anticipated by the framers of the measure. As its defects became more apparent in operation, the lack of any co-operation between the units in the districts or any co-ordination between the districts themselves became the cause of a great deal of friction, whilst the allocation of quota (which became a marketable asset) to the inefficient collieries at the expense of the efficient was a further cause of trouble.

The coming into force of the Act synchronized with a heavy decline in the export trade (see pages 95 and 183). The exporting districts, deprived of their market abroad, turned their attention to the home market, and taking full advantage of the low rates of freight for sea-borne coal by coastal shipment captured quite a considerable share of the home trade, to which, they claimed, they were not only entitled on economic grounds, but also as compensation for the loss of their overseas trade.

Between 1929 and 1933 the output fell by 51 million tons and the lack of demand greatly enhanced the difficulty of bringing the new schemes into operation. With supply in excess of demand, prices failed to rise —there was in fact a slight fall; competition for orders in a restricted home market and a fiercely competitive one abroad led to wholesale evasion of the minimum-price provisions of the Act.

In June 1933 the Secretary for Mines indicated in the House of Commons that his Department was quite aware of the fact and gave a list of the methods adopted for the purpose. The evasions were due to the lack of effective control in the districts, to dissatisfaction in some of the districts because of the differing levels of the minimum-price schedules, and to the absence of any measure of co-ordination of prices between the districts.

In 1934 the Government decided to tighten up the machinery of the Act in order to prevent these evasions and to ensure co-ordination of minimum prices between the districts. The Bill was introduced, but on the colliery owners undertaking to amend their schemes in the required directions it was withdrawn. The central scheme was amended, and came into operation on January 1, 1935. At the same time inland quota was separated from export, and the Central Council was empowered to make separate allocations to the districts for special classes of coal.

In July of 1935 a big step towards eliminating unnecessary competition in their own district was taken in Lancashire by the setting up of a voluntary central selling organization. Later in the year the demand of the Mineworkers' Federation for increased wages led to a general recognition of the fact that any advance in wages was impossible without some form of centralized selling and a substantial rise in the level of prices.

On October 31, 1935, the colliery owners gave an undertaking to the Government that by the middle of 1936 an organization for the complete and effective control of the sale of coal would be set up in each coal-mining district, with central co-ordination. The Government stipulated that the district schemes must:

(1) "Cover all the coal-owners in each district and must have a measure of permanency."
(2) "Effectively prevent inter-colliery competition."
(3) "Be so drawn that evasions cannot exist."

On June 10, 1936, the Central Scheme Amendment Order was presented to the House of Commons and on June 24th received the approval of the House. The order not only gave the Central Council wider powers, but also laid it down that those powers must be used.

On the same day the draft orders for the amendment of the district schemes were presented to the House and on August 1, 1936, the new selling arrangements came into operation. These and amalgamations are dealt with separately.

As happens so frequently in the case of legislation which has aroused fierce controversy, this Act of Parliament neither realized the hopes of its friends nor justified the fears of its opponents. Thoroughly unsound in principle economically, it established a system which limited and impeded private enterprise and at the same time embodied the worst features of State intervention and control.

The best that can be said for it, as it operated during the period 1931 to 1936, is that by the quota system it "spread the work", and by its minimum-price provisions, evaded though they were in many cases, it helped to prevent a much bigger fall in the price of coal in the years of the depression which followed immediately on its enactment, when the prices of other products tumbled very heavily indeed, and coal declined only slightly in its average selling price.

As a matter of general interest it should be noted that a General Election took place in 1931 before the Act had been long in operation. The Socialists were heavily defeated and a National Government has been in office ever since.

CHAPTER XII

DISTRICT AGREEMENTS

SINCE 1926 the conditions governing the relationship between owners and men have been settled by representatives of the two parties in the districts, subject to the two governing principles laid down by Parliament in respect of minimum wages and maximum hours of labour. The terms are embodied in a series of district agreements. There are twenty-one districts.

The same general principles are incorporated in all the agreements, with variations to suit the conditions of each. Whilst other matters are covered by the agreements, the most important of them all are the provisions made for the disposal of the proceeds and the regulation and payment of wages. In this connection the features common to all are:

(1) A basis rate of wages which is the foundation on which is built up the figures of actual wages paid.
(2) A fixed minimum percentage added to the basis rates whether the proceeds permit it or not.
(3) An agreed method of ascertaining the amount of the proceeds, certified by two firms of independent accountants acting for owners and men respectively.
(4) A provision for dividing, in agreed proportions, the proceeds, and any surplus remaining after adding the minimum percentage to wages.
(5) The creation of a "deficiency account," being the amount paid in wages under (3) in excess of the amount permitted by the proceeds.

(6) A "subsistence" wage payable to the lower-paid workers irrespective of proceeds or any other consideration.

The differences in the agreements are:

(1) In the amount and terms of the basis rates.
(2) In the amount of the minimum percentage to be added to the basis rates whether proceeds permit it or not.
(3) In the figures governing the division of the proceeds and surplus proceeds between capital and labour.
(4) In the period covered by the ascertainments.
(5) In the method of dealing with the "deficiency account".
(6) In the amount of the subsistence wage.

The Basis Rates: These have been fixed as the result of many years' experience of local conditions in each district. The rates in Northumberland and Durham were fixed in 1879; that of Scotland in 1888. The majority (12) date from 1911, and the most recent (Forest of Dean) from 1919.

The Fixed Minimum Percentage: This has also been fixed in the districts as the result of experience. It varies with the districts, and can be raised or lowered by mutual agreement.

The Ascertainments: Proceeds are determined by the joint accountants, the books of every colliery undertaking being open for inspection for the purpose. Wages are the amounts payable under the basis rates plus the fixed minimum percentage. Other costs are included on a mutually agreed basis. If the proceeds are not sufficient to pay wages on the basis rate plus the minimum percentage, the difference is made up by the owners and carried forward to the deficiency account. If the proceeds are more, the surplus is divisible between wages and capital. The result of the ascertainments governs wages for the next ascertainment period.

Ratio of Wages to Profits: The district agreements provide that the proceeds shall be divided in certain proportions between wages and profits. In the majority of the districts the ratio is 85 per cent to wages and 15 per cent to capital. In the others it is either 87 to 13 or 86 to 14. In two districts there is a slight difference in the ratio when applied to the "standard" proceeds and when applied to the "surplus" proceeds. Kent, as a new coalfield, has a formula of its own for determining the ratio. Where there is a surplus after allowing for wages on the basis rates plus the fixed additional minimum percentage, the agreements provide for its being divided in varying proportions, but the arrangements made for the recoupment of deficiencies have prevented any increase in the minimum percentage in most districts.

Ascertainment Period: The period covered by the ascertainments varies. In nine cases it is three months, in six it is one month, in two it is two months, and in two it is twelve months.

Deficiency Account: This is the term applied to the difference between the amount actually allocated to wages under the fixed-minimum arrangement and the amount actually available from the proceeds when the latter do not provide sufficient money to pay the minimum agreed on. The deficiency is made up to the minimum by the owners and carried forward in the "Deficiency Account". Thus if the wages paid in Durham under the previous ascertainment were £1,000,000 for a month in which the proceeds fell short by £100,000 of the amount required to pay the wages due on the basis rates plus the fixed additional minimum of 65 per cent, the £100,000 is provided by the owners and added to the amount of the "Deficiency Account". The district is then "on the minimum". In every district this deficiency is carried forward. In about half the districts it is carried forward indefinitely; in four or five it is cancelled annually; in others part of the surplus is applied for recoupment. The total of deficiencies in all the districts now amounts to many millions, and is never likely to be repaid in full.

The Subsistence Wage: This is the daily wage paid to the lowest class of labour. No definite information is available as to the number of men paid on this basis. Neither basis or rates of payment are the same in all the districts. In some it is a fixed figure per day. In others the wages paid are made up to the "subsistence level" by an allowance of so much per shift, which also varies. In many cases there are allowances for children, for youths who are the sole support of the family, for dependants, etc. All these allowances are merged in the wages bill, and according to the Samuel Commission absorbed less than 2 per cent of the wages bill. As to the subsistence wage itself the Commission reported: "No serious problem arises . . . it affects in any case a small proportion of all the workpeople employed."

It will thus be seen that the core and kernel of the wages question in the district agreements are the available proceeds and the minimum percentage. Once the former are sufficient to pay the latter, the sharing of the surplus comes automatically into operation, and if that position is maintained there can be no additions to the deficiency account. The accumulated deficiencies should be got rid of on some agreed principle capable of application, as far as is practicable, to all the districts.

As for the basis rates themselves, they must always be settled in the districts, where the local knowledge makes it easy. The basis rate may be a piece one or a day one. It varies from district to district, from pit to pit, from seam to seam, and even in the same seam. It is fixed on the spot and can be adjusted on the spot to meet changing conditions. The method of fixing it is well understood by the workers, and, complicated as it may appear to the outsider, it works quite smoothly. New basis rates are often required, for conditions are always changing. A new pit may be opened, a new seam worked, or an old one reopened, working on time rates may be altered to working on piece rates, new types of machinery may be introduced for the first time, or the entire pit may be closed for a period, and the whole method of winning coal revolutionized by the installation of new equipment throughout. In all these cases, the basis rates are agreed between the representatives of the owners and the men on the spot, and provision is made for settling any differences which may arise in fixing them.

These are matters which can only be settled in the districts, for their bewildering variety makes anything approaching uniformity impossible. Even all the changes which have come over the industry in recent years have left unaffected the fundamental fact that the problem of making a pit an economic productive unit is a district problem, and the terms under which it can be achieved are best settled in the districts by those who know local conditions.

The new Joint Standing Consultative Committee may be able to agree upon "general principles applicable to the determination of wages by district agreements", but it is inevitable that the basis rates must be fixed locally. Co-ordination of prices, the "sharing of trade", and the new selling agencies may do a great deal to make conditions more uniform throughout the coalfields, but it is very doubtful whether, in this industry, there can ever be the conditions which permit of either complete uniformity in earnings or in wages variations. The addition of a uniform 13⅓ per cent increase on the minimum percentage in 1924 brought immediate trouble, and was one of the chief causes of the stoppage of 1926, while the demand for a flat-rate increase of wages in 1935 was one which it was found impossible to concede. The workers in the industry acknowledge the lack of uniform conditions by their insistence on the retention of the cavilling system in some districts. This is a method of roughly "ironing out" the unequal opportunities for wage earning which are created by the geological differences in the seams. Lots are drawn at stated intervals, so that all the piece workers have the same chance of securing a working-place in the best seams. When the "cavils" are drawn and the hewers and coal cutters have to move to a new working-place, the whole work of the pit is disorganized, and the net result is the loss of a day's, or even two days', output in every cavilling period, which is generally a quarterly one.

This again is a district question. It is an old custom, and old customs die harder in the mining industry than in any other. If the miners' leaders, however, are in earnest in their desire for increased efficiency, they should consider the abandonment of this and other out-of-date district or county customs which reduce efficiency, and in doing so reduce wages also.

The difficulties in the way of equalizing the rates of pay of the workers for the same class of work in the different districts are inherent in the industry, and some elasticity must be permitted in the application of the "general principles" to the settlement of wages in the districts.

A good illustration of the difficulty was afforded in 1921, when the "national pool" was under discussion. It was suggested that the principle might be carried a stage further by its application to the earnings of the piece workers in each pit, so that those who had the luck to draw a "good cavil" should share that luck with their less fortunate workmates by pooling all earnings, but the proposal met with a very cool reception indeed.

Great as are these district variations they need not prevent the application of the "general principles" to wages, but the differences should be more frankly acknowledged by the Mineworkers' Federation by discouraging the frequent demands for uniform rates of pay on a national basis applicable to all the districts, and by ceasing to make claims for flat-rate increases for all workers in all districts, irrespective of economic position, or geological differences, or present earnings, claims which are not only unfair to the poorly paid workers, but must inevitably lead to disappointment and recrimination when, as in 1935, they cannot be granted on a uniform basis.

There has been already a substantial rise in the general level of miners' wages since the settlement of January 24, 1936. There is hope of a further increase, but if the best results are to be obtained from the selling agencies and the new spirit which has been evident in the recent negotiations due regard must be paid to all the varying factors in the conduct of the industry.

The results of the working of the agreements so far as wages and output are concerned are set out in the quarterly and annual summaries issued by the Mines Department, and in these, for purposes of convenience, the twenty-one districts are grouped into nine.

CHAPTER XIII

Wages—Short-Time Working—Overtime

WAGES

THE mining industry is the only great industry in which there operates the principle of the sharing of profits between employers and employed. It is of little use, however, having profit-sharing if there are no profits to share. Off and on, this has been the position of the mining industry since the scheme was initiated. Wages and profits, even when shared, can only come out of the proceeds of the industry, and the selling price of coal has been so low, during the period that the system has operated, that there has been no margin worth speaking of between the costs of production and the proceeds to divide in the agreed proportions. Wages, for the past few years, have thus become almost stabilized, and stabilized, in the case of the lowest-paid workmen, on a scale which, when short time is worked, means real hardship and privation. In the case of the better-paid workers the wages paid compare favourably with those paid in other industries, and when measured by that standard, or the cost of living index figure, are not inadequate for the maintenance of a reasonable standard of life, but even in their case are not sufficient when short time has to be worked. A full week's work in the pits means either five and half or six shifts per week. If all the workers in the industry were fully and regularly employed on this basis they would not be so badly off, except for the subsistence-wage men and the men engaged in the uneconomic pits which ought to be closed down, but are artificially kept alive, and in which the seams are so thin, or the working conditions in other respects so difficult, that it is not possible for the piece workers to make a decent living, and they drop back on to the minimum, with possibly the added hardship of short time.

In the official reports dealing with the industry the wage earners are referred to as the workers "in and about" the pits. In the public mind, however, they are all "miners", thanks very largely to the popular Press and the publicity given to their industry during the last quarter of a century. As a matter of fact, the men engaged in the coal industry cannot and ought not to be lumped into one bunch or category and all loosely described as "miners".

At every colliery there is employed a greatly diversified assortment of labour, some of it skilled, some semi-skilled, and some unskilled. There are skilled craftsmen who are not "miners" at all, but without whose services the wheels would never revolve. There are surface workers with multifarious duties, all necessary to the successful working of the pit, but who rarely or never go below. And even below ground, there are many employed whose services are essential, but who are not "miners" in the sense that they are coal getters. The Samuel Commisson reported that for every hundred workers at the coal face, one hundred and forty-five were at work elsewhere.

The earnings of all, however, are lumped together in the summaries of results issued by the Mines Department, and the total divided by the number of men employed over a given period. The result is then given as the "average earnings per man shift worked".

Average Earnings

Like averages in many other spheres of human activity, "average earnings" in the mining industry are useful in that the figures serve as a rough guide to the general economic situation of the workers in the industry, as an indication of whether it is getting better or worse, and as a basis for comparison with the average earnings of the workers in other industries.

They show the variation in the average earnings in the districts but they conceal the differences in the earnings of the individual workers, and in particular they do not show the earnings of the low-paid worker, which was really the cause of the 1935–1936 dispute.

The average earnings per man shift worked vary from 10s. 9¾d. in North Derby to 9s. 0½d. in Cumberland, the average for the country being 9s. 7½d. (including allowances in kind) (1935 figures, Ministry of Mines Summary). The earnings of the hewers or coal getters are much higher than this, rising in good seams to as much as 20s. per shift, so that these averages must hide a number of cases where wages are much too low. There are two other factors which cannot be overlooked in an endeavour to get the picture right. The miners complain that these averages include the wages of all officials below the under-manager. These officials, however, are not paid much more than the well-placed coal hewer, and as their numbers are comparatively small, their effect on the average cannot be appreciable.

On the other hand, these averages include the earnings of the boys and the youths under 20.

According to the Ministry of Mines there were employed "in and about" the mines in 1934 (97 per cent of the industry) 738,000 persons, of whom 30,000 were boys between 14 and 16, and 80,000 youths under 20 (Mines Department Summary).

This leaves a total of 628,000 adult workers. The total number of man shifts worked was 186,385,000, an average of 252 per person employed. The total wages bill was £85,289,000. If we allow a weekly wage of 15s. per week for the boys and 25s. for the youths, the total wages bill for the 110,000 is just £6,000,000 for the year. This leaves £79,000,000 for the 618,000 adult workers. A simple calculation will show that by excluding the boys and youths the average earnings for the adult workers is not 9s. 1·82d. as shown in the summary (all workers) but exactly 10s. per man shift. This is 10d. per shift more than shown. The average number of shifts worked (252) is 4·84 per week and this multiplied by 10d. gives an addition of 4s. per week to the average earnings of the adult worker.[1]

In a speech at Ashbridge on July 21, 1936, Mr. W. A. Lee, Secretary of the Mining Association, gave some interesting figures for the first quarter of 1936. He said average gross earnings of all wage earners, including juveniles, was 10s. 3½d. per shift. For all adults underground the average figure was about 11s. 9d., and for adults at the coal face about 12s. 9d. The average cash earnings (all wage earners) were £2 10s. 9d. per week. The corresponding figure for all adults underground was £3 0s. 0d., and for adults at the coal face £3 5s. 0d., all three figures being exclusive of allowances in kind.

Even these good averages, however, do not get over the fact that there are still too many low-paid workers.

[1] The 1935 figures are slightly higher. See Appendix VI.

Averages do not interest them. What they are concerned with is the amount of money in the pay packet which they receive each week.

The curse of the industry as at present organized is short time. When told that the "average" earnings per man shift are a certain figure the tendency of those unacquainted with the facts is to multiply that figure by five and a half or six and from the resulting amount conclude that the miners cannot be so badly off after all. For a full year's work on this basis, the number of shifts worked would be 280 or 306 respectively, allowing in each case six days for holidays. In 1934, however, the total number of shifts worked averaged only 252, or 4·84 per week, and in some districts it was less. In the first six months of 1935 the average was only 4·84, and for the year 4·92. These averages *must* include a fairly large number of cases in which the number of shifts worked was only four or just under four. If he is on the minimum, or worse still, on subsistence rates, a man's earnings for that week will be four times the minimum to which he is entitled, or four times the subsistence rate prevailing in the district. In the county of Durham, for example, the minimum is 7s. 1½d. and the subsistence rate is 6s. 6½d. This gives for four shifts in the case of the minimum, 28s. 6d., and in the case of the subsistence rate, 26s. 2d., and from this there are the "offtakes" to be deducted. The effect on wages of working short time is thus severely felt, and it must be remembered also that the wage earner who works four days per week is not entitled to draw unemployment benefit.

In an enquiry which I made in 1936 at six collieries in the Notts and Derby coalfield, I found that the average earnings of the piece workers fluctuated between 15s. 5d. and 20s. 5d. per shift, whilst the datal workers (including boys) averaged 12s. 8½d. per shift.

The value of these very satisfactory "earnings per man shift" was, however, completely lost because the average working time of the collieries was just a little over four days per week.

The actual average "cash earnings" in 1934 were, for the year, £115 11s. 6d. per person employed for the whole country, the highest being in Scotland, £133 2s. 8d., and the lowest in Durham, £104 19s. 2d. These are exclusive of allowances in kind, which vary from 0·36d. in Lancashire and 0·39d. in Scotland, to 1s. 1·10d. in Durham, per shift. The high figure in Durham is due to the fact that there and in Northumberland free houses (or rent allowance in lieu thereof) are part of the agreement, as well as free coal.

If the same basis be taken for the "cash earnings" of the boys and youths as taken for the "earnings per man shift" and a similar calculation is made, then the corrected average figure of "cash earnings" for all adult workers "in and about" the mines for the year 1934 is £127 16s. 7d., or about £2 9s. 0d. per week, exclusive of allowances in kind (1935 was a little higher).

These figures show quite clearly that the worst feature in the wages position in the industry is the low cash earnings of a number of the men (an unduly large proportion in the poorer districts and in particular in the exporting districts), due in part to the low selling prices, the working of uneconomic pits, and short time. All these factors operate most harshly in the case of the lowest-paid men and result in many cases in pitifully low cash wages. A few weeks' short time may be borne patiently, as it often is in these cases, but when it becomes a regular feature of the industry it becomes insupportable and calls for drastic remedies.

The core of the problem being the cash earnings of the lowest-paid grades of labour, the demand for a flat-rate increase of 2s. per shift for adults and 1s. for juveniles in 1935 was a great mistake on the part of the Federation. The wages costs of the districts vary from 6s. 11d. per ton to 10s. 4d. per ton, and in addition there is in every district a big gap between the earnings of the well-paid coal getter and the datal worker on the subsistence wage. There are other varying factors, such as a difference of 8 cwt. in the output per person employed per shift, to which attention has already been drawn, and their combined effect is to make the just application of a flat-rate increase in all the districts a quite impracticable proposal. The Executive of the Federation in asking for it probably had in mind a previous occasion on which a flat-rate increase of 2s. per shift was conceded. This was in 1919, immediately after the Sankey Commission, but they have overlooked the fact that the mines were then under State control. Wages and profits were guaranteed by the taxpayer, which made it easy, too easy, in fact, for the efficient conduct of the industry, as subsequent events proved.

SHORT-TIME WORKING

The selling agencies ought to result in a fair and reasonable increase in prices, now too low, and thus correct the first of these features. The two second are interlocked. The industry is too large. Its output capacity under existing conditions is about 260 million tons. Demand is stabilized at 220 to 230 millions and there is little hope of any substantial increase. For good or evil a deliberate policy of "spreading the work available" has been adopted, each district being allotted the task of producing a certain quantity and no more, without the special authority of the Central Council. Each colliery has its "quota" and must not produce more without the sanction of the district council. In this respect the modern, up-to-date, well-equipped mines, with thick seams easily and economically worked, are no better off than their less efficient neighbours. They are thus deprived of one of the greatest incentives to cheap production, the right to work to 100 per cent capacity. If they exhaust their quota before the end of the quota period they must apply to the district board for a further allocation. If it is refused they must buy quota from those who have not been able to dispose of their allotted quantity. If no quota is available for purchase they must cease production until they receive their new allocation or be fined 2s. 6d. per ton for over-production. If they do succeed in buying quota the charge (3d., 6d., 9d., or 1s. per ton) must be charged against their production costs.

This is a policy deliberately embarked upon under the 1930 Act in the national interest. It keeps open the uneconomic units and prevents the expansion of the economic. The less efficient are kept alive and the result is short time at some period through the year at nearly all.

If it is in the national interest that these mines should be prevented from going out of production with all the social consequences involved, then the nation must accept the situation so created and be prepared to meet it. If the alternative policy were adopted—the survival of the fittest—there would be a considerable addition to the number of unemployed miners, and the burden of maintaining them would fall first on the unemployment insurance fund, i.e. partly on the State, and ultimately, in the event of long-continued idleness, wholly on the State. The industry working at full capacity in the most up-to-date pits can give employment only to a certain number of men in view of the fact that the demand is not likely to expand greatly, even with reduced costs of production and lower prices. There are those who, like Lord Snowden, are continually telling us that the extended use of machinery reduces costs, that reduced costs lower prices, and that lower prices increase the demand and therefore swell the volume of employment.

The theory is quite sound when it is applied to a new and expanding industry like the motor-car industry. It was true of the mining industry in days gone by under totally different conditions to those existing to-day. It is not true of the mining industry to-day, or if true, only to a very limited extent. Even a substantial reduction of production costs, with a corresponding reduction in price, would not to-day stimulate demand to any appreciable extent. The home market can absorb little more, and the market abroad is not now governed by the economic forces which would permit of a market being found for the increased output.

If, therefore, we are to continue with the policy of "spreading the work", and short time is to be a permanent feature of the industry, the nation, having enacted the policy through the House of Commons, should accept responsibility for its victims. In this connection consideration might be given to their position under the unemployment insurance scheme.

Their position is exceptional. No other industry is

subject to brief stoppages affecting all its employees at such short notice as the coal industry. The workpeople have insured themselves against unemployment, yet they may go on losing a day's, or two days', employment every week throughout the year without becoming eligible for benefit.

Consideration should be given by the Ministry of Labour as to whether, in this industry, claims for unemployment pay should not be admissible for any day for which the employer is willing to certify that the pit was idle through lack of trade or some other cause outside the control of the worker, and be payable on receipt of such a certificate. Such a system could hardly be open to abuse, for no colliery owner has any interest in voluntarily laying his pits idle without good reason, and trade disputes could be expressly excluded from any such scheme. The cost would not be high, and there should therefore be no risk of its endangering the solvency of the National Insurance Fund. Not nearly enough consideration has been given to this question of short time and its effect on the weekly pay packet. Its unwilling victims are the workers, and if the balance of advantage to the nation lies in continuing it, some means of relieving them of its consequences on their standard of life must be sought and found. Averages are deceptive, but it is obvious that if an industry can only give an average of 4·92 shifts per week to its workpeople though they would all gladly work 5½ or 6, there must be too many people engaged in it. This despite the fact that the number of persons employed has declined from 1,225,929 in 1920 to 769,474 in 1935. It would have declined still further but for the Act of 1930. That Act had many defects, but it did spread out the work available. It has enhanced, however, this evil of short time. Short time was nothing new in the industry, but since 1930 it has become a permanent feature in a majority of the districts, as the official reports show. The nation, having through the legislature perpetuated the evil, ought to accept its consequences, and in the manner suggested, or some similar national method, shoulder at least a part of the financial responsibility accruing from it. Parliament has intervened in the national interest to prevent the free play of economic forces in the industry. From the point of view of national efficiency it would be better if that freedom were restored. It would result in the industry employing, as full-time workers, as many as it could absorb and maintain in employment. It would mean that production would be concentrated on the economic pits, but that, in its turn, means a large reduction in the number of workers engaged in the industry. It means the survival of the fittest, and that again means a still heavier burden of unemployment on the nation.

Concentration on the best pits is not something easily accomplished. In the first place no one has ever yet succeeded in defining exactly what is an "uneconomic pit." Conditions vary so much that an economic pit in one district may be uneconomic in another. A small pit may be more efficient than a large one. An old pit with thin seams highly mechanized (as in Scotland) may be for many reasons a more remunerative economic unit than a newly sunk pit elsewhere. An increase in selling price will turn a marginal colliery into an economic and remunerative one. Except for the incorporation in the West Yorkshire scheme of a proposal to get rid of the redundant pits by purchase and closure, as in the case of Shipbuilding Securities Ltd., no method of closing them down has ever been worked out. It can only be done by purchase, for no colliery owner will close down his pit voluntarily without compensation, nor should he be expected to do so.

Should a number of pits be closed down on the grounds of redundancy without any regard for the social consequences, there would probably be a public outcry similar to that which followed the adoption of this policy in the shipbuilding industry.

OVERTIME

In 1934 and 1935 there were frequent complaints about the working of overtime and as a result two enquiries were held by the Mines Department, one in Lancashire and one in Scotland. The reports were issued in June 1934 (Lancs, Cmd. 4626) and in July 1935 (Scotland, Cmd. 4959). The Lancashire report showed that the ratio was only 0·41 per cent to the number of hours worked, and there was no "appreciable evidence" that the amount of overtime being worked was excessive.

In the case of Scotland the report said that where mines were largely mechanized overtime working was unavoidable, but even allowing for the greater proportion of machine working in Scotland the ratio, 3·28 per cent, was too high. More could apparently be done to reduce overtime and owners and managers were strongly recommended to give the matter their "careful and continuous attention". This it is understood is now being done.

Both reports express the view that the total abolition of overtime would have little appreciable effect on the total volume of employment available.

CHAPTER XIV

THE SURVIVAL OF THE FITTEST

THE survival of the fittest may be brought about in two ways—by ruthless competition which will drive the weakest out of business, or by a deliberately planned policy of extinction of uneconomic units. Whichever line is adopted the results are the same. Either is bound to involve hardship. The problem the nation is faced with is whether a policy of rationalization should be embarked on with the declared intention of placing the industry on a sound economic basis, making the best use of our greatest national asset (next to the land itself), giving regular employment to its workers, paying good wages, returning a fair dividend on its capital, and supplying its product at just and reasonable prices to all consumers alike. Such a policy involves concentrating production on the most favourably situated districts, and on the best of the pits in all districts. The full implication of this policy should be realized.

The Royal Commission of 1925 reported that: "If all the undertakings could come up to the level of efficiency of the larger ones, the problem of restoring prosperity to the industry would be a long way nearer to a solution." Efficiency and size are not synonymous.

The Commission, however, did not visualize the emergence of a situation such as that in which the industry now finds itself, with a demand almost stabilized at a figure well below its productive capacity and any expansion of an appreciable extent highly improbable. Under the new conditions the improvement indicated by the Commission as desirable would bring a solution, but it would not be the solution its members had in their minds.

A simple calculation will show what is involved. In 1935 a total of 754,000 wage earners, employed for 4·92 shifts per week, produced 222 million tons of coal. What would they have produced if fully employed for 5¾ shifts per week, or 300 per annum? The answer is 260 million tons, which, *under existing conditions*, represents the maximum output capacity of the industry. In the March quarter, 1936 (winter quarter), output was just over 60 million tons (Mines Department Summary, 58·55 + 3 per cent), or at an annual rate of 240 millions. The workers, however, were not even then working full time, the average number of shifts being 5·2 per week. The margin of flexibility for expansion to meet increased demand is, therefore, *under existing conditions*, only 20 million tons, or less than 8 per cent of capacity. This calculation is based, of course, on the existing system, under which each pit is producing its alloted quota of the output. The *potential* capacity of the industry is another and entirely different matter. It is much greater, but greatly increased output is not needed and will not be needed unless there is a greatly increased demand. With improved trade the home market may absorb an additional seven or eight millions, but there appears to be little immediate hope of any increase in exports, and it would be foolish, under present world conditions, to count on it. The 1935 output being 222 millions, it would not be wise to count on a stabilized demand greater than 230, or 30 millions below capacity, unless we can get back to the 1930 level in exports.

This 230 millions can be produced *under existing conditions* with short-time working (greater in summer than in winter) and giving such employment to about 750,000 wage earners. If new conditions are to be created by concentrating production on the economic units only, then a new calculation is necessary, and one showing the gravity of the issue.

As mechanization proceeds, the output per person employed increases. It has gone up steadily since 1920 and is still increasing. Some of our best pits are in North Derbyshire and Nottinghamshire; yet this district works systematic short time. In the March quarter, 1936, the average number of shifts there was 4·8. The output per man shift worked, however, was 28¾ cwt., against an average of 24 cwt. for Great Britain, and the output was at the annual rate of 360 tons per person employed, against an average for Great Britain of 323 tons. If the North Derbyshire and Nottinghamshire miners worked the full week of 5¾ shifts, their average output per man would be 430 tons for the year.

Concentration on the best pits will not raise the average output per man shift in Great Britain to 28¾ cwt., or not speedily, at all events. But increased efficiency, so loudly demanded, means reducing costs by increasing the output per person employed. If, therefore, concentration is to be of any value, it must be assumed that the latter figure will rise. An addition of 2 cwt. (only 8⅓ per cent) would bring the average output per man shift in Great Britain to 26 cwt. Full-time working on this basis (300 shifts per annum) would mean a yearly output per wage earner of 390

K

tons, or an average of 96 tons more than the average of 1935. Taking the figure of 230 millions as the annual output, this new figure resulting from increased efficiency by concentrating on the modern, well-equipped collieries means that employment on full time would be available for 600,000 wage earners. Add 15,000 for the "clerks and salaried persons" and we arrive at a total figure for persons employed of 615,000 against 769,000 in 1935, a reduction of 154,000.

These figures are not conclusive, for they are open to the objection that the poorer districts can never come up to the standard of production per worker of the richer districts. Even they, however, are increasing the individual output under the existing conditions, mainly because of increased mechanization, and this, combined with concentration on the modern well-equipped collieries, must inevitably lead to a substantial reduction in the volume of available employment.

In a matter of this kind no estimate could possibly be strictly accurate, but making full allowance for all the varied factors involved, a fair conclusion would appear to be that any policy of reorganization involving full-time occupation for the workers in the industry by closing down the poorest of the pits and concentrating production on the best, must result in the displacement of at least 134,000 workers, and the stabilization of the number of wage earners to whom the industry will give full-time employment on an output of 230,000 million tons, at about 620,000 and no more. *It should be noted that even if there were no concentration and no increase in the individual output figure* (24 *cwt. per man shift*), *the effect of the abolition of short-time working alone would be to reduce the number of wage earners from* 754,000 *to* 640,000.

If we add the 15,000 clerks and salaried persons to the 620,000 we get a total of 635,000 persons employed against 769,000 in 1935, that is 134,000 fewer.

The problem is a serious one. The addition of 134,000 to the live register of the unemployed is in itself a grave enough matter. In the case of the mining industry it is doubly so, for the social consequences of closing down a mine are much more serious than in closing a factory. The community is an isolated one, dependent entirely on the pit, and all the social services cluster around it. A dismantled colliery means a dead community.

Yet rationalization is the only alternative to the existing system and in the interests of national efficiency both the nation and the industry must face the new situation which has arisen, the nation paying willingly its share of the price which will have to be paid, by assisting in the transfer of labour, the establishment of new industries, and by encouraging the setting up of by-product plants on a bigger scale than hitherto attempted, while the industry makes its contribution by increasing efficiency, reducing its costs, and paying good wages to its workers. Then, with an industry resting on a sound economic foundation, the number of workers engaged in it stabilized and in regular employment, it may be possible to discuss the difficult question of some reduction of hours by international agreement, if and when the standard of life in other coal-producing countries is raised to the level of that of the British miner.

CHAPTER XV

The 1935 Dispute—Terms of Settlement, January 24, 1936

THE 1935 DISPUTE

SINCE the year 1920 there have been three national stoppages in the coalfields of Great Britain—in 1920, 1921, and 1926.

Like the 1935–1936 dispute, they were all brought about by the differences between owners and men on the two questions of wages and a national wages agreement.

To take the latter first. Up to 1921 the regulation of wages had always been a matter for the districts and all differences regarding wages had been a matter for adjustment between owners and men in the districts.

The settlement after the 1921 stoppage provided for the setting up of a National Wages Board, and this remained in being for five years until the stoppage of 1926. That long and disastrous dispute ended in the defeat of the miners. Towards the end the Executive of the Federation lost control of the situation, the men drifted back to work in large numbers, and eventually the Federation found itself forced to recommend the districts to enter into negotiations with the coal-owners in their respective districts for a settlement on district terms. The owners had always objected to the national agreement and had only given a reluctant consent to it in 1921. They now refused to continue it and the Government found it impossible to compel them to do so. The industry reverted to district settlements, the Miners' Federation lost something by which it set great store, and since 1926 all questions affecting wages have been dealt with in the respective districts.

The Mining Association is the central organization of the colliery owners. It is a body on which all the districts are represented. It deals with many aspects of the problems of the industry, but it does not deal with the regulation of wages, which is regarded by the districts as being a matter for district negotiation and district adjustment.

It is not possible to enter here on a full explanation of the grounds on which they base their view, but they may be summarized. These are that no two districts are alike, no two pits alike, that this industry is in a different category from any other, inasmuch as the geological and geographical differences make uniformity quite impossible. The quality of the coal, the cost of producing it, and the purposes for which it is sold, vary from district to district. The cost of production varies as much as 4s. per ton produced, and the output per man shift worked from 19½ cwt. to 27½ cwt. A pit may be an economic productive unit in one district, but a similar pit in another district quite the reverse. The differences in the thickness of the seams, the quality of the coal, the access to markets, the varying cost of transport, the vital importance of the export trade, which is so different from the inland trade, all these, added to the factors already mentioned, the owners contend, make it exceedingly difficult, if not impossible, to regard the industry as one productive unit and to make uniform wages regulations for governing it, through a single national authority, entirely out of the question.

The Mining Association has consistently refused to revert to a national wages agreement. It maintains that it has no authority to conclude such an agreement with the Federation. Wages, for this Association, are a matter for each district, and the organization indicates quite clearly that it believes the experience of five years of a national agreement to have been so profoundly unsatisfactory that, even if it could, the Association would not voluntarily renew it.

In arriving at this decision the Association has been largely influenced by the extent to which politics dominated the industry in the years 1921–1926 when a national agreement was in force.

The owners hold the view that during the period it was in operation there was continual strife in the industry—in short, that a national wages agreement led directly to national disagreement; that since 1926 the district agreements have worked satisfactorily and without leading to any great upheaval in the industry; that the demand is inspired more by political than economic motives, and that they can, therefore, see no good grounds for reverting to a form of agreement which has been already tried and failed to give satisfactory results to either of the parties who signed it.

The Mineworkers' Federation, on the other hand, have never wavered in their belief that there will never be a settled peace or a satisfactory standard of wages for the workers engaged in it until there is established a permanent National Wages Board with powers to regulate the level of wages throughout the whole of the coalfields of the country.

They quite frankly acknowledge that there are very great differences between the collieries and between the districts; they agree that there are these differences in the geological conditions of the pits, in their standards of equipment and organization, in the quality of the coal mined, in the purposes for which it is required, and in the cost of getting it to its intended market, all of which must lead to substantial variations in the cost of production.

They say, however, that: "Under the present separate ownership of the mines, these differences cannot be ignored, and the miners have no desire to ignore them; but they do not make impracticable the kind of agreement they desire."

That form of an agreement is one which would take out of the hands of the districts the final fixation and control of the basis rates of wages in each district, which vary under the present system, and would continue to vary under a system of national regulation and control.

These base rates have been agreed in the districts as a result of many years of experience. They are in two parts, one for those workers who are paid by results (piece workers), and one for other classes of workmen (datal workers). The former are payments for the coal actually won,[1] and the rates vary, not only with the district but in the same colliery and sometimes in the same seam of coal. The base rate for the datal workers is a flat rate of so much per day. This flat rate varies with the class of labour. It is pretty much the same in any district for the same class of

[1] Piecework is not strictly confined to coal getting.

labour at the different pits, but is not the same in all districts for the same class of labour.

Under the existing agreements a minimum percentage is added to the basic rates, irrespective of the results disclosed by the monthly ascertainments in each of the districts. This minimum percentage comes into operation whether a profit or a loss is reported by the joint accountants acting respectively for owners and men. This minimum percentage is a district percentage. It is settled in the district in relation to the economic position of the industry in that district. It varies from district to district, and may be adjusted in the district if the economic position requires it. Additions to the minimum percentage are determined by the results in the working of each district, as certified by the joint accountants, and the proceeds, after allowing for the payment of wages on this minimum basis, plus "other costs", mutually agreed upon, are divided between wages and profits on the basis set out in the agreements, and which has been already described.

The miners contend that the system is unsound because of the lack of co-ordination of the wages level between the districts. They demand that the minimum level of wages in each district shall be fixed and maintained by a National Wages Board, representative of owners and workers in all the districts. They desire this because they hold the view that: "The level of wages in any particular district is not the concern of that district only, but the concern of other districts also, for the level of wages in one district vitally affects other districts" (M.F. Statement of Case).

The percentage of labour cost in the production of coal is very high (nearly 70 per cent), and as wages can only come from the proceeds of the industry, the miners claim that it is illogical to attempt to co-ordinate district prices, as is now proposed, and to leave wages to be settled in the respective districts, unco-ordinated and unrelated to one another, even on a minimum basis.

Output and price being already under a form of national control, the miners contend that the third vital factor governing the success or failure of the industry—wages—should be brought under national control also, as these three factors cannot and ought not to be dissociated from one another if it is to prosper. To leave wages unco-ordinated is, in their view, merely to intensify competition between the districts; if one district reduces wages others feel compelled to follow, or risk losing the orders. In the owners' view the co-ordination of prices will itself remove any incentive to cut wages.

And finally, they repudiate the suggestion that the demand for a national wages agreement has any political significance at all, asserting that the claim is based on economic considerations alone. Such a method, they are convinced, would be better for both owners and men, would lead to greater co-operation between them, and hasten the day when the industry will be treated as one national unified entity, the ultimate objective which they frankly acknowledge they desire to achieve.

Here, then, are the views of the two parties to this aspect of the dispute. The question of a national agreement is one of principle and one on which neither side appears disposed to give way.

All that need be said about it here is that, unless the existing minima can be raised through the medium of a national wages organization the latter will be of little value to anybody. The setting up of such a body would undoubtedly strengthen the hands of the men's organization at the centre, but it would not, of itself, bring more money into the proceeds, and that is what is the first essential if wages are to be increased.

An important point that in general is either overlooked entirely or not given sufficient prominence, is that in 1933 wages absorbed 97·57 of the net proceeds, and in 1934, only slightly less, 95·4 per cent. The figure for 1935 was 94·3 per cent.

In 1932 the Government obtained from the coalowners a definite pledge that the existing level of wages would be maintained for one year. This, the miners hold, was, in actual fact, conceding the principle for which they are contending. The pledge, however, was given separately and independently by each of the districts, whereas the miners are demanding that any such agreement should be concluded between the two national organizations. This is the bone of contention.

The varying fortunes of the industry, its position during and at the end of the five years from 1921 to 1926, when a national wages agreement was in force, and the differences between owners and men which led to its termination in the latter year, are dealt with elsewhere (see page 38 et seq).

TERMS OF SETTLEMENT, JANUARY 24, 1936

The original demand of the miners was for a flat-rate advance in all the coalfields of 2s. per shift for men and 1s. per shift for boys. The estimated annual cost was about £18,500,000.

The ballot vote taken in November on the question of striking in order to enforce this demand resulted in an overwhelming majority in favour of the men withdrawing their labour. On December 18th a Delegate Conference in London decided on this course, and notice was duly given to the owners by the men in all districts to terminate their engagements unless their demand was conceded. The Secretary for Mines intervened, and as a result of negotiations between owners and men the unacceptable offer referred to was made and rejected. A slightly revised one was then submitted and accepted.

The terms of the settlement were not at all satisfactory to the miners, but they were regarded as an instalment and accepted as such. The decision was doubtless influenced largely by the national circumstances at the time of the Delegate Conference called to consider the terms. H.M. King George V had died only a few days before and the miners' leaders were naturally reluctant to bring about a stoppage at a time of national mourning.

In the settlement the Miners' Executive waived the claim for a uniform flat-rate advance in all districts. They recognized also that the industry could not afford to pay the cost of the increase demanded. The Government, through the Secretary for Mines, had firmly, definitely, and unequivocally refused the request of the Mineworkers' Federation for a subsidy, and the Conference undoubtedly acted wisely in accepting.

The increase in wages, as finally agreed upon for men, with corresponding advances for boys under the terms of settlement were:

Northumberland, Durham, and Cumberland	6d. per day
Scotland, Forest of Dean, and Derbyshire ..	9d. per day
Yorkshire, Lancashire and Cheshire, North Wales, South Derbyshire, North Staffordshire, Cannock Chase, South Staffordshire, Warwickshire, Leicestershire, and Shropshire, all	1s. 0d. per day
Somerset	8d. per day
Kent	5d. per day

South Wales: An increase in the minimum percentage on basis rates of $2\frac{1}{2}$ ($22\frac{1}{2}$ to 25) and an increase in subsistence allowance of 5d. per day (7s. 8d. to 8s. 1d.).

The agreement includes arrangements for a corresponding increase in the basis rates of payment for piece workers. It will be noted that the smallest increases are in the exporting districts, and there very strong dissatisfaction was expressed with the terms. These were, however, accepted by a large majority, despite the fact that they fell far short of the original demand. There was an important factor in the agreement which had a very powerful bearing on the decision. This was that part of the owners' communication which dealt with the question of national relationships. In many quarters this has been mistakenly construed as conceding the principle of settling wages and other terms of employment nationally, instead of, as hitherto, in the districts. This may, quite conceivably, contain the germs of future controversy, and it is well, therefore, to quote the actual words. These were:

"The owners' representatives informed the representatives of the Mineworkers' Federation that the coal-owners in all of the districts had accepted the recommendation which they had made with regard to future relationships.

"They were, therefore, authorized to say that, if there is full continuity of work and no notices given, the coal-owners will be prepared to co-operate with the Mineworkers' Federation in setting up a Joint Standing Consultative Committee for the consideration of all questions of common interest and of general application to the industry, not excluding general principles applicable to the determination of wages by district agreements.

"The coal-owners make this proposal in the earnest hope and belief that it will conduce to the maintenance of good relationships in the industry and to the benefit of all those engaged in it."

After the settlement, Mr. Joseph Jones, the President of the Mineworkers' Federation, said:

"A further reason for the decision was the acceptance by the owners of the necessity for national negotiations, for it is our profound conviction that a national handling of our problems is essential to progress and to the peace of the industry in the future. Every development within the industry in recent years provides a powerful reason for adopting a national, as opposed to a district, conception of the industry's problems, and we are delighted to think that the coal-owners are at last showing signs of appreciating our point of view."

It will be observed that the owners' communication spoke of a Joint Standing Consultative Committee "for the consideration of all questions of common interest and of general application to the industry, not excluding *general principles* applicable to the determination of wages by *district* agreements".

In the interpretation to be applied to these words there lies all the germs of a very serious difference of opinion as to their exact meaning. It is to be earnestly hoped that there has been no misunderstanding between the parties as to the powers and duties which will devolve upon this Committee.

CHAPTER XVI

"Offtakes"—Notes on "Offtakes"

"OFFTAKES"

In considering the question of miners' wages, nothing puzzles the student unacquainted with the method of payment more than what are called "offtakes".

These are deductions made each week by the colliery company at the pay office from the earnings of the worker for that week.

It should be clearly understood that they are chiefly voluntary or agreed deductions made at the request and with the consent of the worker, payments for which he receives something in return, and are not in any way deductions made for the use or profit of his employer. On the contrary, the owners do the book-keeping and collect the individual payments, thereby saving the men the trouble of paying their subscriptions direct, and their organizations the trouble of collecting the money. The coal-owner cannot tap the workers' earnings at the source for his own advantage, for the mineworker, like the wage earner in every other industry, is adequately protected against illegal deductions by the Truck Acts.

Unlike other industries, mining is, in the main, carried on in self-contained communities; the life of the community depends on the pit. The social services grow around it and are largely dependent on it for their efficiency. By voluntary agreement between employer and employed deductions for many services outside the scope of the State or the local authority are made at the pay office, an arrangement which is convenient to the workman and ensures a regular income for the particular purpose intended.

The only compulsory deductions from earnings are those for sickness, health, and unemployment insurance (the national scheme) on exactly the same basis as in other industries.

The nature, purpose, and amount of these "offtakes" varies from district to district, from pit to pit, and even from individual to individual. It is, therefore, impossible to give an exact list of the deductions or their amount for the country as a whole. The following list, however, will serve as a guide to those interested. It is based on the system operating in the counties of Northumberland and Durham.

Purpose for which deduction is made:

(1) Doctor.
(2) Coal Leading.
(3) Miners' Permanent Relief Fund.
(4) Aged Miners' Homes.
(5) Infirmary.
(6) Band.
(7) Nurse.
(8) Institute.
(9) Powder and Explosives.
(10) Checkweighman.
(11) Improper Filling.
(12) Pick Sharpening.

From time to time there may be other deductions of a special character, such as a special levy for the dependents of the victim of a fatal accident, repayments to public assistance authorities, priest, local ambulance or special charities fund, rent arrears or trade union contribution, but with the exception of "improper filling" they are all made with the workman's consent.

The total of the "offtakes", excluding State insurance, varies very considerably, not only in the districts, but also in the pits, as well as with the class of worker. For example the explosives deductions will apply only to a small section of the workers, whilst at some pits there may be no deductions from anyone for band or institute or other local service.

The total, including State insurance, may be in some cases as high as four or five shillings. The average earnings per person employed (this includes boys) are given by the Mines Department at 9s. 3d. per shift (excluding allowances in kind). For a full week of 5½ shifts this gives a weekly wage of £2 10s. 10½d.

One fact, however, must not be overlooked. In these difficult times many collieries have to work short time. The "offtakes" are automatic, the employer having no alternative to deducting them each week, even if the employee has worked only one or two shifts. In such a case the deductions make a very big hole in a man's earnings and this explains, in part, some of the cases of pitifully low cash earnings which are given publicity from time to time.

The following brief notes on the various "offtakes" may make the matter clearer.

NOTES ON "OFFTAKES"

(1) *Doctor.*—The miner himself is insured against sickness and ill health under the national scheme, and has always available the services of his panel doctor. His wife and family are, however, not so insured. In order to provide

medical attention for them, he authorizes his employer to deduct a stated amount (usually 6d. per week) from his wages. The employer, having retained these subscriptions, remits at regular intervals to the doctor, so that the whole family is assured of skilled attention in case of sickness. It is a system which works satisfactorily to all concerned. The doctor is paid and the miner has no doctors' bills to meet.

(2) *Coal Leading.*—Every colliery worker receives a supply of coal either free or at a nominal cost. He pays, however, for delivery and agrees to a small deduction from his earnings for this service.

(3) *Miners' Permanent Relief Fund.*—This is a voluntary contribution for the men's own purposes. It is only deducted by the owners at the workers' request, and for the convenience of their organization.

(4) *Aged Miners' Homes.*—This is a similar contribution for a very worthy object, which has been admirably supported by both the owners and the men, and is a credit to both.

(5) *Infirmary.*—A voluntary contribution to the local hospital. Where it is levied on any considerable scale the workers have their own representatives on the committee.

(6) *Band.*—Colliery bands are a feature of almost every mining district, and some of them have made musical history. They are largely maintained by these voluntary subscriptions, deducted at the pay office for the purpose.

(7) *Nurse.*—In some villages a nurse is maintained and paid for by the miners themselves, a small levy being made for defraying the cost. This is a service of great value to the community, especially in maternity cases.

(8) *Institute.*—A centre for social intercourse, formerly provided and maintained by the joint local effort of employer and employed. Under the aegis of the Miners' Welfare Fund, these centres have been greatly extended and improved in many of the coalfields. The Fund bears the cost of constructing or improving the building, but the

cost of maintenance is borne by the men by means of a small levy on their earnings. An account of the excellent work being done in this direction will be found in the admirable report of the Miners' Welfare Committee.

(9) *Powder and Explosives.*—Ever since explosives were used in coal mining the miners have paid for what they use. The workers who use them are paid by results (piece work), and prefer to buy through the employer and have the cost debited against their earnings. They thus buy both better and cheaper. The cost of the explosives is taken into consideration when the piece-work rates are fixed. The fact that the miner pays for them direct acts as a deterrent against wasteful use or careless working.

(10) *Checkweighman.*—This official is the representative of the workmen. His duty is to see that the output of the coal getter is accurately credited to him, and for this purpose he acts with, and sits side by side with, the owners' representative. His wages are paid by a levy on earnings, and as a matter of convenience the agreed amount is deducted from the miners' wages each week.

(11) *Improper Filling.*—This is the technical term for loading tubs with stone instead of coal. Deductions are made where the amount of the former is excessive, the owners naturally objecting to paying for unsaleable material. The amount to be deducted is agreed on between the owners' and the workers' representatives.

(12) *Pick Sharpening.*—Where miners have to find and sharpen their own picks they find it inconvenient to do the sharpening themselves. They arrange, therefore, with the colliery company to have this done by the colliery blacksmith, and to have the charge deducted from their pay notes.

CHAPTER XVII

Amalgamations—Compulsion and the Rights of Minorities

AMALGAMATIONS

As indicated on page 100, one of the main objects of the 1930 Act was to enforce amalgamations of existing coal-producing undertakings so as to reduce the number of operative units in the industry, increase efficiency, and eliminate wasteful competition. The formation of combines for large-scale production with low operating costs has been a feature of almost every industry in the post-war period. Not all of them have been successful, for in the little boom which followed on the end of the war the craze for amalgamations reached its zenith; many of them became unwieldy, and in the financial crashes which ensued millions of capital was irretrievably lost, a very large portion of it by humble folk who had invested their life savings in industry. Others have been quite successful. All, however, have been *voluntary* amalgamations, entered into willingly by those engaged in the industry concerned, and in the mining industry the most successful and most profitable have been those of moderate size, undertakings producing under one million tons per annum.

In the case of the mining industry, the 1930 Act introduced an element of compulsion by giving to the Reorganization Commission power to call upon the coal-owners to submit schemes of amalgamation, and, where they failed to do so, to prepare such schemes itself for submission to the Board of Trade for approval. Any such scheme having been approved by the Board of Trade must then be brought before the Railway and Canal Commission for confirmation or rejection. A very serious view was taken by Parliament of the need for adequately safeguarding the interests of the undertakings affected by any such schemes, and in the Act definite and explicit directions are given to the Railway and Canal Commissions as to when they must refuse their sanction.

In view of the situation which has arisen it is as well to give here the actual words of the Act. In Part 2, Section 13, Subsection 2, it is laid down that the Railway and Canal Commission: "(*a*) Shall not confirm a scheme unless satisfied—

"(1) that it would be in the national interest to do so; and

"(2) in the case of an amalgamation scheme, that the scheme

(*a*) will result in lowering the cost of production or disposal of coal; and

(*b*) will not be financially injurious to any of the undertakings proposed to be amalgamated, unless the scheme contains provisions for the purchase at a price to be fixed in default of agreement by arbitration of any such undertaking; and

(*c*) that the terms of the scheme are fair and equitable to all persons affected thereby."

The task imposed on the Reorganization Commission, with the limited power conferred upon it by this Act, was a difficult and thankless one. The colliery owners did not believe that the solution of their economic difficulties was to be found in amalgamations. The owners had no objection to amalgamation in suitable cases, but held that where it was necessary or desirable voluntary agreement would bring it about, as in other industries, and they objected most strongly to having anything in the way of amalgamation forced upon them.

In the early stages (1930–1932) the Reorganization Commission concentrated upon assisting, rather than promoting, amalgamations, but even in this direction its efforts evoked little enthusiasm. For many months, and in face of strong opposition in every district, the Commission continued its endeavours to induce the owners to embark voluntarily on schemes of amalgamation, always with the threat of compulsion in the background; but beyond giving a stimulus to some which the latter had had in contemplation or already embarked upon, the results were so meagre as to be practically negligible. Although received everywhere with courtesy and listened to with patient attention, the Commission could make little progress. The extremely disappointing results led the Government to seek to strengthen the hands of the Commission, and on May 31, 1932, the Attorney-General made a very important pronouncement in the House of Commons on the intentions of the Government regarding the future of that body. He said:

"I say that when this Bill is out of the way, the Reorganization Commission set up by Part 2 of the 1930 Act can take up the task that was committed to it by Parliament with energy and a certainty that the Government not only hope, but intend, that it should proceed with its task. There is certainly an opportunity, now that we have set up this industry in comparative stability for twelve months, for the Commission to undertake its task with a vigour and an assurance not possible as long as they thought it was practical politics that Part 2 of the Act might be repealed. The Minister for Mines and the President of the Board of Trade will do anything that is necessary to encourage the Reorganization Commission to put into force the powers they have already, and the passing of this Bill will help to create the conditions in which reorganization can take place" (Official Report, H. of C.).

Fortified by this authoritative pronouncement, the Commission persevered in its attempts to persuade the coal-owners to embark voluntarily on schemes of reorganization, concentrating now on what was known as "partial amalgamation", as distinguished from "total" amalgamation, the former meaning the co-operation of, or co-ordination of, the activities of financially independent units, and the latter complete amalgamation in the sense that all the units composing it were absorbed entirely in the new concern, financially and otherwise.

In December 1933, however, the Commission was compelled to report to the Minister of Mines that it was making no progress whatever, even along this line, and that they had informed the owners that they could not much longer defer "putting in motion the machinery provided by Section 13 of the Act in places where nothing is being done".

Having reminded the Minister that the Government announced in 1930 that it was intended to pass "without delay" a measure for the nationalization of royalties, the first part of the report concludes with the definite pronouncement that "the present system of mineral ownership would stand in the way of effective and lasting organization", even if other changes were successfully made.

The second part of the report consists of a series of "narratives", giving, separately, an account of the work of the Commission in each of the districts. In every case, leaving aside the slight assistance the Commission was able to give in the formation of voluntary amalgamations, the story is one of complete failure. Owners would not agree to the form of amalgamation desired by the Commission, and the latter, believing that voluntary amalgamations were better than compulsory, was reluctant to even attempt to put in force the powers which the 1930 Act was presumed to have conferred upon it.

Faced with these almost insuperable difficulties, the Commission proceeded to exercise those powers which the Act definitely conferred upon it—that of instituting enquiries, calling for schemes, and formulating itself schemes where they were not forthcoming. All this expenditure of labour, time, and money, however, led nowhere, for the Commission had not the authority to insist upon the schemes being put into operation when completed, and whenever opposition was encountered (and this was in every district) the only means of securing adoption lay in an appeal to the Railway and Canal Commission, the duly constituted court under the Act of Parliament.

In addition to the opposition of the owners, the uncertainty of its own powers, and the difficulties arising from multiple ownership of the mineral, the Commission had to contend with another factor of great importance. This was that the Act of 1930 undoubtedly embodied two principles of a contradictory character, as the owners pointed out repeatedly. The quota system established under Part 1 of the Act was expressly designed for the purpose of spreading employment and production, and, as has been shown in the preceding pages, it has achieved this result.

Part 2, however, was formed for the purpose of promoting amalgamations between productive units in order to increase efficiency by concentrating production on the best pits and closing down the redundant ones, and the Commission itself was established in order to carry this out. Buttressed by the "quota", many "marginal" collieries have remained alive, refusing to be either amalgamated or squeezed out. This is in the "national interest" from the point of view of "spreading the work" and the grave social consequences which follow on the permanent closing down of a colliery. It is, however, inconsistent with the policy of concentrated production which the Commission was created to promote, for success in that direction, as shown on page 131, involves the dismissal of at least 134,000 men from the industry. This, in turn, brings another problem for the Government, for it is their duty, and not the duty of any industry, to make the necessary provision for the maintenance of superfluous workers.

Throughout 1934 the Commission continued to struggle with the opposition of the owners, and persevered in its endeavours to reconcile the irreconciliable. Finding all its labour fruitless, the Commissioners decided to clarify the situation and obtain guidance as to the real extent of their own powers by bringing a test case before the Court.

The case selected was that of West Yorkshire, where a partial amalgamation scheme had been drawn up by some colliery owners, but had failed to secure the full support of all. The Commission therefore drew up a scheme which was substantially the same, and in May of 1935 submitted it to the Railway and Canal Commission for confirmation. The Court rejected the scheme, "both on merits and on law", without even calling on counsel for the objectors. The Court found that the "partial amalgamation scheme" was not an amalgamation scheme at all, and fulfilled none of the four requirements, without which, as set out in Part 2, Section 13, Subsection 2, of the Act of 1930, the Court was bound to reject it.

This legal decision having made it clear that the Commission was wrong in assuming that the Act of 1930 empowered the Court to enforce, as a "partial amalgamation", any co-operation between financially independent concerns, the Commission was driven back on "total amalgamations", a clear-cut form of combination which the Act gave the Court the power to confirm or reject. A beginning was made at once, and enquiries set on foot "as to the most appropriate groups to choose for the purpose of total amalgamation".

Before these could be concluded, however, and any action taken, the Commission was requested by the Government to suspend them and refrain from instituting others pending consideration by the Government of the whole situation and the powers vested in the Commission (July 28, 1935).

This was just when the House of Commons adjourned for the summer recess. Immediately afterwards those in the industry were busily engaged in the negotiations arising out of the miners' demand for an all-round increase in wages of 2s. per shift, and in November the country was in the throes of a general election.

During this period the Reorganization Commission was in a state of suspended animation, but in the middle of January 1936, the new Government having settled down, it presented another report to the Secretary for Mines, formally advising him of the result of the West Yorkshire case, and intimating that as a result of the decision their only objective must be total amalgamation, that they had still to discover how far compulsion could be applied in such a case, and that in the meantime they were "practically at a standstill" (Cmd. 5069 of 1936).

The Mines Department and the Government were now faced with a new situation and compelled to give serious consideration to the question of whether to abandon altogether the idea of compulsory amalgamation or strengthen the powers of the Commission so as to enforce it; and, if the latter, how best to provide for it.

For some months, except for a formal announcement that the Government proposed to promote legislation for strengthening the powers of the Commission and that a Bill was being drafted to meet the situation created by the decision of the Court, little was heard of the course which the Government had decided upon until, early in May (1936), the Coal Mines Bill, 1936, was launched, without warning, on a startled industry and a bewildered House of Commons.

No consultations had taken place between the Mines Department and the parties most interested, the Mining Association and the Mineworkers' Federation. Both organizations were reoccupied with the effects of the selling agencies which were to come into being on August 1st, and if their attention was being closely directed to any other matter involving legislation it was to the expected measure for dealing with royalties. In point of fact, the Minister of Mines did not consider that the introduction of a measure designed to enforce compulsory amalgamation "was a suitable occasion on which to consult with the Joint Consultative Committee". This latter is the body set up by owners and men as a result of the negotiations which terminated the 1935 dispute (see pages 140–41), and its function was the consideration of "all questions of common interest and of general application to the industry", and one would naturally have thought the Minister would have welcomed it and been glad to consult it even if the propriety of parliamentary procedure compelled him to do so unofficially.

When the Bill appeared, early in May, members of the House of Commons and those familiar with the industry throughout the country could scarcely believe they read aright, for the Government, having decided to add to the powers of the Reorganization Commission, had evolved a very arbitrary, even if speedy and effective, method of overcoming opposition to its proposals.

Stripped of its legal jargon and expressed in language easily comprehended by the man-in-the-street, the Bill, in its original form, provided for these things:

(1) Gave power to the Reorganization Commission to formulate a scheme of amalgamation for every coal mine, with legal authority to impose it on every undertaking concerned, whether it was desired or not, and irrespective of the financial, economic, or technical position of any of them.

(2) Abolished the safeguards provided in the Act of 1930, which established the Railway and Canal Commission as an outside independent tribunal charged with the duty and responsibility of deciding whether any such scheme should be confirmed or rejected. (Section 13, Coal Mines Act, 1930, see page 148.) The Commission was thus constituted the supreme authority in deciding an issue to which it was a party—judge and jury in its own case.

(3) Provided for total amalgamation in two stages: (*a*) By means of a "reorganization" scheme imposed on the constituent concerns by the Commission. From this there was to be no appeal to the Courts except on a point of law. (*b*) By means of a "participation" scheme in which all the productive units in the "reorganization" scheme would be absorbed. Objections in this case were to be heard by the Commission itself, and from the decisions, when confirmed by the Board of Trade, there was the customary provision for appeal to the higher courts both on points of equity and of law.

(4) Empowered the Board of Trade to sanction the withdrawal of any reorganization scheme drafted by the Commission provided the "transferor" companies, before the order was made approving it, submitted a voluntary scheme which satisfied the Board that it would be effective in achieving the desired amalgamations.

(5) Enacted that in the "participation" schemes, provision should be made for "alterations with respect to the membership, the control and management and the capital of the transferee company" (Second Schedule, Section 5).

(6) Provided that when a "participation" scheme is confirmed and made effective, the owners of, or shareholders in, the "transferor" companies shall receive payment for their property in the form of shares in the "transferee" company, and in no other way.

(7) Permitted the Commission, in the framing of any "reorganization" scheme, to separate the coal mines owned by a "composite" concern from its other activities and to amalgamate them with purely coal-producing concerns.

No. 1 represents a new and dangerous departure

in the relationship of the State to British industry. It constitutes a very big step forward to that complete bureaucratic control beloved by Socialists. It gives a blank cheque to the Government of the day, *and to any future administration,* to impose its will on the mining industry without consulting Parliament, and subject only to a departmental order laid before Parliament for a period of twenty-one days not receiving the assent of the House of Commons.

This enthronement of bureaucracy is a precedent establishing a principle which it would be quite easy to extend to other industries. It is therefore not surprising that when the Bill came before the House the Socialist Opposition could find no other means of condemning it than by moving an amendment regretting that it did not go much farther and concede the whole principle of nationalization of the mines.

No. 2 is an even more astonishing departure than No. 1. Not content with giving a branch of the Civil Service the power to enforce its policy on a great industry, the Bill swept away the safeguards against arbitrary action which were inserted in the Act of 1930 by a Socialist Government, the most important of which was that all schemes had to satisfy an outside independent tribunal that they were in the national interest, etc. (see page 148).

Under the Bill, not only was the independent tribunal abolished, but it was enacted (Clause 5, Subsection 2) that in any proceedings instituted after the approval of a "reorganization" scheme by order of the Board of Trade, in order to test its legality, such approval should be regarded as "conclusive evidence that the provisions of the scheme are in the national interest".

The chain of bureaucratic control was thus complete.

The measure gave the Commissioners power to frame the "reorganization" schemes, abolished the independent appeal tribunal, and limited the power of the Courts to rejection of any scheme only on the ground that it did not comply with the provisions of the Act itself.

The Reorganization Commission is an appanage of the Mines Department. The Department of Mines is a subordinate department of the Board of Trade. The Board of Trade is the Government department with which rests the final authority, subject only to Parliament. The three are thus links in the one chain. The Commission reports to the Mines Department, and the Mines Department reports to the Board of Trade, so that with the elimination of the Railway and Canal Commission the bureaucracy was supreme except for a totally inadequate measure of parliamentary control.

No. 3(*a*). This means, in effect, that the Commission could proceed to draw up, in secret if it so desired, and without consulting the firms concerned, a "reorganization" scheme for their compulsory amalgamation into one productive, operative, and financial unit. The Commission was to be the sole judge of the suitability of the companies concerned for amalgamation, and was under no obligation to even inform the latter of the terms of the amalgamation until after the scheme was completed.

No. 3(*b*). Under the provisions of the "participation" schemes the terms of transfer were to be settled by the Commission. The owners were not to be consulted as to the value of their property and were to be left in ignorance of what they would receive for it during the whole period that the schemes of amalgamation were being prepared. The only safeguard provided in the Bill lay in an appeal to the High Court *after* the scheme was confirmed and the terms fixed by the Board of Trade.

No. 4. This was obviously intended as a "lever" to induce the coal-owners to embark voluntarily on "total" amalgamations in preference to having such schemes forced upon them by the Commission. As any such scheme had to be approved by the Board of Trade, there would be, in practice, little difference except that it would evolve in its final form as the result of consultation and negotiation between the owners and the Commission.

No. 5. The powers vested in the Commission by the Bill itself and the schedule attached for the framing of the "participation" schemes were so vast as to be almost unlimited. They enabled the Commission to decide the form of management, the personnel of the boards, the amount of the capital required, the extent and class and place of priority in any new capital issued, and the number of undertakings to be included in any such scheme. These far-reaching provisions would establish the Commission as autocrats in the industry, legally empowered to dictate on all these matters to those in control of the amalgamated undertakings, to remove them if dissatisfied with their conduct of the business, and, armed with authority, after the confirmation of the "reorganization" scheme, to demand the infliction of penalties in the form of heavy fines or imprisonment, or both, on any individual who, being the owner of, or responsible official in, any transferred undertaking, refused to give to the Commission such information as it might consider necessary for the preparation of the "participation" scheme.

There seems to be little doubt that if Parliament

were to agree to these proposals the result would be the establishment for the first time in British industry of a form of bureaucratic control not far removed from complete State control; in short, what was described at another of the crises in the coal industry as a "bastard form of nationalization".

No. 6. The delegation of authority to dispose of other people's property to a Civil Service Commission is hardly likely to commend itself to those who have built up the businesses concerned, or those who have invested their money in either coal mining or any other industry, while the method adopted in the Bill for paying the owners or shareholders of the "transferred" undertakings would inevitably lead to grave injustice in many cases, and very probably to costly and long-drawn-out litigation in others.

Amalgamation of coal mines is a totally different matter from the amalgamation of factories. The mining industry is an old-established one; geological differences are so great that no two productive units are alike; coal is a wasting asset, subject to the law of diminishing returns, and this law cannot operate similarly in any two cases; geographical considerations play a big part in the economics of the industry, and these govern largely not only the policy of a district, but the policy of individual undertakings, the interests of which are not always identical and whose product may be quite different from that of its neighbours. Some concerns have pursued a wise and prudent financial policy, and, knowing that the life of a mine is limited, have set aside out of revenue each year reserves for meeting the bad years, for the repayment of capital when the pit is worked out. Others have pursued a quite different policy, that of paying everything earned out in dividends in good times, and, when bad times came along, have accumulated heavy overdrafts.

These are not by any means all the differences in the productive units in this complex industry, but, leaving aside all the others, no compulsory scheme which amalgamated the efficient with the inefficient could ever be expected to satisfy all interests involved. To combine the provident with the improvident is even more difficult. This problem has been discussed again and again, whenever, in fact, amalgamations have been "in the air", but no one has ever been able to produce a scheme for amalgamating them compulsorily which would satisfy all concerned. The rough-and-ready way of adjusting the financial differences adopted in the Bill—by the proportionate allocation of shares in the amalgamated concern—cannot in justice be regarded as an equitable solution of this difficult aspect of the amalgamation problem. The immediate effect must inevitably be to depreciate the value of the property of the efficient and provident undertaking. In all the discussions no answer has ever been given to those who question the right of the State to embark, in a selected industry, on a policy which has this result, except that it is in the national interest. If it be in the national interest and the community is to reap the benefit, then the community should bear that portion of the burden due to its own policy, and not impose it on their fellow citizens, whose only offence is that in the national interest, as well as their own, they have conducted their businesses on sound and efficient lines, both technically and financially.

The method proposed in the Bill was not made any more attractive by the fact that, in addition to being empowered to formulate the "participation" scheme

M

entirely "on its own", the Commission was to be the sole judge of the consideration to be given to each transferred undertaking for its property, not in cash, but in shares of the totally amalgamated concern, guided only so far as the amount was concerned by the very elastic provision that it should be "the value thereof at the date of transfer as between a willing buyer and a willing seller". This, presumably, would be decided by the Commission alone, and the only remedy provided in the Bill was recourse to the High Court. All these perfectly legitimate objections not only reveal the difficulties in the way of enforcing compulsory amalgamations, but also the injustice inseparable from the method proposed by the Government in the new Bill.

No. 7. Nothing could be more unjustifiable or calculated to arouse more bitter controversy than the proposal in the Bill to give power to the Commission to separate the coal mines owned by a "composite" concern from its other activities, and to transfer them to some other company without the owner's consent and at the Commission's own valuation. There is a large number of these "composite" companies, most of them large concerns engaged in a variety of industries, such as iron and steel, tinplates, brickmaking, pipe manufacture, etc., and in some cases their coal mines are operated almost entirely for the purpose of supplying coal to their other works. It is true that the Bill provided that "due allowance shall be made for any injury suffered by the company by reason of the separation of any property of the company from other property belonging to it", but no monetary consideration could compensate for the tearing away of a part of a composite company's equipment which is vitally essential for the successful carrying on of their enterprise.

It is no answer to assert that the Commission would not be so foolish as to handicap important industrial undertakings by severing their coal mines from the other parts of their business. The Bill gave them the power to do it, and it is not in the national interest that any Government department should be endowed by Act of Parliament with power to interfere to this extent in the conduct of any industry. This was recognized in the 1930 Act, and a clause inserted (Section 13, Subsection 1) definitely providing that no coal mine should, in any amalgamation scheme, be separated from the parent undertaking to which it was ancillary without the consent of the owners. In the new Bill this very wise restriction was removed and the Commission left an entirely free hand to separate the coal-mining operations of any company from its other activities if it thought fit.

These were the most serious objections to this very unfortunate measure, and it is a formidable list. The most surprising feature about it was that it should have been introduced by a National Government pledged to oppose Socialism and composed of ministers who only a few years before not only strongly condemned compulsory amalgamations but insisted on the safeguards which they now proposed to remove. One can only assume that with the pressure of business arising from the negotiations on wages and selling agencies and royalties the measure was hastily drafted and inadequately considered, a view to which its sudden and unexpected appearance lends some credence.

Nobody appeared to want this Bill. The Mining

Association was strongly opposed to compulsory amalgamations, and the Mineworkers' Federation had certainly not asked for it, while the moment chosen for its introduction was generally regarded as most inopportune in view of the other matters involving legislation on which Parliament and the industry were already engaged.

When introduced by the President of the Board of Trade, the Bill had a more unfavourable reception than any Government proposal of recent years. It is not known whether the Government had realized the Socialistic nature of their measure, or whether the Cabinet had been advised of the fierce opposition which had boiled up in the few days which their own supporters had had to consider it, but in any case Mr. Runciman announced, in introducing the Bill, that the Government had decided on amending it in certain directions in the hope of making it more acceptable.

The amendments, when he outlined them, proved to be of vital importance and of such a far-reaching character as to alter the whole structure of the Bill. They are given below. Demands were made from all quarters of the House for its withdrawal and for a new Bill incorporating the full proposals of the Government, and in the end the House never got down at all to a discussion of the Bill as presented. The Prime Minister intervened with a promise to give another day for the discussion and in the interval to issue a White Paper explanatory of the modifications to be introduced in Committee. The storm was over, and the House settled down for the rest of the evening to one more desultory discussion of the problems of the industry, and one entirely unconnected, in any formal fashion, with the measure before the chamber.

The proposed amendments, as outlined by Mr. Runciman in the House of Commons on May 18, 1936, were three in number, embodying:

(1) A proposal to limit the powers of the Reorganization Commission (for two years) so that no scheme of compulsory amalgamation could be enforced before July 1, 1938.
(2) A modification providing that the coal mines ancillary to undertakings which were not primarily engaged in the production or treatment of coal could not be included in any compulsory amalgamation scheme without the consent of the owner concerned.
(3) A provision for the setting up of an outside independent impartial tribunal to go into the objections to schemes and report to the Board of Trade.

All three were vital amendments, and made such extensive alterations in the structure of the Bill that it was withdrawn and never discussed in the House. It should be noted that the only satisfactory amendment is No. 2. The first one is open to the very grave objection that it creates a period of uncertainty bound to retard development. The third is open to the even graver objection that the tribunal proposed is merely a consultative one, with the authority to make recommendations but no power to enforce them.

A few days afterwards the Prime Minister announced in the House of Commons that, whilst adhering to the principle of compulsory amalgamation and the main provisions of the Bill as amended by the changes outlined by the President of the Board of Trade, the Government had decided, in view of the opposition shown to the proposals, to withdraw the measure and submit a new one in the autumn. The promised White Paper was not issued, and it is not possible, therefore, to comment on it. It had been made clear by the introduction of the Bill that no measure conferring such extensive powers on a Government department would ever be acceptable either to the industry, to the House of Commons, or to the country.

It is imperative that when the new Bill does appear it must, above all, provide for:

(1) The setting up of an outside independent appeals tribunal.
(2) A definite instruction in the Act of Parliament itself, that no scheme shall be sanctioned unless it is proved that it will result in lowering the cost of the production and distribution of coal.
(3) Adequate safeguards for the composite undertakings to which the mining of coal is only ancillary.
(4) A limitation of the powers granted to the Board of Trade.
(5) A stricter measure of control by Parliament than in the original Bill.

This is the least the industry and the House of Commons has the right to expect.

COMPULSION AND THE RIGHTS OF MINORITIES

In every walk of life, when men are voluntarily associated or seek to unite for some common purpose, there arise questions on which there appear legitimate differences of opinion. They may be questions of principle or questions of policy, but inevitably there comes a time when those comprising the association are divided into groups. In any country which enjoys the priceless gifts of individual liberty such associations are built on a democratic foundation and the policy determined by the elementary democratic principle of majority rule. The application of the principle, however, carries with it the obligation that the power enjoyed by a majority shall not be exercised tyrannically, or in such manner as to inflict grave injustice on the minority.

It is in the nature of things that "minorities must suffer", but it is equally true that "minorities have rights", and the trouble which arises, and always will arise, in voluntary combinations of men and women, is how to safeguard those rights without sacrificing the principle that the will of the majority must prevail, or inflicting undue hardship on the dissentient minority.

Opposition to a line of policy which is approved by a majority can only be overcome in one of two ways—by persuasion or by compulsion. A negligible minority carries little weight, and is dependent on the spirit in which the decisions of the majority are implemented. A large minority can often succeed in effecting a change or partial change in the policy or proposals to which they object. In between these there are minorities which may exercise an influence more or less powerful. In all these cases, by argument and persuasion, by compromise and by goodwill on both sides, a solution of the difficulties satisfactory to all concerned may be evolved.

When, however, persuasion, conciliation, compromise have all failed, compulsion in some form is inevitable if the will of the majority is to prevail, for there is no other course open except to leave things as they are. It is always unfortunate, for, firmly rooted in the hearts and minds of all men who recognize the rights of minorities to freedom of thought and speech and action, within the limits essential to the existence of civilized communities, there is a deep-seated repugnance to the adoption of compulsory methods and a strong dislike towards being forced either to adopt them or to submit to them.

Amongst the British people, accustomed for generations to the widest measure of individual freedom, this trait is highly developed. Shakespeare knew it and emphasized it when, in one of his plays, he makes one of his characters say: "Give you a reason on compulsion! If reasons were as plentiful as blackberries, I would give no man a reason upon compulsion, I."

Every organization or association of individuals encounters the difficulty of deciding at what point the minority should be "compelled" to accept the will of the majority, and many of them provide for it in their constitution or the rules governing their procedure.

Looked squarely in the face the problem is: "What majority is necessary to justify compulsion?" Has a "majority" of 51 the "right" to "dictate" to a "minority" of 49? If the "right" is questioned, is it established if the majority figure is 60 and the minority figure is 40? Have those who have fixed the figures at $66\frac{2}{3}$ and $33\frac{1}{3}$ (the popular "two-thirds" majority) arrived at a solution fair to all concerned, inflicting no hardship on any which cannot be justified in the interests of all? Should the figure be four-fifths, or even nine-tenths, before compulsion is applied? These are questions which can only be answered with assurance in the circumstances of each case, and best answered by those responsible for the activities of the body concerned and the persons composing its membership. One thing is common to all, however; that is, that in the interests of all the liberty enjoyed by a minority ought not to be allowed to degenerate into license, so that the action of a resolute minority should be permitted to impede or arrest the progress desired by a substantial majority.

In the case of the coal-mining industry it is generally acknowledged that amalgamations of the productive undertakings are desirable *in certain circumstances*. What those circumstances may be in actual fact is hotly disputed in every case, as it is almost bound be to in such a varied and complex industry.

During the last ten years voluntary amalgamations have taken place on quite a considerable scale in a number of the districts, with the result that out of the total output of 220 million tons, 165 millions are produced by under 150 undertakings.[1] They have not been numerous enough, however, or on a big enough scale to satisfy the requirements of the Reorganization Commission appointed by the Government after the passing of the 1930 Act, for this and other purposes. Instead of strengthening the powers of the Commission in the direction of encouraging voluntary amalgamations, with some compulsory power held in reserve, the Government decided to give to the Commission the power to mark out amalgamations, to abolish the right of appeal to an outside independent tribunal on the actual amalgamation scheme, and to permit appeals to the High Court by the undertakings to be amalgamated only in the terms of participation. The storm of protest which ensued led to the withdrawal of the proposals (May 1936), with the promise of a new Bill in the autumn embodying the amendments outlined by the President of the Board of Trade.

In making the announcement, the Prime Minister said that the Government adhered to the principle of

[1] See Appendix X, page 362.

compulsory amalgamation, so that the only thing to be decided is the method of applying it.

Everyone connected with the industry, including the Reorganization Commission, agrees that, where they can be brought about, voluntary amalgamations are greatly to be preferred to compulsory ones. This being so, it would appear that, with the breathing space provided by the withdrawal of the first measure, there is both ample room for compromise and time for more careful consideration of the nature and extent of the compulsory provisions which are to be included in the new one.

Bearing in mind the rights of minorities, a solution fairly satisfactory to all concerned might be found on these lines or on lines approximately close to these suggestions:

(1) The power to call for schemes of voluntary amalgamation to be still vested in the Re-organization Commission.
(2) An outside independent tribunal (preferably a lay one with some legal members) to be appointed to hear the case for amalgamation and to determine whether the scheme ought, in the national interest, to be confirmed, rejected, or amended.
(3) In cases where a voluntary amalgamation scheme has been approved by the Re-organization Commission and the minority objecting is responsible for only 15 per cent or less of the output, the onus of proof that the scheme is not in the national interest to be placed on the objectors.
(4) The right to determine what is an "area" or a "district" suitable for amalgamation and what undertakings included or excluded, to be vested in the tribunal, and not in the Commission.
(5) Where the Re-organization Commission has called for

a voluntary amalgamation scheme and no such scheme is forthcoming after the expiry of one year, the Commission to be empowered to apply to the tribunal for a declaration that a stated area is a suitable one for amalgamation. On such a declaration being obtained, notice to be given to all undertakings in that area, that unless a voluntary scheme be formulated within one year, the Commission will frame its own scheme and submit it for approval. The tribunal would, of course, have power to refuse to grant the declaration asked for.

(6) A clause to be inserted in the Act of Parliament for the protection of composite undertakings, providing that no coal mine, being the property of any such undertaking, should be detached from it, unless it was shown to the satisfaction of the tribunal that less than 50 per cent of the coal produced from that mine was used for the undertakings' own business, and that it was in the national interest that it should be separated.

(7) In cases where the objectors to a scheme of voluntary amalgamation were responsible for 15 per cent to 33⅓ per cent of the output, the tribunal to be directed to decide the issue on the question of the national interest with the onus of proof on the promoters, and if confirmed, to have the authority to vary the terms and conditions (including finance) of the scheme, in order to safeguard the rights of the minority.

(8) No scheme of amalgamation to be confirmed by the tribunal unless it has the approval of, and is sanctioned by, undertakings in the area which are responsible for at least two-thirds of the output in that area, already defined by the tribunal as being one suitable for amalgamation.

(9) The Commission to have the right to appear and to

be heard by the tribunal when any scheme of amalgamation is being considered.

(10) The decision of the tribunal on questions of fact to be final, and appeals to be permitted on questions of law only to the Court of Appeal.

A small minority with a "nuisance value" ought not to be allowed to thwart the majority in industry any more than in any other sphere of life. Some form of modified and suspensory compulsion such as that outlined above ought to bring them into line and enable the amalgamated units to work out a common policy in the interests of all. Any such solution is much to be preferred to compulsory amalgamation imposed on all by any oligarchy.

It is not only on the owners' side of the industry that the rights of minorities arouse interest and invite comment. The impartial critic may be pardoned if he points out that there is a parallel on the workers' side.

In the 1935–36 dispute, when a ballot of the members of the Mineworkers' Federation was taken on the question of a strike, the voting was 409,351 for and 29,215 against, a total of 438,566. At the time the number of workers on the colliery books was 747,500. Thus the question whether the whole industry was to be stopped was decided by 409,351, or 54·7 per cent of those at work, while 45·3 per cent were either opposed or had no voice in deciding whether there should be a stoppage or not.

But that is not all. Under the Unemployment Insurance Acts there are a quarter of a million persons classified as miners who are unemployed. This brings the number of persons in the industry, working and unemployed, to just under a million. So that the 409,351 who voted for a strike represented just 41 per cent of those engaged in the industry, while nearly 600,000, or 59 per cent, were either against a strike, did not vote if entitled to do so, or were not consulted at all.

The Federation has a membership of just over 500,000, so that 80 per cent were in favour of striking. Some of the unemployed are members and some are not. With its membership of 500,000, it speaks for nearly two-thirds of those actually at work; but if the unemployed are taken into account and the positive vote regarded as the decisive factor in the result, the issue was decided by a minority vote and the majority committed to a strike because of the strength of the organization behind the demand for a stoppage. Thus, in that case, it becomes not a question of the rights of minorities, but the question of the right of an organized minority to force its will on an unorganized majority.

If the right to decide the issue be confined to those actually at work, there remains the difficult problem of the rights of the very substantial minority of 45·3 per cent, composed of 29,000 members of the Federation, who voted against a strike, approximately 60,000 members who did not vote, and approximately 250,000 who do not belong to the Federation and therefore had no say at all, making a total of 339,000 against a positive strike vote of 409,351.

Here is a problem in "compulsion and the rights of minorities" even more difficult than that on the owners' side of the industry, for the minority is numerically large, but, being in the main both unorganized and dumb, no one knows to what extent it would support the Federation in such a case or how far it would go in opposing it.

The only safe conclusion is that in the organization of labour it is the active, zealous workers in the cause who "collar" the machinery and dictate the policy, and so long as minorities, however powerful in numbers, remain both unorganized and silent they must be prepared to submit to the will of the majority, how ever narrow the margin may be between them.

CHAPTER XVIII

THE SELLING AGENCIES

THE new district selling agencies have been established for the purpose of ensuring that no coal shall be sold at or from any coal mine at prices below those fixed for each class of coal by the Executive Board for the district in which the coal mine producing the coal is situated.

There are seventeen of these districts, with a scheme for each, embodied in the draft order laid before Parliament in pursuance of Subsection (4) of Section 3 of the Coal Mines Act, 1930. The districts are:

- Scotland
- Northumberland
- Durham
- Cumberland
- Lancashire and Cheshire
- Midland Amalgamated
- Shropshire
- North Staffordshire
- South Staffordshire and Worcestershire
- Cannock Chase
- Warwickshire
- Forest of Dean
- Bristol
- Somerset
- Kent
- North Wales
- South Wales and Monmouthshire

Although the object aimed at in setting up these agencies is the same in all the districts, the method adopted is not the same in every case.

In four districts the system adopted is one of complete centralized selling on the Lancashire model, which was established in 1935. These districts are Lancashire,

Shropshire, South Staffordshire, and the Forest of Dean. Under these schemes the whole of the coal produced is transferred to the Executive Board; the Board does the selling for the whole district, and the individual undertaking no longer sells its coal at all.

The arrangements as to prices and credits are made within the district between the various undertakings and the Board.

In the large Midland Amalgamated district, which has an output of 70 million tons, a system of group selling has been adopted. In this district the collieries are divided into groups, each with its own selling agent. The work of these selling agents is to be co-ordinated by a co-ordinating committee for the whole district. There is one selling agent only for each group, who sells on behalf of the individual undertakings, each of which receives the proceeds of the sale of its own coal and retains its own profits. This method is really a combination of control of sales with central selling.

In the remaining twelve districts (the majority), including the four exporting areas, the method adopted is that of the central control of sales. There is no transfer of coal to the Executive Board, each undertaking continuing to sell its own coal. The prices and conditions of sale, however, are under the control of the Executive Board. Permits for sale are required, and selling without a permit involves penalties. In the permits it is stipulated that the coal shall not be sold below a specified price, and also that it shall not be re-sold below the same price.

The central draft order, which required a resolution of Parliament, gives to the Central Council statutory authority for the co-ordination of all these district schemes, with power to enforce penalties on the districts if they fail to comply with its directions.

The variety of system, due in part to the geological and economic differences between the districts, has the advantage that it will enable the industry to see which of them works out best. As the Minister of Mines said in commending the schemes to the House of Commons: "The whole of the schemes are really measures of experimentation. This is not the last word in organized selling; in fact, it is only the first" (Hansard, June 24, 1936).

The schemes should eliminate wasteful competition between collieries; should lead to inter-district agreements, and possibly to a system of zones of delivery. They should bring increased revenue to the industry by strengthening the position of the seller, and, as under all the schemes every colliery has a definite share of trade, as distinct from quota, they should give a stimulus to voluntary amalgamations where these are likely to be of either technical or financial advantage. And they should lead speedily to some sort of organization for distribution, which is admittedly defective and in far too many hands for the good of either the industry or the consumer.

So far as the latter is concerned, he is adequately protected by the Committees of Investigation provided for in the 1930 Act and which have now been reconstituted so as to include persons with legal training and qualifications.

CHAPTER XIX

EXPORTS

THE export of coal has been for a hundred years one of the most important factors in the economic life of the nation.

In that wonderful era of industrial expansion which made Great Britain the "workshop of the world", the latter half of the nineteenth century, her industrial supremacy was largely due to coal, the basis of all her manufacturing activities. In the remarkable progress made in those fifty years the part played by the exportation of British coal may be gauged by the fact that in 1850 the total exports were just over 3 millions; in 1900 they had increased to 44 million, and in 1913 had reached the very high total of over 73 million tons. (Including bunkers, etc., over 98 millions.)

The export of coal provided our ships with the bulkiest of outward cargoes, and the freights earned by its transportation reduced the freights on the homeward run, when they returned to these shores with their cargoes of food and the raw material required for our great industries, for which the coal sent abroad helped to pay. The commanding position attained by our mercantile marine in the days before the war was largely due to the fact that there were always these bulky outward cargoes to cheapen the homeward freight or enable the ships to act as the world's carriers between foreign ports. In those days, when coal was the only fuel used by ocean-going steamers, British coal was not only shipped abroad for the use of other countries in their manufacturing processes, but, on account largely of its qualities, was stored at depots all over the world for the refuelling of British and foreign steamers. Before oil became such a serious competitor in the field of marine propulsion more than half the coal shipped abroad was used for navigation purposes, and a large proportion of that half was taken up at the depots abroad by our own vessels.

In the welter of confusion caused by the transition from war to peace and the fierce controversies which have since raged within and around the industry, the almost inestimable service rendered to the nation by those responsible for the establishment of this extensive and profitable business has been almost forgotten.

It gave a new lease of life to old ports; it led to the opening up of new ones; it brought profit to coal-owners, land-owners, railway companies, dock and harbour authorities, ship-owners, shopkeepers, and others; it gave employment to miners, dockers, seamen, ship-builders, engineers, and a host of workers in ancillary businesses.

Up to 1913 it was a business which had been founded and built up by the coal exporters. It was one of great value to the coal-owners, for it was superimposed on a demand for coal in the home market which was in a state of continuous expansion. The producers had no worries at all so far as the foreign market was concerned, either technical or financial. They mined the coal and sold it to the exporter, either *ex*-colliery, delivered at a nominated port, or free on board at such port. The exporter was responsible for the obtaining of the orders, the quality of the coal supplied, the transport by sea, and delivery at the port designated by the buyer. He paid cash to the colliery in sterling, within a month, and received payment from the purchaser in sterling, generally at ninety days' settlement. (Now, in cases such as Italy and Spain, under the changed conditions, he has to wait for payment through a clearing office, with payments in arrears from six to twelve months.) There were, of course, as was natural in such a business, family, social, and sometimes financial associations between the producers and the exporters, but as a general rule the two businesses were quite separate and distinct. The exporter bought his coal where he chose, sought out his own markets, established his own connections abroad, and had his own representatives in every important coal-purchasing country or coaling station in the world. It was his job to meet the competition of other coal-producing countries, and to meet it on the basis of quality and price. Such was the system in operation at the outbreak of war in 1914.

The war brought about tremendous changes in this branch of our overseas trade; in fact, it may truthfully be said to be primarily and mainly responsible for the major part of the troubles which have befallen the export trade in coal. During the war nations which had been dependent on British coal turned to other sources of supply or other sources of power. Where they had coal measures of their own they exploited them to the full, being no longer bound, in war time, by normal economic considerations;[1] where water-power was available a great stimulus was given to the

[1] Holland increased her output from 2 million tons in 1913 to 12½ million in 1934. Spain from 4 million to 6 million. Russia from 29 million to 90 million tons.

utilization of water-power for the generation of electrical energy; new uses were found for lignite or brown coal, a low-grade fuel, particularly in Germany; and oil, wherever available, took the place of coal. Thus the war, and our inability, as the result of the war, to supply our customers, had the dual effect of driving some of them to the use of other forms of power and strengthening the competitive power of other coal-producing countries, Poland in particular, in the struggle for what markets remained at the end of it.

Another very important factor in the decline of the export of British coal since the war is to be found in the largely increased use of oil for marine propulsion. The navies of the world, including our own, have abandoned coal almost entirely, and war vessels are to-day driven either by steam generated in oil-fired boilers or by internal-combustion engines of the Diesel type. The mercantile marines of every country are following rapidly in the steps of their navies, and the increase in the number of passenger and cargo-carrying vessels driven by oil since 1913 is phenomenal. Almost every ocean-going passenger vessel is now oil-fired or oil-driven. It is now truer than ever that "the liner she's a lady", for her dainty appearance is never spoiled nor her passengers inconvenienced by the clouds of dust which smothered her when bunkering with coal. The "intermediates", carrying both passengers and cargo, are following in the wake of their big and luxurious sisters, and even the cargo tramps on some routes and little coasters are turning from coal to oil. The effect of this change on the British coal-exporting industry will be understood from the figures given in the table on the following page.

It will be seen that of the world's tonnage there is

a reduction of no less than 11 million tons in the vessels using coal.

In the British mercantile marine the tonnage of vessels using coal has been exactly halved—18 million tons to 9 million.

While the world's tonnage has increased by 40 per

WORLD'S TONNAGE (Vessels over 100 tons)

	July 1914	July 1935
Tonnage of Steamers and Motor-ships	45,403,877	63,727,317
Tonnage of Motor-ships	234,287	11,304,691
Tonnage of Oil-fired Steamers ..	1,310,209	19,885,070
BRITISH TONNAGE (Vessels over 100 tons)		
Tonnage of Steamers and Motor-ships	18,892,089	17,298,432
Tonnage of Motor-ships	32,000	2,886,495
Tonnage of Oil-fired Steamers ..	457,000	5,244,082

cent, the tonnage of coal-fired vessels has fallen from 96·6 per cent to 51 per cent.

Of new vessels built to Lloyd's rules in 1935 only 20 per cent was coal-fired—150,000 tons out of 750,000—whilst of 1,800,000 tons under construction in the shipyards of the world in March 1936 over 1,000,000 tons were vessels fitted with internal-combustion engines. Exports of coal have fallen from 73 millions in 1913 to 38·7 millions in 1935, and bunkers from 21 millions to 12·5 millions.

One of the most remarkable features of the post-war

period has been the growth of economic nationalism. The desire, and in some cases the need, for producing as much as possible within their own borders has led in many countries to the imposition of tariffs, import quotas, licensing and currency restrictions, all of which have affected British exports, coal in particular. The same spirit has led to the subsidizing of their exports by other coal-producing countries, and this form of competition the British industry has had to meet without any similar measure of Government assistance.

In addition to assisting in other ways, Germany subsidizes her export trade to the extent of 6s. per ton, derived from a levy on coal consumed in the home protected markets. Great Britain is the only coal-producing country in which the home consumer is not levied in order to help the export trade.

Polish coal, which is sold at the pit-head for 18s. per ton, is carried 375 miles by rail to Gdynia at a charge of 3s. 3d. per ton; port charges are 1s. Yet the export price f.o.b. is only 13s. 6d. per ton. In Great Britain 13s. 6d. would not pay the carriage for a similar distance. Exports from Poland are thus subsidized directly by a levy on the home consumer and indirectly by a phenomenally low rate of transport.

The three national stoppages of 1920, 1921, and 1926 helped the foreign exporter very considerably at the expense of his British rival, especially that of 1926, when we lost markets which we have not regained and may never regain.

The decline in the export of British coal is believed by many to have been accelerated by the Act of 1930. That Act provided for the setting up of a scheme in every district to be administered by the district coal-owners for dealing with all matters connected with the industry, and one of the chief features of each scheme was the fixation of minimum prices for each class of coal, both in the inland and the export market, with penalties for selling below the agreed schedule prices.

These prices, though issued confidentially, could not be kept altogether secret, and unquestionably our competitors abroad were able to secure a vast amount of information concerning them. Coal-owners were unable to reduce their prices even when told that a penny or twopence reduction would secure a contract. Exporters thus found their difficulties increased in meeting competition abroad, difficulties which they had to find their own means of overcoming.

In addition, there was no elasticity in the schemes. The same minimum price had to be quoted for 100 tons as for 100,000 tons, so that the big buyer had no advantage over the small one. Wholesale evasion of the minimum price restrictions ensued, and a coach-and-six was everywhere driven through the Act of Parliament.

Keen controversy has always raged around the question of the extent, if any, to which our export trade in coal was affected by the provisions of this Act. Wherever the truth may lie, there can be no gainsaying either the rapidity or the magnitude of the decline. 1929 was a comparatively good year; in the early months of 1930 exports were well maintained on the 1929 level; in the summer there came the debates on this Act, with the threat of increased and regulated prices; before the Act was on the Statute Book the fall commenced; by the end of the year we were down by over 5 million tons. In 1931 the fall continued, and by the end of that year another 12 millions had gone; 17½ million tons in two years. In 1932 there was a further drop of 4 millions to 39 million tons, at round about which figure exports have since remained. In the same period bunkers shipped for the use of steamers engaged in the foreign trade decreased by over $2\frac{1}{2}$ million tons per annum. The total fall (exports and bunkers) was from $76\frac{1}{2}$ million tons in 1929 to 53 million tons in 1934, a loss of $23\frac{1}{2}$ million tons. The figure for 1935 is under 52 million tons. These figures leave out the coal equivalent of exported coke and manufactured fuel.

The other factors already mentioned have each in great or lesser degree been responsible for part of this heavy fall, but all the evidence seems to indicate that the restrictions imposed by the Act of 1930, which ought never to have been applied in the manner they were to the export trade, have also contributed their "quota" to the very regrettable decline.

The position might have been even worse but for the trade agreements entered into by the Government with other nations, particularly the Scandinavian countries and with Canada. Even in this direction, however, there was little real gain. Other coal-producing countries, particularly Poland and Germany, had expanded their productive capacity, and, driven out of these markets, they turned, aided by their Government subsidies, direct and indirect, to others, with the result that what we "gained on the swings" we "lost on the roundabouts".

The quota for export coal has now been separated from the inland quota, but even with this there appears to be little hope of any great expansion in the present position of world trade.

Recently, an agreement has been arrived at with Poland for quantitative regulation of exports to avoid ruthless price-cutting, and it would seem that it is in this direction, as in the case of the iron and steel industry, that there lies the chief hope of placing our export trade in coal on a really profitable basis, even if it is not on such a large scale as in the days of its former glory.

The changed conditions under which this trade is now carried on has brought about a demand for a change in the method of conducting it. The demand from coal-importing countries is now substantially lower than in pre-war days, while the productive capacity of coal-exporting countries is substantially higher. There is to-day little in the way of a "free market" for coal abroad. The total quantity imported into nearly every coal-importing country from all sources is limited by Government control, and in some countries is further controlled by the granting of licences permitting to each individual or firm the right to import only a certain fixed tonnage, and these licences may be used by the holders for bargaining purposes with the producers or exporters of the various coal-supplying nations. In others the quantity of British coal which must be taken is fixed by the respective Governments under the terms of their trade agreements, and the producers or exporters make their own arrangements with the importers as to who shall supply it and the price at which it shall be sold. In some cases the difficulties created by currency fluctuations and restrictions have led to a system of barter, in which a certain amount of coal is exchanged for an agreed quantity of some other commodity, in order to avoid what are known as "frozen credits", or, in plain language, in order that the supplier may receive reasonably prompt payment for the goods he delivers.

Agreements entered into by the ship-owners of the various maritime nations (voluntary agreements) have standardized freights to some extent, and thereby reduced somewhat the speculative element in the conduct of the business.

All these far-reaching changes in the field of international exchange, coupled with the restrictions on export imposed by the Act of 1930, make it evident that the methods of marketing British coal abroad which were so successful in pre-war days are no longer suited to the new conditions.

After the passing of the Act of 1930 a recognition of this fact led some of the coal-owners to embark on schemes for eliminating the intermediary or exporter and selling their coal direct to the consumer, either by the formation of subsidiary companies or by establishing their own selling agencies both at home and abroad; in short, a direct "producer to consumer" system, under which the coal producer, or combination of producers, would themselves undertake the duty of marketing the coal, a task which had hitherto been left mainly to the merchant or exporter. The largest of these organizations was formed in South Wales, and, along with one or two other "producer to consumer" associations, this is still in existence, and dealing with a very large proportion of the export trade from South Wales ports.

The proposal to oust the exporters from a field in which they had been supreme for so long naturally aroused very strong opposition, and in 1932 and 1933 led to a somewhat bitter controversy. Into the merits of that controversy we do not propose to enter. The arguments "for" and "against" are fully stated in two small pamphlets issued in 1932, the first, *I Fight for*

Coal, by Mr. H. H. Merrett, and a reply entitled *We Fight for Facts,* issued on behalf of the British Coal Exporters' Federation, where anyone interested may "read, mark, learn, and inwardly digest" them, and although the latter may severely tax his mental and intellectual powers of digestion, the reader will find in both a great deal of information and much to arouse controversy concerning this very important and highly complex branch of our export trade.

CHAPTER XX

Selling Prices—Transfer Prices—Association with other Industries

SELLING PRICES

THE selling price of coal is of primary importance to both owners and men, for it is the only source from which either profits or wages can come. Pithead prices should be adequate to enable the industry to give both a fair return to capital and to pay fair wages to its workpeople.

The consumer in the home market is vitally concerned also, however, in the selling price. Some of our industries, particularly the iron and steel industry, depend for their success at home and their competitive power abroad on cheap coal. Care must be taken in any raising of prices that this and other industries are not handicapped in the markets of the world by any unwarranted increase in their production costs through dearer coal, for the export trade is of vital importance to this country.

Leaving these industries aside, however, there is a very large volume of production the price of which per ton at the pithead could be raised without doing any serious injury to anyone.

Chief among the consumers who can afford to pay more are the public utility concerns—gas, water, and electricity. They have been getting their coal far too cheaply for many years owing to the fierce competition for their orders. They are all, or nearly all, prosperous concerns, paying good wages to their employees and returning a handsome dividend to their shareholders in the case of those privately owned. Where municipally owned the same is true, wages being good and the undertaking nearly always showing a substantial margin of profit. All of them could afford quite easily to pay an additional 2s. per ton for their coal. The charge in their case is one which can be widely spread, so widely, in fact, that in the majority of cases the effect on the price of the gas or electricity or water would be almost negligible. It is estimated that if the price of coal were increased by 10s. per ton it would add no more than a tenth of a penny to the cost of electricity per unit. A shilling per ton on all coal used by the gas industry would only increase the cost of gas by one-sixth of a penny per therm.

In the case of coal for household use there is without a doubt a margin which is far too wide between producer and consumer. The coal for the domestic fire passes through far too many hands before it reaches the home, and every one handling it takes something in the shape of profit. In those areas which are fortunately situated near or comparatively near to the coalfields consumers are not so much exposed to exploitation in this direction. In London and the south of England, however, the toll levied between the pit and the kitchen is very heavy and without doubt excessive. Even granting that the railway charges are excessive (round about 12s. per ton) there is far too big a margin for fair dealing.

On the south coast much of the household coal is sea borne and the cost of transport is thus only about half that of rail transport. Yet there also prices are as high as 53s. or 54s.

The Samuel Commission enquired very exhaustively into the selling prices of domestic fuel, particularly in the post-war years, and amongst other things said "the increase in the total margin required by the retail merchants and in their expenses is disquieting".

They reported that retailers' costs are excessive, and that if all the retail trade could be conducted as economically as that of the Co-operative Societies, a very substantial margin would be available either for reducing prices to the consumer or increasing them to the colliery and so adding to the miners' wages.

In London, "best" coal is being sold now (1936) to the unfortunate householder at 57s. 6d. per ton, plus 1s. 6d. per ton for delivery in sacks. "Best" coal varies in origin, quality, and price, and no one except the original buyer and seller, in each case, knows what it costs at the pithead. Average quality bright household coal, however, is retailed at 51s. to 53s. in sacks, delivered. It comes from different coalfields, but the average pithead price is about 26s. or 27s., a difference of 25s. to 26s. between the pit and the cellar. This is much higher than it should be, and it is evident that the margin for distribution is too great and has increased since the Samuel Commission made its report.

An examination of the distribution return from the Ministry of Mines will show the annual quantities consumed by the various users. The prices to the iron and steel and some other industries cannot be unduly increased without danger, and the export trade is in an entirely separate category. Foreign buyers are not swayed by sentiment, and in a competitive market prices are already sufficiently under control to ensure that exporters get the best prices obtainable. If the exporting districts are to pay increases of wages some means of compensating them for the increased cost of production will have to be found.

The general conclusion at which it is quite easy to arrive on an impartial examination of the facts is that with proper organization the price at the pithead, which is the chief thing that matters, could be substantially raised over a volume of production totalling at least 100 million tons with great advantage to owners and men alike and without doing any great injury to any section of the community, provided adequate safeguards against unduly high prices are forthcoming, particularly in the case of domestic coal.

TRANSFER PRICES

Many coal-producing companies are either composite concerns, or are associated with other undertakings which purchase coal, such as iron and steel companies, coke ovens, and by-product plants, and many coal-owners are either directors or otherwise connected with similar coal-buying concerns.

In the minds of the miners there is a deeply rooted suspicion that where such a connection exists between a coal-producing and a coal-consuming undertaking, coal is transferred to the buyers at figures below the market prices, with the result that in the ascertainments the wages fund is reduced and wages depressed.

Whilst it is probable that there have been, and may now be, cases of this kind, there is no evidence that the practice is a general one. It is the duty of the joint accountants to see that coal so sold or transferred is entered in the books at the proper market price, and as a matter of fact these prices are sometimes raised by the accountants during the ascertainment. The Samuel Commission paid a tribute to "the thoroughness of their methods and the spirit of fairness in which they approached their task".

At the same time the Commission reported that, despite this, "a radical change in the treatment of transfer prices is needed to place the wage ascertainments beyond suspicion". No definite conclusion could be reached that the transfer of coal under associated conditions did actually depress prices, but the fact that it could do so prevented the Commission from giving the miners an assurance that it did not and could not happen.

Recognizing the difficulty that would be created if, as a solution, the joint accountants had to be given power to examine the books of all the associated companies, as well as that caused by the differences in quality and price of the many grades of coal produced by the collieries, the Commission recommended that a solution might be found by ignoring altogether the transfer prices entered in the colliery company's books, and from time to time publicly and officially declaring "through some impartial authority in each district what shall be taken as the market price at that period of every kind of coal sold in the district".

In any event the establishment of the central selling agencies which are now to be set up should end this controversy once and for all.

As a matter of fact the effect of transfer prices on wages has been greatly exaggerated. The Samuel Commission reported that only 20 to 23 per cent of the output was so transferred and this could not, with the safeguards provided, affect the general level of wages. Such transfer, in any case, is confined to a few districts.

ASSOCIATION WITH OTHER INDUSTRIES

The question of transfer prices raises at once that of the relation of the mining industry to other industries either directly connected with it or dependent on it for their supplies of raw material.

In this connection the demand of the miners is that they should be allowed to share in the profits derived from the by-product industry. There is here involved a fundamental question of principle. That question is the extent to which the principle is to be applied. Science is making rapid strides in the discovery of new methods of utilizing raw coal. While some of them are associated with the coal-producing undertakings, others are quite independent, and look to the mining industry only to supply them the raw material most suitable for their processes.

The Samuel Commission recommended that the mining industry should be "intimately associated with several other industries—with gas, electricity, smokeless fuel, oil, chemical products, blast furnaces, and coke ovens." The extent of the association, however, was not defined, and in another part of the report the claim of the miners to have the revenue derived from the manufacture of coke by firms in which colliery companies were financially interested included in the ascertainments for wage fixing was definitely rejected—"any direct inclusion of coking labour with mining at the same rates of net proceeds would be manifestly absurd".

The chief reason for this conclusion, undoubtedly the right one, is that there is a fundamental difference in the proportion that wages bear to the total cost of production. If the claim will not bear examination in respect of those undertakings associated with coal-producing concerns it must be still more "absurd" if made in respect of independent undertakings. The same argument will apply in the case of the production of benzol, smokeless fuel, petrol, heavy oils, or chemical products, no matter what the process employed—hydrogenation, low-temperature carbonization, or any other.

The whole weight of argument is against the claim. A boundary line must be drawn somewhere. The producer of wheat does not share in the profits derived from his product in all its stages from the earth to the breakfast table, nor the producer of cotton in the profits obtained from the use of his product from the cotton field to its final form as a shirt on a man's back, or part of an explosive used in the extraction of coal or the slaughter of men in the interests of peace and civilization. The interests of the miners should be safeguarded by a strict supervision of transfer prices, but the very desirable expansion of the new industries now being established for the utilization of coal can be best promoted by leaving them to develop in complete independence and freedom, with a free market in which to purchase to the best advantage those commodities (not only coal) they require for the success of their undertakings, and which they deserve for their enterprise.

CHAPTER XXI

Mining Royalties—State Acquisition and Method of Leasing—Mining Wayleaves

MINING ROYALTIES

In redemption of the pledge given to the electors last year, the Government will shortly introduce into the House of Commons a Bill for the unification or nationalization of mining royalties. Such a measure is long overdue, and when introduced the Bill will be the most important piece of legislation in connection with the coal industry since the Act of 1930. It is, therefore, very desirable that the public should understand clearly what is the existing situation, the new situation which the Government will endeavour to establish, and the method by which the desired results are to be attained.

The position as it exists to-day dates back to the time of Elizabeth. For nearly four hundred years English law, in regard to the ownership of ungotten minerals, with the exception of gold and silver, has been based on a decision of the courts in 1568 that, with this exception, all minerals are the property of the landowners, i.e. that his ownership is not confined to the surface, but extends to the centre of the earth. Broadly speaking, Great Britain and the United States are the only coal-producing countries where this principle obtains. In almost all other countries the State owns the coal, and either works it or grants concessions to do so.

There can be no denying the fact that private ownership of the minerals has operated greatly to the disadvantage of the mining industry. Every tribunal which, in recent years, has enquired into the condition of the industry has condemned it and stressed the need for unification. Even the Sankey Commission, which issued seven separate reports, and the members of which differed on almost every issue on which they had to report, were unanimous in this. In recent years the difficulties under which the industry labours because of this private ownership of the mineral have become widely recognized. The principle of public ownership has been accepted by the Government and endorsed by almost everybody except the royalty owner himself.

The chief disabilities which the private ownership of the mineral imposes on the industry are:

(1) The layout of a minefield is governed largely by surface boundaries and surface rights. These are the least-important considerations in planning for efficient production.

(2) A colliery owner sinking a shaft has often to obtain leases from a multiplicity of land-owners. The average number is five. One only may, if he chooses, cause untold trouble and expense, and gravely hinder much needed development, by refusing to lease or demanding unreasonable or exorbitant terms.

(3) Under the existing system it is not possible to plan ahead for the best development of the coal seams in an area. This results in increased costs of production and waste of both physical effort and valuable time by compelling the miner to travel long distances below ground to the coal face.

(4) The necessity for leaving barriers of coal between

the property of one royalty owner and that of another. This is both wasteful and unnecessary. Many millions of valuable and easily won coal have had to be left underground for this reason.

(5) The colliery owner has no prompt and effective means of redress when suffering from these grievances. Recourse to the courts, as the law stands, is expensive, dilatory, and unsatisfactory, so that in the majority of cases he prefers to suffer—and to pay.

(6) The very heavy charge levied for royalties and way-leaves, both surface and undergound. The average royalty charge is 5·86d. per ton (1934). The highest is 1s. 9d. per ton (in South Wales) and the total sum paid £4,840,594 (1934).[1]

(7) The psychological effect produced in the minds of the workers by the knowledge that very large sums of money are paid every year to fortunate individuals who contribute nothing to the carrying on of the industry.

The Acquisition and Valuation of Land Committee appointed after the war gave a list of fourteen defects in the existing system, all of which militated against the efficient working of the coal seams, but the above list may be regarded as summarizing them all.

In every other field of human activity moneys paid as royalties are payments made for service rendered or work done by the recipient. In the case of mining royalties no service is rendered. The royalty owner receives payment of these large sums solely because Nature planted the coal under his land, because the State in less enlightened times allowed the system to grow until it became firmly established, and a coal royalty as much a form of property in the eyes of the

[1] The 1935 figures are practically the same.

law as any other. The system, however, is bad for the industry and bad for the nation. In these times it is morally and economically indefensible, and ought therefore to be ended as speedily as possible.

Before considering unification, let us examine the results of the continuation of the pre-war system in the post-war period, the evils which the change is intended to eradicate, and which are daily becoming more irksome under the new and infinitely more difficult conditions.

Evils of the Existing System

Post-war changes in the economic position of the industry have not only emphasized the seriousness of the burden of royalties in general, but revealed also the inequalities and injustices of the existing system, which imposes the heaviest charges on the exporting districts, those least able to bear them. In the main, royalty rates were fixed during a period of phenomenal expansion in the industry. In the forty years from 1874 to 1914 production increased from 127 million to 287 million tons. A remarkable feature of this increase was the growth of the export trade, for while home consumption had increased from 109 millions to 189 millions, the export figures rose from 17 millions to 98 millions. Whilst the increased output of 160 million tons was evenly divided between the home and export trade, the percentage increase in the former was only 73 per cent, and in the export trade no less than 470 per cent.

The owners of the mineral were thus in a position of great strength particularly in the exporting areas, and as the demand from abroad increased in the years immediately before the war, royalty rates in these districts were steadily raised and more onerous terms imposed on the colliery owners by the mineral owners, who were virtually in a position to dictate their own terms. Thus, while the general method of making payment for royalty charges is that of a fixed sum per ton of coal produced, or an equivalent charge based on the area and thickness of coal worked, other liabilities for payment were introduced into mining leases and still persist. These include "fixed rent", a minimum charge which must be paid whether coal is worked or not; a fixed sum per foot thickness of coal worked, and a sliding scale based on the selling price of the coal produced.

These different methods of payment, the varying conditions of the leases, and the economic changes in the position of the industry, have brought about grave injustices and inequalities in the incidence of the burden which have long called for redress.

The chief method of payment is that of a fixed sum per ton of coal produced, and a glance at the annual summary issued by the Mines Department shows at once the extent of the charge and the uneven nature of its distribution. The average charge is 5·86d. per ton, but, like most averages, this figure conceals great variations. The most striking of these is the difference between South Wales (mainly exporting) and South Derbyshire (mainly inland). The average in South Wales is 8·67d. per ton, and in South Derbyshire 3·83d. per ton (1934). Yet South Wales is one of the most depressed areas and South Derbyshire one of the most prosperous.

Broadly speaking, the incidence of royalty charges is heaviest where trade is bad and lightest where it is good. Thus in 1934, Yorkshire, North Derby, and Notts, South

Derby, Leicestershire, and Cannock Chase produced 72½ million tons and paid in royalties £1,429,000. South Wales produced 31 million tons and paid £1,115,000. On an output greater by 135 per cent only 28 per cent more was paid in royalties. The average per ton in the first case was 4·73d. per ton and in South Wales 8·67d., or nearly double. It should be noted that these three inland areas have not only a sheltered market, but that they have benefited largely by the tariff policy of the Government, which has greatly stimulated demand in the iron and steel industry, and also increased it in other industries through the improvement in trade in general. South Wales and other exporting districts, on the other hand, have had to face the full blast of foreign competition, much of it subsidized, the competition of oil (in the Navy and Mercantile Marine particularly), and other forms of motive power, as well as the fruits of economic nationalism in the form of the intensive development of their own coal measures by other countries (irrespective of all economic considerations) and the safeguarding of their own interests by the imposition of tariffs, licences, quotas, currency restrictions, and even prohibition. Compared with 1913, total production in 1934 fell by 66 million tons, and of this, no less than 41 million tons, or 62 per cent of the total, was due to the decline in exports, which fell from 98 million to 57 million tons. Thus, while total production dropped by 23 per cent, exports fell by 42 per cent, and inland consumption by only 12 per cent, from 184 million to 162 million tons. The heaviest losses have thus fallen on the exporting districts, and in so doing have completey reversed the relationship of the coal-producing areas.

In pre-war days, the exporting districts were not only prosperous, but made the greatest profits. In the five pre-war years, the annual profit of the whole industry was roughly £13,000,000 per annum, or about 1s. per ton. In the five years 1930–1934, the profits were £3,000,000 per annum or about 3d. per ton. The whole of the 1930–1934 profits, however, were earned by the inland districts, and over this five years period the exporting districts show a loss of nearly a million pounds, whilst the inland districts had a credit balance of £14,000,000. The exporting districts, producing nearly 40 per cent of all the coal, had an annual loss of nearly £200,000, while the inland districts had an annual gain of nearly £3,000,000.

While profits in the whole industry were thus divided by four, the royalty owner was on velvet. None of the adverse factors already mentioned affected him except the reduced output. The average royalty in the five pre-war years was 5·64d. and in 1930–34 it was 5·43d., a reduction of 3·7 per cent. IN THE FIVE PRE-WAR YEARS, PROFITS WERE MORE THAN TWICE AS MUCH AS ROYALTIES. IN THE LAST FIVE YEARS ROYALTIES WERE NEARLY TWICE AS MUCH AS PROFITS. While profits have been reduced by £10,000,000, the sum total of royalties has been reduced by only £1,000,000, and this reduction is attributable to one cause only, the fall in output. The royalty owner's £5,000,000 has been secure, whatever might happen to profits or wages.

In the mining industry nearly 70 per cent of the proceeds go to wages. In pre-war days the ratio of profits to wages was as 17 to 100. In the last five years it has been 3·3 per cent. While profits have thus declined generally and vanished altogether in the exporting districts, the mineworkers also have had to bear their share of the misfortunes which have befallen the industry. Wages have fluctuated violently and until recently were practically stabilized at pre-war levels, allowing for the increased cost of living. The number of wage earners has fallen from 1,080,000 in 1913 to 754,000 in 1935, in round figures, so that with the shrinkage in employment, the total wages paid in the industry are at least £30,000,000 less per annum, an appalling loss of purchasing power to the nation. Through all the changes, while capital and labour, the wealth creators, have had to adapt themselves to new conditions and shoulder the burden of the losses due to them, nothing has disturbed the serenity of the royalty owner, who could afford to smile through it all, sure of his payment on every ton of coal produced, and in some cases if none at all were produced. His is the first charge on the industry. The colliery owner must provide for it before sinking his shaft and pay it whether he makes a profit or a loss.

In the prosperous pre-war days, with a rapidly expanding industry, these royalty charges, even though unjustifiable, and in some cases extortionate, were not generally sufficiently onerous to handicap enterprise or to hinder development. The industry could afford to pay them. To-day, the position is entirely different. Expansion has ended; output is stabilized with little hope of any substantial increase in demand, either at home or abroad. The number of workpeople is growing steadily less, and those still engaged in the industry are demanding higher wages, while competition grows fiercer and any return on invested capital becomes more difficult to obtain.

Evidence of the unequal and excessive nature of

these royalty charges was forthcoming in the House of Commons on April 11, 1934, when the Secretary for the Mines Department said that in nine cases in South Wales, the royalty paid exceeded 1s. per ton in 1925, and the highest rate was 1s. 9d. per ton. At the time of the post-war boom in cases where the royalty was based on the selling price, the coal producers were actually paying as high as 3s. 9d. per ton of output.

The lack of uniformity is not confined to the amount of the royalty. It extends also to the length of the lease, to the method of payment, and other terms or conditions imposed in the lease by the mineral owner, varying only with the power he possesses through the need of the lessee. Some of the latter constitute an even greater grievance than the financial burden of the royalties or wayleaves themselves, and the power to impose them on any industry is not one which should be allowed to remain in the hands of private individuals.

Amongst these is the form of royalty known as "dead rent". This is the method of payment already referred to as "fixed" or "certain" or "minimum" rent. It is levied on the area of the surface acreage and may be as high as £5 per acre per annum. No definite principle has ever governed this form of levy, and each case has been determined by local conditions and the attitude of the mineral owner. The worst feature of the system is that the royalty must be paid whether the coal is worked or not. In some cases this annual charge is merged in the royalty charge for the full period of the lease, and in these cases the coal producers are able to average their payments. If in any year they do not produce enough coal to meet the "dead rent" charge, this can be carried forward and set against the total amount due to the mineral owner. In many cases, however, this is nullified by the fact that the "average" clause in the lease may be for only one, two, or three years. If, within these limits the colliery owner is unable to recover his short workings, the "dead rents" are forfeited. In such cases the colliery owners are actually paying royalties twice over. During the last few years hundreds of thousands of pounds have been forfeited through this unjust method of collecting royalties, because the condition of the industry prevented colliery owners from recovering shortages within the period stated in the average clause. The coal being still unworked, absolutely nothing has been received by the colliery owners in return for these large payments. In justice to the colliery owners, they should be regarded as part payments for the ungotten coal, and in the valuation which will be made under the forthcoming legislation, they should be brought into account for that purpose.

Unification

Whilst it is no longer seriously contested that the private ownership of the minerals is opposed to the national interest, it is no easy task discarding a system which has governed the production of coal for nearly four hundred years and replacing it by another more suited to our day. It is one which bristles with difficulties, and this is the main reason why successive Governments have been reluctant to deal with it, despite the recommendations of numerous Royal Commissions and Courts of Enquiry. These difficulties must be faced, for no matter how great they may be, they are neither as great nor as important as the difficulties imposed on the industry by the private ownership of the ungotten coal. Once boldly grappled with, and overcome, the former are done with, whilst unless they *are* overcome, the industry can never be freed from the difficulties under which it has laboured for so long and is still suffering to-day.

Before dealing with the methods to be adopted for the State acquisition of existing royalties, there are two aspects of the problem which call for attention, and which must not be omitted from the new legislation. These are the questions of unsuspected or undiscovered coal deposits, and known deposits at such deep levels as to be unworkable. In both these cases the coal should become State property by a declaration of State ownership. The principle has been accepted in the case of the Petroleum Production Act, and there is no reason why it should not be made applicable to coal in these cases. It inflicts no injustice on any landowner and effectively shuts out the possibility of any recurrence of existing evils in the event of such seams being worked in the future.

A decision to apply this principle in these two cases would remove them from the realm of controversy, and by preventing any possibility of complicating the issue, confine legislative action strictly to the vital part of the problem, i.e. the method of dealing with the existing deposits of coal, both those which are now being worked and those at present unworked at normal levels.

Even in regard to the latter, there is one direction in which the matter of unification might be simplified. This is in dealing with that section of mineral ownership in which the freehold of the coal measures is the property of the colliery owner or undertaking working them. It is unthinkable that any undertaking mining coal should be placed in a worse position either financially or otherwise under State ownership of the mineral than under the existing system, and as the undertaking is now working its own property, the simplest way to deal with this part of the problem would be to grant to it a perpetual lease at a nominal or peppercorn rent, with the option of purchase by the State where preferred. This would remove them from the ambit of the proposed legislation except so far as the minerals which are not their own property are concerned, and to that extent reduce the amount of work involved in valuation and in fixing the amount of compensation to be awarded in such cases.

The fundamental reason for unification being the necessity for increased efficiency and economy in the production of coal, the new proposals must be so framed that they not only bring technical advantages to the industry, but also some measure of financial relief, particularly in those cases where the royalty and way-leave charges have hitherto been so high as to constitute a real burden on the undertaking compelled to pay them.

The State having for so long recognized the right of private ownership, cannot now be justified in claiming possession by confiscation of those rights. Such action can no more be morally justifiable in this case than in the case of any other form of property, a legal right to which has been established and recognized by the State, and is indeed not now advocated except by a small section of extreme Socialists. Acquisition by purchase is, therefore, the only legitimate method of acquiring these properties, making the State the only royalty owner and relieving the colliery owners of the disabilities consequent upon multiple ownership.

The Samuel Commission made an exhaustive examination of this subject, and came to the conclusion that the probable price to be paid for all existing royalties and underground wayleaves in "just and fair compensation" to the existing owners was £92,000,000 and adding £8,000,000 for contingencies, accepted £100,000,000 as a maximum figure. The calculations were based on figures supplied by the Board of Inland Revenue, and taking into account all relevant factors such as diminished income-tax yield, loss of mineral rights duty, provision for interest and sinking fund, the Commission expressed the view that the transaction would have practically no effect on the National Budget.

In these calculations it was assumed that the royalty charge would remain at existing figures, and the total burden of £6,000,000 remain a charge on the industry but be paid to the State instead of to private individuals. The Commission, however, foresaw the possibility of excessive claims and this is the danger which will have to be faced when the valuations are made under the new Act which is to nationalize the royalties. In the intervening ten years the value of money has changed, and this is sure to bring a demand from the royalty owners for a substantial increase in the purchase price. *It must be resisted.* The chief interest of the nation is not the royalty owner, but the industry itself. The royalty owner neither toils nor spins, while the colliery owner contributes his capital, knowledge and technical skill, the miner contributes his labour in the most hazardous of all occupations, and the consumer bears the burden of the royalty charge in the price he pays for his coal.

Under State ownership of the minerals the chief object to be aimed at should be the relieving of the industry of any and every impost or impediment which hampers development, handicaps enterprise, or hinders efficient and economical working. Unification will remove the technical disadvantages, but this is not enough. The existing charges are too heavy for the industry to bear, and when the State resumes the ownership of the mineral the eventual objective should be to reduce them to a "peppercorn" figure paid in recognition of the right of control by the State and so relieve the industry of the greater part of the financial burden. It is the duty of the State to encourage industry, not to hamper it, or to make profit out of it. "Fair and just" compensation should be paid for the existing royalties, but there are many cases where there has never been any justification for the very high charges; there is a great deal less to-day. To base the purchase price on prevailing figures in the latter cases would be neither "fair" nor "just". To do so would merely stabilize the existing burden and delay inordinately the time when any relief could be given to the industry by a reduction.

The mining industry is passing through a very difficult period; it cannot afford to make these large payments with nothing in return, and it is against the national interest that coal producers should be asked to do so.

Coal is the bedrock foundation of our whole industrial life, and at a time when shipping, sugar beet, and agriculture are being financially assisted by the State, the colliery owner and the miner may justly demand that in the financial provisions of the new Act of Parliament, such provision will be made as will rapidly and progressively reduce the royalty charges, even if it involves an annual contribution from the Exchequer, until such time as the debt is extinguished and the cost per ton is merely nominal.

STATE ACQUISITION AND METHOD OF LEASING

It is to be presumed that in the forthcoming Bill the Government will make provision for taking over the whole of the minerals comprising the coal measures, including those ancillary to the winning of coal. Some authority, to be called the Coal Commissioners or Royalty Commissioners, will then be appointed and in this body will be vested the administration of the national mineral estate.

In the light of past experience there are four considerations to which great importance should be attached in setting up this body. These are:

(1) That if statutory powers are to be conferred upon it, those powers should be clearly and definitely set forth in the Act of Parliament, free from the ambiguity which has marked some of the legislation of recent years in connection with the coal-mining industry.

(2) That it should be a body composed of business men with some legal members and independent technical experts, but without representation of either the coal-owners or the workers in the industry.

(3) That as far as possible it should be free from any kind of political influence or possibility of political pressure, but as in the case of the Import Duties Advisory Committee, either the Board of Trade or some other Government department should be responsible to Parliament for its exercise of the very extensive powers conferred upon it directly or indirectly by the legislature.

(4) That irrespective of whether the powers given to it are conferred by statute or delegated to it by some Government Department, there should be a right of appeal by an aggrieved party to the arbitrament

of an outside independent tribunal, whose judgement shall be final, so as to avoid the possibility of lengthy and costly litigation.

Having "entered into possession" it will be the duty of the commissioners to grant the necessary leases. In the case of existing leases several points of outstanding importance will require very careful consideration. These are:

(1) *Consolidation of Existing Leases.* The main reason for unification being to increase efficiency the leases now held by any undertaking should be merged into one on terms not more onerous from the start than those of the present multiple system.

(2) *Length of Lease.* A point to be determined will be whether leases should be granted in perpetuity to those now working the mineral or whether they should be limited. If the former the rights of the two parties to terminate even a nominally perpetual lease will have to be clearly defined. If the latter, the rights of reversion at the end of the lease will have to be clearly stated as between the two parties, as well as the position of the lessee in relation to the owners of the surface lands. In determining the length of the lease regard will have to be paid to the length of life of the seams, for coal is a wasting asset.

(3) *Terms of Lease.* Whilst it is out of the question that in this industry uniform conditions could be embodied in all leases, the worst of the anomalies and inequalities of the existing system must be removed. Owing to less favourable conditions a number of leases have already been renewed on better terms, and it is certain that in many others reduction in the charges would be made as they fall due for renewal, even without unification. In

> this connection it should be noted that the disposition to grant more favourable terms is not so marked as it was before the proposals of the Government were announced. Some leases were arranged when trade was good and some when it was bad, so that the inequalities exist not merely between the districts but also between leases in the same area.

Another point which is certain to arise is the question of the relationship between the new owners of the mineral and the owners of the surface lands in cases where both are at present the property of one proprietor. In such cases it frequently happens that the owner refrains from building in order to work the mineral fully. If under the new conditions he is to be made liable for surface damage where no such liability exists at present, the terms of the lease will have to be modified to meet the new situation.

The Method of Valuation and Purchase

From time to time various methods of fixing the amounts to be paid to the royalty owners have been propounded, and there can be little doubt that this will prove one of the most difficult aspects of the transition from private to State ownership.

Reference has already been made to the fact that the Samuel Commission estimated the total cost of £100,000,000. The value of money has changed in the interval, so has the economic position of the industry; it is probable that to-day a slightly larger sum will be required, but the increase in the capital charge should not be sufficient to give rise to any anxiety.

The difficulties will arise when the royalty owners file their claims and the Commission, as an impartial administrative body, finds itself faced with the delicate task of fixing the amount of compensation to be awarded in each case with even-handed justice to the claimant while jealously guarding the interests of the State.

It is impossible within the limits of my space to go into all the details of the different methods proposed, but one or two may be mentioned.

It has been suggested that in every individual case the value of the royalty should be determined by Government valuers appointed for the purpose. Another suggestion is that a general basis should be fixed of fifteen years' purchase of the amount received by the royalty owner on a five-year average, less mineral rights duty. A third proposal is that in each case the valuation should be that adopted by the Commissioners of Inland Revenue for the purpose of fixing death duties less mineral rights duty. Another is that as the districts are clearly defined, a total sum should be allotted to each district and the amount to be awarded to each individual claimant settled by a specially appointed tribunal in each district.

Whatever method may be adopted, however, the variations are so great that nothing like uniformity can be, or ought to be, expected. Very careful consideration will have to be given to the changes in the volume, nature, and direction of the demand, to the inequalities of the royalty charge not only as between mine and mine, but also as between district and district; to the fact that some landowners have exploited the needs of the producer whilst others have not; to cases where the more valuable seams have been exhausted as compared with those in the earlier stages of production; to the need, in fixing the charges, for new machinery and plant, requiring fresh capital in order to reduce the costs of production at what is probably the most difficult period in the history of the industry. It is essential that in fixing the amount of compensation the payments made in advance to the royalty owner should be set off against the total awarded. In cases where the royalty charge has been excessive (as in South Wales) due regard should be paid in fixing the amount of compensation to the very large sums taken out of the industry in excess of a "fair and just" payment over a very long period of years. Account will also have to be taken of the royalty owner's liability for surface damage in many cases on the termination of a lease. And lastly, though this does not by any means exhaust the many considerations involved, there should be no compensation paid for underground wayleaves, a form of levying toll on the industry which ought never to have been permitted.

The task of framing a satisfactory measure to deal with all the complexities which have arisen during the operation of this hundreds of years' old system is not an easy one. The task of the new authority charged with the duty and responsibility of administering the Act will be a heavy and difficult one. The evils of the existing system, however, make the long-deferred change necessary, and its complexities make it imperative that in drafting the measure and altering or amending it in its passage through the House, the exact meaning of its various provisions should be laid down in terms which are crystal clear, and the statutory powers of the newly constituted authority defined with equal clarity in the Act itself. With this, and appeal to an outside independent tribunal provided for, the road should be open for a great improvement which has been strenuously advocated for many years in many quarters, but which will fall short of general expectation unless it lightens the financial burden carried for too long by the industry, and from which it is now, in very difficult circumstances, entitled to some measure of relief.

MINING WAYLEAVES

Another grievance calling for redress, and one which must be dealt with in the new Bill, is the heavy toll levied on the industry for surface and underground wayleaves. It is of little use a colliery owner putting his brains and capital into the sinking of a shaft unless he can get his coal to the shaft, to bank, port of shipment, or to a railway without paying heavily for the privilege.

For many years and in every coalfield, the industry has suffered from the extortionate prices insisted on by the owners of surface land for the right to convey coal from the seam to the shaft, or up the shaft, from the pit to the railway, blast furnace, coke oven, or loading wharf. These landowners are monopolists; the coal *must* pass over or under their land in most cases, and they have, therefore, a power which they do not fail to use. The manner in which it is used and the effect on the coal and iron and steel industries cannot be better illustrated than by giving the facts of a case which came before the courts in 1934 and 1935. This was the case of the Consett Iron Company Ltd. and the Trustees of the Clavering and Towneley estates.

The facts in this case were:

(1) The Consett Iron Company applied for relief from excessive rents charged for wayleaves for use of surface land used as a railway.

(2) The railway was constructed by the Consett Iron Company, and is maintained and worked by them.
(3) There is no other way of transporting the coal.
(4) The land concerned comprises an area of about 27 acres of a maximum letting value of £5 per acre per annum.
(5) The landowners will not sell the land.
(6) From January 1, 1890, to December 31, 1931, the Consett Iron Company paid, for the use only of these 27 acres, a total of £164,473, or £6,092 per acre (without interest).
(7) As long as the pits are working, the company which has supplied the brains, the capital, the enterprise, and the workers who have provided the labour, must submit to paying £6,000 per annum for permission to use this small piece of land, and pay it to those who do nothing to assist, but receive it in full, whether there is a profit or a loss, and no matter how low the wages the company can afford to pay its workers.

The case was brought before the Railway and Canal Commission in 1934, under the provisions of the Mines (Working Facilities and Support) Act, 1923, and the Mining Industry Act, 1926. This court found in favour of the company and ordered the rent to be reduced to £10 per acre or £270 per annum. The lessors appealed and in 1935 the judgement was reversed in the Court of Appeal. There is no appeal to the House of Lords. The decision of the Appeal Court caused great surprise, for there can be no doubt whatever that the *intention* of Parliament was to give the courts the power to grant relief in this very type of case.

The Railway and Canal Commission in Scotland had previously come to the same conclusion as the similar body in England; had granted the relief asked for, and there was no appeal.

The position now, therefore, is that the law means one thing in England and another in Scotland.

The Consett case is a typical one. In no circumstances whatever should any industry be subjected to "stand and deliver" treatment of this character. The landowners have, in most cases, received in rent the full value of their land over and over again, and it is the duty of Parliament, in the new legislation, to see that the errors in the Acts of 1923 and 1926 are rectified, and the industry relieved of charges for which, in the twentieth century, there can be neither justification nor excuse.

Commission after Commission has reported that as in the case of royalties, landowners have demanded as wayleaves rates of payment which are exorbitant and bound to impede development. These rates vary from 0·09 per ton to as high as 4½d. per ton. These higher rates are caused by the fact that the coal producer is sometimes compelled to make separate leases with a large number of landowners and each of these takes as much as he can get in the form of a levy on each ton of coal that passes over his strip. He is a monopolist and can dictate his own terms. In a recent judgement Mr. Justice McKinnon said that the lessor of a wayleave had nothing to sell except his unwillingness to grant. "The value of the land can only be fixed by the factor of his own cupidity and the necessity of the lessee, who is the only possible purchaser." In one case, no less than 4½d. per ton was charged as wayleave for coal transported less than half a mile from the pithead.

Other illustrations of the disabilities imposed on the colliery owner are:

Payment of wayleave charges on coal transported from

the pit to the colliery boilers and from the pit to the coke ovens associated with it.

Payment of wayleaves where they do not merge in the dead rent in respect of exhausted properties.

Payment of a surface wayleave for coal on which no underground wayleave is charged.

Payment of shaft wayleaves in addition to high rates of royalty.

Payment of underground wayleave on coal brought through an exhausted area. This means that the landowner having received payment for his coal, can demand and receive payment for the right to bring other coal through the exhausted and valueless area left behind.

The history of the royalty and wayleave system has been one of exploitation by the landowner at the expense of the industry, under expanding and monopolistic conditions so favourable as to enable him to make his own terms.

While enormous changes have taken place in the technique of the industry both above and below ground, while mechanization has increased tremendously and very large sums of money have been expended by the coal producers on the installation of washing, breaking and sizing machinery, and the establishment of by-product plants, the royalty and wayleave owner has not only contributed nothing to the expansion or prosperity or preservation of the industry, but the method of exacting payment for royalties and way-leaves and other conditions in mining leases has remained, in the main, entirely unaltered throughout.

In the post-war period the trading conditions under which the industry has been carried on have been much less favourable than in the pre-war period of expansion. Parliament recognized this and the Acts of 1923 and

1926 were intended to give some relief to the producer by safeguarding him *"in the national interest"* against excessive and extortionate charges. These Acts of Parliament gave him the right of appeal against them to the Railway and Canal Commission. The power which Parliament undoubtedly intended to give to the Commission was taken away from it so far as existing leases are concerned by the decision in the Consett case already referred to. It is important that in the forthcoming legislation that power should either be restored or vested in some other independent tribunal so that some safeguard may be provided against the excessive charges now levied by private landowners for wayleaves as well as to afford the producer some protection against any possible exploitation by the State itself when the royalties become the property of the nation.

CHAPTER XXII

Mechanization—Accidents—The Miners' Welfare Fund

MECHANIZATION

THE changes which have been taking place and are still taking place in the industry cannot be better illustrated than by the great increase in the amount of coal produced by machine mining. The following table gives the total of machine-got coal for each year from 1925 to 1935, with 1913 for comparison.

To the nearest million

	Million tons		Million tons
1913	24	1930	76
1925	48	1931	77
1926	*28	1932	80
1927	58	1933	88
1928	61	1934	104
1929	72	1935	113

* National stoppage in 1926.

In 1935, a total of 92 million tons was mechanically cleaned, mostly by washing, nearly twice as much as in 1927.

The amount of coal won by machine mining has increased from just over 8 per cent to just over 50 per cent since 1913. This accounts to a large extent for the reduction in the numbers employed. The reduction will continue, for we are still behind some other countries in mechanical mining, and this as it extends will reduce the number of workers still further. The German mines in the Ruhr are winning practically all their coal mechanically, and one of the results is that the output per man shift has risen since 1913 from 18·6 cwt. to 33 cwt. in 1934, compared with 24 cwt. in Great Britain (March 1936). Largely for the same reasons the output in Poland has increased from 23½ cwt. to 38½ against our 24. If the output per man shift increased in this country to 30 cwt. (it is already 28 in Derbyshire) the annual output of the worker, on a full-time basis of 5½ shifts per week, would rise to 420 tons, and this, on an output of 220 million tons, would give employment to only 550,000 wage earners, a reduction of 200,000. So far as mechanization is concerned, however, it must be remembered that geological conditions are different in this country.

The march of science is enabling every coal consumer to get more out of every ounce of coal, so that unemployment in the actual getting of coal is being caused to an ever increasing extent by improved methods of both production and utilization.

Since 1929 the output of coal has declined by 14 per cent, but the volume of employment has been reduced by 22 per cent.

ACCIDENTS

The mining of coal is the most dangerous of all industrial occupations and its toll of human life is greater than that of any other industry. For many years mine-owners and the legislature together have been working steadily towards an increasing standard of safety in the mines. The first Act of Parliament providing for the inspection of mines was passed in

1850, and since then many others have been placed on the Statute Book, all with a view to the safeguarding of life in this hazardous occupation. As a result of increased inspection, extensive research work and greater precautions in minimizing the unavoidable risk, the fatal accident rate above and below ground declined steadily from an average of 2·24 per 1,000 persons employed in the ten years 1873–82, to 1·05 in the ten years period 1923–32. In 1920 a low record was reached of 0·88 per 1,000. Since that date, with the exception of 1934, the death-rate has fluctuated but little, being almost stationary at about 1 per 1,000, despite the fact that the fatal accident figures were swollen by explosions in every year except 1921, 1924, and 1929. Whilst causing a serious and regrettable loss of life, none of these was on a big scale, each involving a death-roll of between ten in the smallest and fifty-two in the case of the largest, and almost everyone connected with the industry had come to believe that in British mines, at all events, the big explosion was a thing of the past, when, on September 22, 1934, the country was terribly shocked and deeply moved by the appalling disaster at Gresford Colliery, in which 265 persons lost their lives, the worst in the industry for over twenty years. This made 1934 a bad year, the number of killed being 1,073 against 820 in 1933 (1,066 and 815 for coal mines alone), and the death-rate per 1,000 1·35 in 1934 against 1·03 (all mines under the Coal Mines Act) in 1933.

In 1934 explosions were responsible for the death of 296 persons, including the 265 victims of the Gresford disaster. Four hundred and thirty-five were killed by falls of ground, 156 by haulage accidents, 16 by shaft accidents, and 89 by causes of a miscellaneous nature, making a total of 992 below ground. Seventy-four were killed on the surface, the main contributory factors being railways, sidings, and tramways (34), and machinery accidents (18), and the remainder in accidents of various kinds. In addition 3,216 were seriously injured.

The big explosion, with its appalling sacrifice of life at one fell swoop, strikes the public imagination, stirs the social conscience and rouses the nation's sympathy, as was abundantly shown in the magnificent response to the appeal for funds for the relief of the dependents of the victims of the Gresford disaster. These figures, however, show that while these happily rare disasters result in a heavy loss of life at one blow, it is the normal, day-to-day work in the pits which is responsible for the greatest number of fatal accidents. The big explosion is now very rare, and it is not too much to expect that with the advance of scientific knowledge and the closing down of the older pits, it will be eliminated altogether. The causes of accidents are well known and are dealt with very fully in the Annual Report of the Ministry of Mines. They are continually under review by the Chief Inspector and his staff, by various committees appointed to consider the different aspects of the problem, by the Safety in Mines Research Board, and a Royal Commission is now sitting to consider the whole question.

Admirable work is also being done in the "safety classes" for boys which have been established in a number of the coalfields.

The whole matter is highly technical, and it is only included here to give the general reader an idea of the dangers inherent in the industry and the increasing efforts made to minimize them. The combined forces at work on research, with concentration on the better pits and increased supervision by the Mines Department, should result in a reduction in the number of deaths from explosions and falls of ground, the most difficult of all the causes to guard against, whilst an extension of the "safety" instruction and a greater appreciation of "safety first" should result in a reduction of the number resulting from avoidable causes. In industry the human factor can never be eliminated, so that it is not surprising to find the Chief Inspector of Mines in his report repeatedly stressing the point that with proper care and attention on the part of the men, the number of accidents could be substantially reduced. In his report for 1935 the Divisional Inspector for the Northern Division says: "In respect of haulage accidents the record of this division is an unenviable one, and the rate is much higher than it should be; 72 per cent of the accidents could have been prevented with ordinary care and caution." It is, moreover, surprising to the layman to find that in this dangerous occupation, the "familiarity which breeds contempt" could be carried so far that in 1934 there were no less than 49 convictions for the improper use of explosives, 49 for smoking or taking matches into the pit, and 20 for "endangering life and limb"—revealing a disregard of danger on the part of the offenders to themselves and their fellow workers which it would require a psycho-analyst to explain.

While there is some evidence that there is need for improvement in the Coal Mines Regulations Acts, as well as for a tightening up of the administration, and the exercising of greater care on the part of the workers, it is satisfactory to know that the coal mines in this country are as safe as any in the world, and much safer than those of the two nearest countries in productive capacity, Germany and the United States of America. "Coal mining in Great Britain is safer than in any other great coal-producing country. Science knows no reason, nor do I, why it should not be made safer still." (Sir Richard Redmayne, *Daily Herald*, December 8, 1933.)

There is no doubt, however, that they could be made safer, and there could be no more worthy object in which the Mines Department, the Mining Association, and the Mineworkers' Federation could co-operate than in a continuous and intensive effort to reduce the accident rate, for only those who have lived in the coalfields know the sorrow and the hardship which comes into the miner's home when the breadwinner is either killed or seriously injured. The swift and unexpected accident which brings death to men working deep in the bowels of the earth can only be guarded against by a realization that the life of the worker is of greater value than any other factor in the industry and the adoption of every safeguard known to science to protect him from unavoidable danger. With the continued improvement of facilities by the owners and the exercise of greater care by the workers, both underground and on the surface, the others should grow steadily less. In this industry eternal vigilance is the price of safety, and when officials and workmen combine in a determination to exercise it *all the time*, there will be no reason why there should not be a substantial reduction in the accident rate in every coalfield in the country.

THE MINERS' WELFARE FUND

No volume dealing with the coal industry would be complete without a reference to the Miners' Welfare Fund.

This fund came into being in 1920 as the result of a universal recognition of the urgent need for a speedy and extensive improvement in the social conditions of the mining communities. There is nothing like it in any other industry in the country, nor indeed on such an extensive scale in any other country.

It was set up in 1920 under the Mining Industry Act of that year, and in the fifteen years of its operation has brought about a transformation in the amenities of life in a mining village which can only be fully appreciated by those familiar with the conditions existing in far too many of them in pre-war days. The work of the Welfare Fund, coupled with the drive against slums or insanitary dwellings, and the post-war standard of housing, has made many of these villages almost unrecognizable to those who knew them twenty years ago.

The activities of the Welfare Fund Committee are so varied and extensive that it is only possible here to summarize them very briefly.

Chief among them is the provision of pithead baths, which have worked a minor revolution in the homes of the miners and come as a veritable godsend to the miners' wives. Strangely enough the proposals for installing these baths met, in the early days of the fund, with very strong opposition, on various grounds, from both miners and their womenfolk in many mining areas. Wherever the innate conservatism of the men has been overcome, however, they have proved to be a triumphant success, and the number of installations is steadily increasing, despite the fact that there are many places where the workers still cling tenaciously to their old customs and habits. The baths are built out of moneys provided by the levies on output and royalties. They are maintained by the men's contributions, and by contributions from the owners which take various forms, either cash or a free heating and lighting service, or the latter in part only, so that the cost varies both with the location of the pit and the size of the installation.

At some of the installations there are canteens attached where the men may purchase food or tobacco or cigarettes, cycle sheds for the storage of their machines, and in several cases boot-repairing shops where they may have their boots repaired at very low charges.

A very large sum has been spent on the building of institutes or halls as a centre for social intercourse, and a Miners' Welfare Hall is now a feature of a large and growing number of mining villages.

The provision of recreation grounds has also been one of the main objectives of the Committee, and in providing these, the need for children's playgrounds has not been overlooked, a large number of them having been laid out. The recreation grounds in most cases provide full facilities for football, cricket, tennis, bowls, and in some cases for putting-greens and miniature golf. Grants have also been made on quite an extensive scale for swimming-baths and to boys' clubs and camps by the Committee.

The other directions in which the Welfare Fund is contributing greatly to the well-being of the mining communities are health and education. The establishment and maintenance of convalescent homes has been one of the main features of the scheme, whilst District Nursing Associations, ambulances, and hospitals have all benefited largely from grants made to their funds by the Welfare Fund Committee. The Aged Miners'

Homes movement in Northumberland and Durham, which has for many years been doing most admirable work with the sympathy, encouragement, and very substantial financial help of the owners, has also received very valuable assistance.

In education the Welfare Fund is doing very useful work in promoting the study of purely mining subjects in mining areas both through the universities and through the medium of other specially assisted instruction centres. Funds amounting to three-quarters of a million pounds for buildings and equipment in the various areas for this purpose have been provided and are being drawn on each year.

For education purposes a scholarship fund was established in 1926 and a special committee appointed to select scholarships for award by the Trustees. This Miners' Welfare National Scholarship Scheme was instituted to provide a university degree course, with allowance for outfit, and an annual maintenance grant is available to successful candidates, who may be either working miners or the sons and daughters of miners. The successful candidates have nearly all made good and taken their degrees in such varied subjects as physics, history, mining engineering, medicine, and chemistry. It should be remembered that these opportunities provided by the Welfare Fund for mineworkers and their sons and daughters are additional to those provided through the normal educational channels. A very large sum has also been devoted to the work of the Safety in Mines Research Board and their safety instruction work in the districts. All this extremely valuable work, however, is so extensive and varied that it is only possible to mention it here. Those anxious for further information will find it fully and clearly set out in the very excellent Report of the Miners' Welfare Committee, the fourteenth issue of which has just been published.

The finance for the Welfare Fund is provided by a levy on the output, payable by the owners, and a charge on the royalties. When the fund was instituted it was financed entirely by a levy of 1d. per ton on the output. In 1926 the money available was supplemented by a levy of 5 per cent on royalties and wayleaves to be devoted to the provision of pithead baths. The 1d. per ton produced approximately a million per annum and the royalties welfare levy approximately £200,000 per annum.

In 1934 the 1d. per ton was reduced to ½d. and made to apply retrospectively to the 1932 output levy (payable in 1933), whilst the duration was extended by 16 years to 1951.

I was one of those who objected to this reduction and in the House of Commons I both spoke and voted against it. I did so, firstly, on the ground that this beneficent work ought not to be retarded or curtailed for the sake of such a trifling sum as a ½d. per ton, and pointed out (only as an illustration and not as a proposal) that the whole of the money saved could have been provided by an increase of only 4d. per ton in the coal consumed by the public utility undertakings, an increase so widely diffused as never to be felt. Secondly, I objected on psychological grounds, for the workers in the industry considered, as I did, that the reduction was unnecessary and the action of the Government in limiting the activities of the Committee by cutting down their available funds was bound to have a bad effect in the coalfields at a time when employment was declining still further, and the general conditions in the industry showed no sign of improvement.

However, the reduction was made, and it is some compensation to know that although the funds available are smaller the scheme has in effect been made permanent, and its work is steadily and continuously bearing fruit in the improvement of the amenities of life among the mining population. The nature and extent of that work may be realized from the following figures of expenditure since 1920:

	£
Pit Welfare	
Baths, Canteens, etc.	3,812,127
Recreation	5,140,888
Health	
Convalescent Homes and Convalescence. Hospitals. Ambulances. District Nursing. Aged Miners' Homes. Special Medical Treatment and Appliances.	3,375,566
Education	1,178,343
Research	892,010
Total	£14,398,934

A very important point so far as the finance of the fund is concerned is that as nearly all the districts have been on the minimum for the greater part of the period during which the fund has been in operation and the proceeds sharing provisions of the agreements have scarcely operated at all, practically all the money derived from the levy on the output has been provided by the colliery owners.

It only remains to be added that the expenses of

administration are only 1¼ per cent of the grants, and that a study of the report of the working of this truly admirable scheme will well repay anyone who is interested in the industry. A full account of the work being done will be found in the Annual Report of the Miners' Welfare Committee (H.M. Stationery Office, 1s. 6d. net).

CHAPTER XXIII

THE MINEWORKERS' FEDERATION

THIS organization, the principal trade union of the workers in the coal-mining industry, is one of the largest of the organized bodies of workers. In common with other trade unions it has suffered a heavy decline in membership during the last few years, but is still one of the most powerful and the largest organization of the mine workers.

There are outside its sphere of influence several other organizations to which a number of the craftsmen, deputies, and other skilled workers engaged in specialized trades belong, as well as one or two miners' industrial unions, the chief of which is that of the Notts coal miners already referred to.

At one time the membership of the Federation amounted to over 900,000, but at present is just a little over 500,000. The decline has been mainly due to the special circumstances of the industry, which have caused a steady and continuous reduction in the numbers employed, and, to a smaller extent, to a dislike amongst a minority of the workers of the policy pursued by the Federation in the troublous years already described. Even so, however, the Federation speaks authoritatively for the great body of mineworkers. The total number engaged in the industry (1935) is roughly 750,000, so that with its 500,000 members the Federation speaks for just two thirds of them.

The history of mineworkers' organizations has been a very chequered and a very stormy one. Many efforts had been made from the middle of the nineteenth century onwards to combine the workers in the pits in one national organization, but all had failed until the formation of the Miners' Federation in 1888. There were, however, a number of local or district associations which, as the trade union movement developed in the country, grew slowly but steadily in strength and activity.

Side by side with them there came into being local associations of coal-owners, and the formation of these bodies led to the establishment of Conciliation Boards in the districts and the discussion of their common difficulties in joint conference and consultation.

With the passing of the Trade Union Act of 1871, the movement gained fresh impetus, and despite numerous setbacks in the years which followed, very considerable progress was made in the formation and enlarging of the workers' unions. The advance was not made without trouble, for in addition to a long series of strikes, mainly concerned with wages, there was disagreement amongst the miners themselves on the trade union question, as well as friction between the rival organizations in the different districts.

Then, as now, the idea of compelling workers to join the unions was very popular with the union officials, and the very questionable methods adopted to bring in non-unionists led to continuous strife. One of the miners' leaders in Durham openly advised his members to ostracize non-unionists and their families. "Regard them", he said, "as unfit companions for yourselves and your sons, and unfit companions for your daughters. Let them be branded, as it were, with the curse of Cain" (Mr. Wm. Crawford).

With the increase in strength, the minds of the leaders turned towards Parliament, and in the election of 1874 Burt and Macdonald were returned as members for Morpeth and Stafford, others being unsuccessful. The return of these two members marked the entry of the miners into the political arena. They were returned as Independent members, no organized political Labour Party having as yet come into existence.

Although still kept apart by differences of opinion on matters of policy, as well as the jealousies of the leaders in the districts, the proposals for combining all in one national organization were continually under discussion, and led finally to the formation of the Miners' Federation in 1888. The bodies originally comprising the Federation were Yorkshire, Lancashire, Cheshire, the Midlands, and Fife, and the total membership in 1888 was only 35,000. In the years immediately following, the district unions added greatly to their numbers, and most of them entered the Federation, so that by 1893 the membership of the latter exceeded 200,000. Durham had joined in 1892, but the county was expelled in 1893 because of a refusal to join in the strike of that year. Northumberland and Durham remained outside for some years longer, mainly because of a difference of opinion on the two questions of political activity in industry and the proposed Eight Hours Act. Hewers' hours at the coal face in these two counties were only six per day. In 1906, however, Northumberland joined up; in 1908 Durham followed suit, and the national structure of the Federation was complete. The same year saw the passing of the Eight Hours Act, the adoption of Socialism by the Labour Party, and the Federation officially linked up with the latter.

Till the year 1902 the primary object of both local and national associations had been the raising of wages and the improvement of working conditions by trade union action in direct negotiation with the employers. With the growth of the Labour movement and an increased representation in Parliament, the demand for political action gained in strength. The declaration of Socialism as the policy of the Labour Party in 1908 and the acceptance of the policy by the miners ended the association of the miners' Members of Parliament with the Liberal Party, to which many of them had hitherto given support. In the early stages of Parliamentary representation, most of the selected candidates were Independent members, although by giving general support to the Liberal Party they became known as Liberal-Labour members. In 1902, however, the Federation levied its members in order to support its own candidates. Even then, all the miners' candidates were not Labour Party candidates. With the decision of the Federation to join forces with the Labour Party, however, support of the Labour group became the first consideration, and only those who undertook unreservedly to give such support had any chance of being selected as official candidates. Some of the older leaders were opposed to Socialism and refused to accept the new conditions. They declined to join the Labour Party, or as it was called at the time to "take the ticket". John Wilson, one of the most respected of the Durham leaders, roundly declared that "he could not vote for a working man who represented the working-class interests only, and he did not think that a man should go to Parliament for that".[1] Burt and Fenwick also refused and retained their independence to the end.

[1] To Keir Hardie (Durham Miners' Assn. Records, 1902).

The great majority of the official candidates took the "ticket", accepted Socialism as the policy of the Federation, and when elected, joined the Labour group in the House of Commons. Since then the Federation has been strongly represented in the House, and political considerations have played a very large part in the shaping of its policy. Indeed, since 1918, it may truthfully be said that political considerations have outweighed the economic and industrial. At the end of the war control of the policy of the Federation had got into the hands of the extremists, men with revolutionary views, lacking those qualities of wise judgement and reasoned outlook so characteristic of Burt, Fenwick, Mabon, Wilson, and others. Having paid small heed to the economic factors governing the prosperity of the industry under normal conditions, they were quite unable to understand or appreciate the difficulties and complexities of the new situation created by the transition from war to peace.

They were completely obsessed by the craze for nationalization, and the only means of securing this being through Parliament, political action became the dominating factor in the policy of the Federation. In the post-war period, Labour representation in the House of Commons has largely increased, and as the party has a virtual monopoly of the purely mining constituencies, mineworkers' representatives form a large proportion of its membership and exercise a powerful influence in its counsels. Being carried on largely in segregated communities, the mining industry enjoys, under a system of universal suffrage, a great advantage over other industries. The miners have been organized to vote for "one of themselves", and as their candidates are nearly always checkweighmen, miners' agents, or lodge secretaries, there is always a powerful mineworkers' or Federation influence at work in the counsels of the Parliamentary Labour Party. In the House, the result is that the coal-mining industry, as one industry, is over-represented on the workers' side, so that it is not surprising that coal looms so largely in the debates there. It is quite fitting that Parliament should decide the main questions of policy in this important industry, that it should regulate and control the hours of labour and conditions of labour on broad lines as in other industries. In the mining industry, however, owing to this political over-representation every petty grievance or minor dispute, which in other industries would be settled amicably on the spot through the normal machinery, is magnified and ventilated on the floor of the House by members anxious to show their solicitude for the welfare of their constituents, whilst on any major issue affecting the industry there is a demand for immediate political action, and any Member of Parliament who dares to differ from them is immediately classified as a "coal-owners' advocate" and an "enemy of the worker".

The objective aimed at by the Federation in this political activity is to induce the Cabinet to compel the colliery owners, by legislative action, to adopt their policy or, alternatively, to force the Government to take over the industry and run it under some form of State control. In the 1926 dispute, a Conservative Prime Minister had to declare emphatically that he was not going to be forced by outside influences to take over this one industry, just as in 1931 a Socialist Prime Minister broke up the second Socialist Government rather than submit, on questions of national policy, to the dictation of an outside body, the Trades

Union Congress, of which the Mineworkers' Federation is a constituent part. There is no doubt that politics had a good deal to do with the three post-war national stoppages, particularly that of 1926, which, beginning with a dispute in the mining industry, developed into a challenge to the Constitution and an attempt to usurp the functions of Parliament by the trades unions involved.

It is equally certain that this insistence on the political aspect of the problems of the industry has been of little benefit to the workers engaged in it, for nothing has been gained which could not have been secured by negotiation, while much has been lost by the attempts to force successive Governments to concede the "whole hog" policy of the Federation by political action. In other industries, the workers' representatives have adjusted their differences with employers without one-tenth of the Government intervention necessary in coal, and in many cases, by the exercise of a spirit of compromise and goodwill, succeeded in obtaining for their members relatively better terms, through the normal channels of negotiation by collective bargaining around the conference table than have been obtained in the mining industry by strikes, threats of strikes, Parliamentary pressure, or Government action.

The stoppages referred to inflicted enormous hardship and suffering on the rank and file of the miners and their wives and families. Thousands of the most thrifty and industrious of them lost the whole of their small and hardly acquired life's savings, whilst many thousands more piled up debts which were a millstone round their necks for years. Yet they endured in 1926 almost to the end.

Those who knew the industry were well aware of those splendid qualities of courage, tenacity, and self-sacrifice possessed by the miners, and to which tribute has so often been justly paid, but even they were surprised by the amazing exhibition of loyalty to the Federation which marked the 1926 dispute in face of the most inept leadership the trade union movement has ever known. The leaders refused to lead; they took their stand on the *status quo*; like the famous French marshal at Sedan, they said "Here we are, and here we stick". They refused all compromise; they rejected every proposal for settlement, no matter by whom it was made; they scorned the advice of their own friends; by their own folly they forced the other trade unions to withdraw their support; they alienated public sympathy and split their own organization from top to bottom; and while the pitiful struggle proceeded, with the miners' case steadily becoming more hopeless and their fellow trade unionists helping to defeat them by handling and distributing millions of tons of imported coal, the only advice vouchsafed from the leaders to the rank and file was to tighten their belts, to "stick it", and live on empty slogans, until at last even the men's loyalty broke under the strain, and drifting back to work under district settlements in which the Federation had no voice, they had to accept terms much worse than they could have secured without the loss of a day's work.

The Federation emerged from the 1926 struggle greatly reduced in membership, impaired in strength, damaged in prestige, its relations with other trade unions embittered, and strife seething in its own ranks, both at the top and among the general body of the members. The "wild men" had had their way, as in

1921, and as in 1921 the price was again, in their President's own words then, "the price of poverty and starvation of their members and the misery of millions of their fellow countrymen". These conflicts were not merely a struggle between employers and workmen over wages and conditions of labour. They were more, and were intended to be something more. They represented what was intended to be the first of a series of assaults on the existing social, economic, and industrial system. In the aftermath of war the conditions were thought favourable and the time opportune, and in the effort to establish the "new social order", the peculiar position of the mining industry led the leaders to regard it as the spearhead in the attack on private enterprise and private ownership. By combining political action in the House of Commons with industrial action in the coalfields, and enlisting the support of the combined workers in other industries, it was hoped to force the Government to nationalize the mines, to eliminate completely the private coalowner, and to establish a system of State ownership with joint control by the workers and the State.

Once attained in the mining industry, the example was to be followed in other industries, "stage by stage until the last stone in the capitalist system crashes to the ground", as it was expressed by one of the chief officials of the Federation in 1919 (Mr. F. Hodges). In order to further this aim, arrangements for mutual assistance were entered into between the Miners' Federation, the National Union of Railwaymen, and the Transport and General Workers Union, a powerful combination which came to be known as Labour's Triple Alliance. It would appear, however, that the leaders of the two other unions had not fully understood or appreciated the extremes to which the miners' leaders were prepared to go in the war against capitalism, despite the fact that the Federation Secretary told the Annual Conference in 1920: "We are going to create a first-class economic crisis which will reduce the nation to chaos", whilst the President declared that they should cut into the Government's policy by progressive demands for higher wages so as to prevent de-control and compel acceptance of nationalization as the only way out. They were not to remain long in doubt as to the full implication of the Federation's policy, for the stoppage of 1921 was speedily to put the new combination to its first test. When the miners decided to withdraw their labour, the other two unions pledged themselves to give their full support. On the eve of the stoppage, the Federation decided to withdraw the safety men from the pits, a course from which the two other unions strongly dissented on the grounds that it meant the destruction of many mines and the means of livelihood of thousands of workers, and must also inevitably involve the employment of the armed forces of the Crown in an industrial dispute for the protection of life and property. Other causes of disagreement arose, resulting finally in such strong resentment at the autocratic and unyielding attitude of the miners' representatives, that on April 15th (Black Friday), the day their strike notices were due to expire, the two other unions cancelled the order for a sympathetic strike and left the miners to fight their battle alone. The new alliance thus failed to stand the strain; it broke down completely at the first test because of the extremist policy of the Mineworkers' Federation[1]

[1] Then the Miners' Federation.

and the dictatorial fashion in which it was sought to force it on the other unions.

In the years which followed (up to 1926) the Executive of the Federation continued to press for political action, particularly in 1924 when the Nationalization of Mines Bill was introduced in the lifetime of the first Socialist Government, and in 1925 when the Conservative Government was induced to buy off an immediate stoppage by subsidizing wages.

In the stoppage of 1926 which followed on the ending of the subsidy period, the history of the Triple Alliance fiasco of 1921 repeated itself, but this time it was the General Council of the T.U.C. which was involved. They authorized the General Strike in support of the miners and were under the impression that from that moment the conduct of the case passed from the Federation to the General Council. Grave differences of opinion manifested themselves, however, almost as soon as the General Strike commenced. The Executive of the Federation declined to endorse the basis accepted by the General Council for the renewal of negotiations. When the T.U.C. got down to a discussion of the terms they found that they were not to be allowed to conduct the case; open rupture ensued when this disclosed the fact that the Federation view of "negotiation" was the granting of their demands in full; that they were not prepared to abate them one jot or tittle; and that they were prepared to use the whole Trade Union Movement and the suffering of the entire nation as a means to obtain them rather than compromise in the slightest degree. When the attitude of the Federation and the full significance of its policy were realized by the General Council, the latter was swift to act; they withdrew their support, cancelled the General Strike, and once again the Federation, owing to its own lack of both wisdom and foresight, landed the loyal and long-suffering miners (worthy of better leadership) in the position of having to fight their battle again alone and unaided.

When work had been resumed in all the other industries, great efforts were made to keep secret the very serious differences which had arisen between the Federation and the T.U.C. One member of the General Council, however, gave a very clear indication of the views of the members of the latter when he wrote: "In our opinion, the miners' leaders have not played the game with their fellow trade unionists." (Mr. Bromley in the *Locomotive Journal*, July 1926.)

The official Report of the General Council on these proceedings was deferred for some months because of the continuance of the coal stoppage, but when it did appear, it contained this striking passage, which speaks for itself:

> "The strike was terminated for one sufficient reason only, namely, that in view of the attitude of the Miners' Federation its continuance would have rendered its purpose futile.
>
> "The Council cannot but regret that so great a demonstration of loyalty by the Trade Union Movement found so little practical appreciation or response on the part of those for whom the sacrifice was made." (T.U.C. Report, 1926.)

The whole policy of the Federation was a mistaken one and its bitter fruits were reaped by the rank and file in unemployment for long afterwards. That the political aim still dominated the minds of the leaders, even after the collapse of the General Strike (i.e. the establishment of the Socialist State by industrial combination and action), was clearly revealed in numerous statements made publicly in the difficult years which followed. A fatal blow had been dealt at the export trade, and it was the exporting districts which suffered most heavily. Short time was the main feature in these areas for long afterwards, and at the time when the melancholy sound of the "buzzer" was heard night after night in the Northumberland mining villages, intimating that the pits would be idle on the following day, the Secretary of the Federation told the workers: "The pits in Northumberland are closing down; let them all close down; we'll get them for nothing then."

And in the Socialist Press the same gentleman committed himself, with all the weight and authority of his official position, to a scheme of nationalization which included not only State acquisition of the minerals, but also State acquisition of the collieries themselves, in both cases without compensation, and as a step towards the complete abolition of the capitalist system.

The obsession of political and legislative methods as the panacea for all the ills of the industry still persists, as was evidenced by the passing of the highly controversial Act of 1930, in the shaping of which, by reason of a Socialist Government being in office, the Federation played a large part.

More recently it was shown again by the clever synchronizing of the ballot for an increase of wages with the general election of 1935; the creation in the minds of the mineworkers of the impression that the question of the 2s. per shift increase in wages would be decided by Parliament; and by the sending of a deputation to the Government to ask once again for a subsidy from the taxpayer in aid of miners' wages.

Federation officials are continually repudiating the suggestion that their aim is in any way political, but all the accumulated evidence shows on what slender grounds the repudiation rests. Certain it is that the political element has obtruded itself in this industry to an infinitely greater extent than in any other, and does so still. Whether "the game is worth the candle" must remain a matter of opinion, but the cold, hard facts of the last twenty years of the history of the industry will not lead any impartial observer to think so. One thing the miner himself would be wise to ponder over. The railwaymen have always subordinated the political element to the industrial, so that it is not without some significance that railwaymen's wages are to-day 122 per cent above pre-war rates, while those of miners were, till recently, only 45 per cent, and even now are only 60 per cent above (1936). The importance attached to political action has led to the miners sending their most capable leaders to the House of Commons. In that chamber their specialized knowledge of the industry is largely superfluous, because there are so many of them to present the case, and their experience of bargaining on behalf of their fellows is lost, for they are debarred as M.P.s from taking part in the routine work of their unions, and are not called into consultation until a crisis is reached.

The mining community has produced many able men with qualifications and experience fitting them admirably for their work as trade union leaders. One by one they yield to the call of the glamour of the House. The miners pay the salaries of their Federation and local officials, and in addition supplement the salaries of their Members of Parliament. Their most experienced negotiators thus gravitate almost automatically to Parliament, where, as the history of the last twenty years clearly reveals, they can render less useful service to their fellows than in the industrial field in which they have been trained. And in addition, the nature of that training, admirable for its own purpose, serves as a handicap in the atmosphere of Westminster, where world affairs occupy the stage. There is thus little gain in either direction.

One other aspect of the Federation's activities calls for attention. Sporadic strikes with the object of forcing non-unionists to join the Federation or for the redress of local grievances are a common feature of all the coalfields, and of late have taken the form of the "stay-in" strike, a method of enforcing a settlement of matters in dispute borrowed from abroad and quite alien to British ideas. These irritating and expensive stoppages over matters with which the employers are in no way concerned are symptomatic, for they reveal a certain amount of discontent with the policy of the Federation. The advantages of collective bargaining to both sides are so obvious that if a reasonable policy of conciliation and goodwill is pursued, there should be no difficulty in securing the 100 per cent membership arrived at, but it is both un-English and undemocratic to seek, by methods bordering on persecution, to compel men to accept and subscribe to a policy with which they are in complete disagreement. A new spirit is manifesting itself, however, in the Federation, which has recently resolutely refused to countenance these "lightning" stoppages, and with this and the wiser leadership now showing itself there should be fewer of these costly and unauthorized stoppages, either on the non-unionist question or for the redress of grievances, alleged or otherwise, and a more regular resort to the properly constituted tribunals in accordance with the terms and the spirit of the signed agreements.

The Federation is a powerful body capable of exercising a very great influence in the affairs of the industry, on the daily lives of the two to three millions of our people who are dependent on it, and on the nation as a whole. The personnel of the officials has changed considerably, and the new leaders have shown that they know how to profit by experience. Their task is never an easy one, for it is the special misfortune of the mining industry that there is always a new generation of "wild men" knocking at the door, eager to force the pace, firmly convinced that they could do the job better, and that their methods would bring quicker and more satisfactory results for the workers. The present officials have shown that they can lead, they have the confidence of the great majority of the members, and to a greater degree than for many years the respect of the owners and the public alike. If they will but continue their wise but firm leadership, rely on conciliation and negotiation rather than on strikes and threats of strikes, and insist on subordinating the politicians in their ranks, the Federation will still play a big part in the service of both the industry and the State.

CHAPTER XXIV

THE MINING ASSOCIATION

As in the case of the mineworkers' organizations many early efforts were made to combine the owners in voluntary association for the furtherance of their common interest, and, like them, the bodies so formed were purely local ones. For the most part they were created for the purpose of maintaining or regulating the price of coal, and in most cases the organizations, such as they were, being formed for a specific and very often a temporary purpose, had only a very short existence.

The efforts to establish large-scale organizations seem to have met with little success either in the case of the employers or the workers until about the middle of the nineteenth century. The remarkable expansion of the industry which commenced about that time, the growth of the miners' unions, and the numerous Acts of Parliament passed for regulating the conduct of the industry, then made apparent the need for closer association between individual coal-owners in the districts and between the various districts in some form of national association. Many questions arose in the districts affecting hours of labour, wages, and conditions of employment, and these were adjusted in the districts by joint consultation between the representatives of the employers and those of the workmen. Indeed, it may be said that the associations of employers grew up side by side in the districts, and until the outbreak of war in 1914 these remained the normal channels for the adjustment of all matters relating to hours, wages, and other conditions of employment, except that in 1908 the passing of the Eight Hours Act, and in 1912 the passing of the Minimum Wage Act, by the legislature established two general principles governing hours and wages in all the coalfields.

The Mining Association, as a national organization of the colliery owners, was formed in 1854. It came into being because of a recognition of the need for joint action in regard to legislation affecting the industry, to promote research work, to encourage the study of the many problems associated with the winning of coal, and for the interchange of views and information between the district associations on all matters of common interest and concern. Up to 1920 the organization was somewhat loosely constituted, membership being open to both district associations and to individual colliery owners, but since that year it has been a federation of district coal-owners' associations only, and all the local associations are affiliated to it, though all of them are extremely jealous of their autonomous powers.

After the passing of the Eight Hours Act in 1908 and the entry of every district into the Miners' Federation in the same year, the latter concentrated on a policy of the abolition of the District Conciliation Boards and the setting up of a National Conciliation Board for the regulation of wages and conditions of employment throughout the whole of the coalfields. This movement made little progress, mainly because the employers' organization regarded these as being the domestic concern of each district and was definitely and strongly opposed to any proposal to attempt to deal with them on a national basis.

This was the position when the war broke out in 1914. With the mines under State control, the Mining Association became, naturally, the negotiating body on behalf of the owners, and equally naturally the Miners' Federation played the same part on behalf of the men. Wages was one of the most important matters the Government, the owners, and men's leaders had to consider; the wages paid were no longer governed by the ordinary play of economic forces; increases were granted on a national flat-rate basis, irrespective of the class of worker and without regard to the ability of any district to pay them. Under war-time conditions the relation between wages and prices was completely destroyed, but the prolonged period during which wages were nationally adjusted and the Federation officials recognized as the responsible negotiating body for the workers in all the districts, gave a tremendous impetus to the demand for a national agreement and the determination of wages levels on common principles applicable to every district. To this, which at the end of the war took the form of a demand for the national pool already described, the Mining Association was still strongly opposed, their spokesman, Mr. (now Sir) Evan Williams, the President, declaring that it would reduce efficiency, destroy incentive, and in the end bring ruin on the industry.

The pressure for a national agreement, however, continued after the abandonment of the claim for the "pool", and finally culminated in the agreement of 1921, the Mining Association giving a reluctant consent to the establishment of a National Board. The functions of the Association were thus extended to include negotiations on wages and other conditions of employment. When this agreement broke down, the principle of national settlement was retained in the agreement of 1924, but at the end of the 1926 stoppage, the colliery owners, convinced by the experience of these five years that national adjustments of wages could never be satisfactory, insisted on a reversion to district agreements, and since then the Mining Association has not participated in the wages adjustments in the various coalfields.

Outside these matters, however, and those relating to the regulation of production and marketing, which are dealt with by the Central Council under the 1930 Act (a statutory body), the Mining Association is the central organization of the British coal-owners, and as such acts for the districts in the negotiations on all questions relating to the industry with the Mineworkers' Federation and the Government.

The policy of the colliery owners has not always been a wise or an enlightened one. In the new post-war world too many of them clung tenaciously to the individualistic conception of their industry, under which it had expanded and prospered so amazingly in pre-war days, ignoring or not fully realizing the far-reaching nature and extent of the changes in world conditions brought about as a result of that vast upheaval. They pinned their faith to competition, not only in the districts, but between the districts, and with other coal-producing countries in the markets abroad. As power to compete successfully under this policy depended on lowering the costs of production, and wages costs in this industry are by far the largest item in such costs, it was inevitable that they should resist any large increase in this direction. Believing still in the theory of a "cheap and abundant" supply of coal, this section of the owners declined to avail themselves of the provisions of the

Act of 1930 for the co-ordination of prices in the districts, or between the districts, with the result that the Secretary of the Mines Department was compelled to admit to the House of Commons in June 1933 that evasion of the minimum-price provisions of the Act was taking place in every district. This failure to maintain the general level of prices at a remunerative level was mainly due to differences of opinion within the Mining Association and resulted not only in the stabilization of wages at figures which in the case of the lower-paid men were quite inadequate, but also in diminished revenue to such an extent that the industry in almost every district was being run at a loss. Diverging views on policy, although honestly and sincerely held on both sides, had the effect of preventing the Mining Association formulating and advocating a clear-cut policy acceptable to all the districts. In the debates in the House of Commons on the coal question, coal-owners spoke with conflicting voices, and members representing mining constituencies, anxious to assist the industry when legislation was pending or being enacted, could get no definite lead on policy from the coal-owners' association in their districts, and were all the time conscious of the fact that, whatever course they advocated, if they pleased one section they would certainly offend another.

In 1935, Lancashire took the lead in setting up a central selling scheme and later in the same year, partly as a result of Government pressure and partly because of the demand by the workers for higher wages, the Central Council agreed to formulate similar schemes for all the districts, with a view to both the increase of prices and their co-ordination between the districts. These schemes came into operation on

August 1, 1936, and should result in the industry being able to pay better wages and a fairer return to capital without inflicting any serious injury on the consumer. It is a change of policy which, if coming rather late in the day, is a welcome one, and one on which the general body of coal-owners is to be congratulated.

There is one aspect of the work of the Mining Association which is in direct contrast to that of the Mineworkers' Federation and which bears very hardly on the individuals who have to undertake it. In the Mineworkers' Federation the men responsible for conducting negotiations are full-time officials of their organization. Their "opposites" in the Mining Association are the heads of large business firms and they complain, with some substance, that they are compelled to devote so much time to the settlement of labour and political questions that they have little left for looking after the interests of their own concerns. This is very largely due to the extent to which politics have dominated the industry.

The Mining Association plays a big part in the conduct of the industry and it is, therefore, vital that in the interests of the nation and of the workers, as well as in their own, the district associations comprising this powerful body should agree upon a policy which, while it may not be acceptable to some, will represent the views of the majority, and having adopted such a policy, will press on to putting it into speedy and effective operation. The Mineworkers' Federation has many representatives in the House of Commons who put forward its policy with all the weight and authority of their organization behind it whenever coal is debated there. Contrary to popular belief, the Mining Association has nobody in the House who can voice its view with similar authority. This is entirely due to the lack of a definite, practical, coherent policy covering the industry as a whole, for the differences within their organization are reflected in the speeches of those who either speak in opposition to the Socialist views or on behalf of some section of the coal-owners. If they fail to produce such a policy they may find, too late, that the demand for still more Government control has become so clamant as to be irresistible, and the House in such a mood, when it is proposed, that no really effective opposition is possible, for the Government will not always introduce proposals meeting with such universal condemnation as those of the Amalgamations Bill recently withdrawn.

CHAPTER XXV

THE MINEWORKERS' FEDERATION AND REORGANIZATION

THE Mineworkers' Federation and the Socialist Party together have produced quite a number of schemes for the reorganization of the mining industry. In all of them the fundamental basis has been some form of nationalization, so framed as to give to the workers' representatives a controlling voice in the conduct of the industry. Apart from *Coal and Commonsense,* which contained a great deal of the former and little of the latter, the only understandable set of proposals they have put forward till recently are those contained in the Nationalization of Mines Bill, which is examined later (see pages 312 et seq.). The effect of State control is also dealt with (pages 306 et seq.).

The latest proposals of the Mineworkers' Federation for dealing with the problems of the industry are set out in a little volume entitled *The Coal Scuttle,* by Mr. Joseph Jones, the President of the Federation, published early this year (1936). It is generally (and naturally) understood to contain not only his own views, but the view of the organization of which he is the head.

(Yet another has just appeared (August 1936). This scheme takes the form of a public utility corporation, but differs only slightly from its predecessors. It is once again "nationalization" or "public ownership", only in a slightly different disguise.)[1]

Mr. Jones differs from some of his predecessors in

[1] *Coal. The Labour Plan.* With a foreword by Sir Walter Citrine. T.U.C. General Council. 3d.

being able to state his case calmly and in moderate language, and if he uses the arts of omission and selection in seeking to make that case he can hardly be blamed. The case, however, beneath the veneer, remains the same, and, in its demand for State intervention and control, goes farther than any previous claims advanced by or on behalf of the workers in the industry. In short, it is a reiterated demand for nationalization—for public ownership, management, and control, not only of the mines themselves, but a form of public ownership leading progressively in an ever-widening sphere to the nationalization of every industry which uses raw coal, and for the proceeds of every such industry to be included in the ascertainments which govern the amount of the wages to be paid to the miners. Under this heading would come all coal used in iron and steel works, in the production of metallurgical and other coke, in the production of gas and electricity, in hydrogenation, in other "oil from coal" processes, in the production of dyes, chemical products, and any other derivatives of which coal is the basis. Of a surety Mr. Jones casts his net wide, and is determined, apparently, to spare no effort in order that the miners may profit by the energy, the enterprise, the ability, and inventive genius of anyone who discovers a new use for coal or improves on any of the old. His theory, quite definitely, is that every process associated with the use of coal should be linked up with the production of coal, and the profits made available for increasing miners' wages.

It is a Socialist conception and, as such, it is as well to have it clearly stated. Those of us, however, who dislike Socialism, and who hold the view that its adoption here would bring nothing but irretrievable disaster, may be pardoned if we refuse to accept the theory as valid and object to its application on grounds of both principle and expediency, whether we are interested in any of the industries concerned or not.

Public ownership of the seams of ungotten coal is sound and justifiable on every ground of public policy, public ownership of such utility services as the Post Office is equally so, and a good case can be made for the extension of the principle to other similar services, transport, for example. There is, however, no comparison between these and the nationalization of a competitive industry, and none of the arguments advanced in support of these cases can be held legitimately to apply to productive enterprises where there is no monopoly and where success depends on that eternal vigilance which is not only the price of liberty, but in modern business the price of prosperity.

British industrial supremacy was built up by the spirit of private enterprise; if we stifle that and replace it by any form of bureaucratic control, with all the enervating influences inseparable from it, the result must inevitably be the same as has characterized nationalization of industry wherever it has been tried; that is, a steady decline in efficiency, enormous financial loss, the eventual abandonment of the system, and a return to private enterprise after great injury (sometimes irreparable) has been inflicted on the industry concerned and all associated with it.

The mining industry, like other industries, needs to adapt itself to the changing conditions of a world which is in a state of flux, but all experience shows that a change from private enterprise to complete State management and control would be, not merely, as Sir Richard Redmayne has said, "A leap in the dark", but a definite change for the worse; a change in which the benefits accruing to the miners are problematical and one which would certainly be against the best interests of the nation as a whole.

If this be true of the proposal to nationalize the production of raw coal, what shall be said of the proposal to apply the principle to the numerous coal-using industries? The mining of coal is a varied and complex process, but is, nevertheless, one industry. Yet unified control is extremely difficult. Many industries, differing widely both in their technique and in the nature of their product, use coal in some form as their raw material. Their methods of manufacture are highly technical and involved, in some cases close secrets, and in others, particularly the newer industries, the processes are delicate and complicated, and their success the result of years of patient research with which the miners have had nothing whatever to do. Yet, under Mr. Jones's scheme, all these are to be "roped in", their businesses run by a series of committees, or "sub-boards" as Mr. Jones calls them (all paid by monies provided by Parliament), their profits utilized to give higher wages to miners who had neither part nor lot in making them. Losses, presumably, would be made good by the State, as has been done elsewhere under nationalization.

Except that it is based on the fundamental Socialist conception of industry, what justification can there be for the application of this very far-reaching principle to one industry? In the chapter on "Association with other Industries" the cases of wheat and cotton were cited. An even more striking illustration is to be found in the steel industry. Steel is the finished product of the steel manufacturer. It is the raw material of a thousand other industries. Are the steel workers to be entitled to share in the profits of all these diversified industries because the latter use their product, and in order that their wages may be increased by the efforts of others? The principle is as sound in the case of steel as in that of coal, and the only possible answer that can be given by Mr. Jones and those who agree with him is "Yes", because the nationalization of the mining industry is but the first step towards the nationalization of all, and the ultimate establishment of the complete Socialist State, with all it implies in the subjugation of the individual, the negation of personal liberty, and that "rigid iron discipline" which Socialists tell us will be necessary when Socialism "comes into its own".

The book is described as giving the "miners' own vision" of the future of the industry. The "vision", when analysed, turns out to be nothing more nor less than our old friend nationalization, or public ownership, whichever term is preferred. Mr. Jones and his friends may believe that to be good for the miners. I believe it to be bad for the miner and bad for the nation, and I believe that the interests of the State are more important than the interests of any section. The Samuel Commission declared against it, and reported that they could find in it "no advantages that cannot be obtained as readily, or more readily, in other ways". Apart from the miners and their Socialist friends, nationalization has few, if any, supporters in the ranks of independent, impartial, responsible men with any knowledge of the industry, with the exception of Lord Justice Sankey, who presided over the Royal Commission of 1919.

In addition, the "other ways" mentioned by the

Samuel Commission are already being applied and are bearing fruit. The iron and steel industry is already closely associated with the coal industry; metallurgical and household coke, benzol, and other derivatives are being produced in ever increasing quantities, while blast-furnace gas is being regularly supplied from iron and steel works to some of our cities. "Oil from coal" plants are in daily production alongside the pits, and more are being put down. A big expansion in this direction is required, and whilst the State can help and encourage it, it is not the duty of the State to undertake it. In the production of gas, the association between the industries is becoming closer and the production of the by-products steadily increasing in quantity and quality. The use of electricity is becoming every day more general and the national grid system, when complete, will supply all our needs in this direction. Scientific research, under private enterprise, is finding new methods of producing many useful derivatives, and in this direction the dead hand of State control would hinder and hamper progress and development, rather than stimulate and expedite them.

There is nothing new in this advocacy of public ownership and control, and any careful examination of its application in the very wide field of operations visualized by Mr. Jones must lead one irresistibly to the same conclusion as that reached by the Samuel Commission, that there is in it nothing that cannot be better achieved by other methods. The whole conception is fantastic and impracticable. Those who have built up successful coal-using industries will never accept its basic principle, and if they were disposed to do so, the workers in those industries would be the first to rebel against a system which reduced their wages for the benefit of the workers engaged in another, only, in many cases, remotely related to it.

Leaving aside the question of principle there are in this volume certain other important aspects of the mining problem which call for criticism and comment. Most of them have been dealt with in the preceding pages, but the following brief notes, supplementing these, and representing another point of view from that of *The Coal Scuttle*, may be useful to those who desire to understand them clearly.

Efficiency: It is good to note that the President of the Mineworkers' Federation now acknowledges that on its technical side the British coal industry is thoroughly wideawake and up to date, and has nothing to learn from any of its competitors. He says: "On its purely mining side, there is nothing wrong with the coal industry. Its mining engineers, managers, and technicians are among the best in the world" (p. 150).

This is very welcome. Mr. Jones makes it clear that he casts no reflection on the technical conduct of the industry. The miners' criticism, he says, is directed against an *order*, and, naturally enough, he adds that it is not directed against that "small minority" of owners who agree with him. He claims that our technicians under the new *order* he desires "would be given far greater scope for the exercise of their technical and scientific knowledge". There is, however, no evidence that they suffer from lack of scope under private enterprise. Indeed, the progress of the last few years indicates quite the contrary. Under State control the incentive would be removed, and handicapped by the formalism of the red-tape methods associated with State activity, the technicians would find themselves enjoying not more scope but a great deal less.

It is to be hoped that this authoritative statement by the President of the mineworkers' organization will put an end once and for all to the wild charges of incompetency and inefficiency so frequently made by the more irresponsible of the miners' leaders against our mining engineers and managers, and repeated, parrot-like, with so much emphasis and misplaced eloquence by Socialist orators who have no personal knowledge of, or acquaintance with, the industry.

Nationalization: Mr. Jones protests strongly against what he calls "insidious and unfair form of propaganda" because those who disagree with him insist that his real motive for advocating these charges is to bring about the nationalization of the mines. Yet on the same page (page 144), paradoxically enough, he frankly acknowledges that they would make this end easier to realize, and in the following page (page 145) boldly asserts that public ownership is the only real solution, no matter what may be done so far as the proposed changes are concerned. This is his objective. His solution is a wholly unified industry under public ownership, with its management and control vested in a series of boards, sub-boards, and committees appointed by the Government, and responsible only to Parliament; in brief, a complete and self-contained bureaucracy.

To the impartial observer there can surely be nothing "unfair" in those who are opposed to nationalization taking every precaution to see that the nation is not committed to far-reaching and irrevocable changes constituting "stepping-stones", as Mr. Jones calls them, to public ownership, when that is the openly announced objective of those who advocate them, and its opponents are firmly convinced that movement in that direction can only make matters worse and not better.

Nationalization of the mines has been the policy of the Mineworkers' Federation for over twenty years. It is still the policy, and Mr. Jones must not be surprised that those of us who believe it to be a wrong policy are determined to see to it that nothing is left undone to prevent its ever being brought into operation.

Transfer Prices: On transfer prices Mr. Jones is as clear as he is on the question of efficiency. Whilst he exaggerates both the extent to which coal is actually transferred and the possible effect on wages, he makes no definite charge that this coal is transferred at figures below market value. His complaint is of the difficulty in arriving at what *is* the market value, particularly in the case of the composite concern, where the class of coal transferred may never come on the market at all. This is, of course, a matter for the joint accountants, and in actual practice little difficulty is experienced. Mr. Jones says: "The miners have the utmost faith in their accountants, men who in many instances have given them long years of faithful service."

It is the duty of these accountants to safeguard the interests of the miners. They are thoroughly familiar with the method of arriving at a fair figure, and there has never been any suggestion that they have failed in that duty. On December 17, 1929, Sir Ben Turner, the Socialist Minister of Mines, said: "Although I have frequently heard the allegation I have no concrete evidence that coal is transferred to associated companies at less than realizable market value" (H. of C.).

Now that the President of the Federation has made it clear that his complaint is against the system and that he makes no charge against the owners of entering this coal at figures below the real value, there ought to be less loose talk of the effect on wages of transfer prices. That effect has always been exaggerated.

There is room for improvement in the method of fixing them, but any gain would be merely in the direction of preventing an occasional difference of opinion between the accountants and dispelling suspicion in the minds of the workers. The effect on wages resulting from an alteration in the method of crediting the prices to the ascertainments would be negligible.

Mr. Jones's real grievance is that the coal so transferred is used in the by-product industries, and he desires the scope of the agreements enlarged so that the profits derived from these industries should be included in the ascertainments. That we have already dealt with (page 192).

The Quota System: One of the most important passages in *The Coal Scuttle* is to be found on page 78, in the chapter on organization. Here the "quota" system established by the Act of 1930, when the Socialist Government was in office, is condemned outright. The author says: "The present practice of giving a quota to every concern irrespective of its economic and geological position is indefensible. It compels the newer, bigger, and better-equipped collieries to march to the pace of the older and less efficient concerns; consequently, there is a great deal of short-time working, a big increase in overhead charges, and a reduction in the wage-paying capacity of the industry. This failure to concentrate output, with its short-time working, is, in fact, just as destructive to wages as competition within the industry."

All this is perfectly true, and it has been pointed out again and again both in the House of Commons and elsewhere. It was pointed out during the passage of the Act, but the policy of "spreading the work" was deliberately forced on the industry by a Socialist Government. Now, after five years, in which the poorer pits have been kept alive at the expense of the richer ones, the policy is condemned, and Mr. Jones advocates, as many of us have been doing for years, concentration on the economic units of production.

Whilst advocating this concentration, however, he has either not realized the full implications of adopting the policy, or he has not the courage to tell the miners all that it involves, for on the next page (page 79) he says: "One must confess that efficiency in the production and sale of coal would not materially increase the number of persons who would be required in the industry."

As a matter of cold, hard fact, concentration on the best pits with the abolition of short-time working, so far from increasing the number required in the industry, would materially reduce it. Nothing is to be gained by evading the issue, as Mr. Jones does, for he adds, "greater efficiency is essential", and if it is essential all the inevitable consequences must be faced.

Mr. Jones cannot make up his mind exactly what he does want. On page 121 he says that the production of 19 million tons of coal would give employment to 75,000 workers. It would, but not full-time employment. With an average output of 24 cwt. per man shift, it would give them employment for four shifts per week only. In full-time work the mining of 19 million tons of coal would mean only the employment of 50,000 men, and fewer when Mr. Jones gets the concentration which he advocates on the best pits. He really ought to face up to this problem, and tell his men, when he talks so glibly about increased employment, whether he means that they must go on working short time for ever in order to "spread the work".

On page 127 this vitally important factor is dealt with in the chapter on "The Survival of the Fittest", where it is shown that the policy, when fully realized, means the displacement of at least another hundred and thirty-four thousand workers.

It is true that in a later chapter on "Unemployment" the author of *The Coal Scuttle* recognizes that unless the causes are neutralized, a reduction in the man power required is inevitable, and suggests three measures for immediate application as at least partial remedies. These are:

(1) Pensions for the older men;
(2) Raising of the age of entry into the industry;
(3) Reduction in hours of work.

The first of these is highly desirable, but the matter is really one for Parliament, for as Mr. Jones himself says, the industry itself could not shoulder the financial burden entailed.

The second would undoubtedly be a step in the right direction and will probably come to pass very shortly, along with the raising of the school-leaving age.

The third is also very much to be desired, but must depend on the economic position of the industry and the hours worked in competing coal-producing countries.

What we are dealing with here, however, is the number of men to whom the industry can give employment. Neither of the two first helps at all in this direction. The only one of any value is, therefore, the third, and this on examination proves to be quite illusory. So far as the immediate situation is concerned, it is mere childish nonsense to maintain that either the British Government or the British coal-owners have opposed the proposal made at Geneva for an international agreement fixing the hours at seven and three quarters, bank to bank. It is even worse to blame the British coal-owners for the fact that the Hours of Work (Coal Mines) Convention has never been ratified.

The position of this country has been stated again and again by the Minister for Mines in the House of Commons. The stumbling-block is now, as it has always been, the question of simultaneous ratification. We have always declared our readiness to ratify when others do so, and as recently as July 2, 1935, the Minister of Labour announced in the House of Commons that "H.M. Government are prepared to ratify the revised Convention simultaneously with the other six countries named in the text of the Convention".

The revised Convention meets all our objections and we are ready to sign when the others agree to do so. To agree to reduce hours in this country and not in others would result in placing the latter in a favoured position so far as production costs are concerned, a consequent further reduction in our export trade, and another increase in unemployment. It is unjust to blame this country for the fact that the Convention has not been ratified, and it is no fault of ours, as Mr. Jones implies, that the field is not "clear for a further reduction all along the line".

Any progress along that line must depend on international agreement and any attempt at isolated action would be worse than folly in the present position of the industry.

The position, then, so far as Mr. Jones's three remedies for unemployment in the industry are concerned is this: No. 1, if adopted, whether with or without State assistance, would merely replace the men over fifty-five by younger men. It would at the same time raise a storm of protest in the coalfields. These men would not accept a "too old at 55" policy, and would strongly object to being thrown on the industrial scrap-heap at that age, even with the pension Mr. Jones suggests. In any event, the number is unknown; it could not be large, and would be smaller still at sixty.

No. 2 would merely raise the age of the young people engaged in the industry, without increasing their number at all.

No. 3 is attainable only by international agreement. If a universal reduction of hours could be agreed upon, it would undoubtedly help employment; but when some coal-producing countries refuse to ratify a convention limiting hours to seven and three-quarters there appears to be little immediate hope of achieving this.

It will thus be seen that when the President of the Mineworkers' Federation states that these three together "would enormously reduce the burden of unemployment", his case breaks down as soon as it is examined.

He seems to realize this himself, for he acknowledges that "they cannot solve the problem of unemployment in the mining areas", and for this he looks to the new industries he would establish there with coal as their foundation.

Whilst it is in this direction that we must look for the future development in the coal industry, Mr. Jones's estimates as to the volume of employment they would create in the winning of raw coal are altogether too optimistic. This matter is analysed on pages 334 and 335, where it is quite clearly shown that not only would the gain be much less in this direction than Mr. Jones estimates, but that the gain will inevitably be neutralized by the displacement of labour due to increased mechanization and concentration on the up-to-date pits. The real gain will be in the additional employment created in the new industries themselves and this should be both varied and extensive.

Mr. Jones's case so far as increased employment is concerned seems to have been built up in the fashion so admirably described in the words of a nineteenth-century English writer:

> "We figure to ourselves
> The thing we like; and then we build it up,
> As chance will have it, on the rock or sand."

The chance in this case has led to building on sand, and the author has, wittingly or unwittingly, helped in the choice. Where the results which he arrives at are based on theory and one differs with him, it is possible to take a tolerant view, for in that field they can be but matters of opinion. Where they are derived from calculations based on authentic figures issued by a Government Department, it is a different matter. On this question of employment Mr. Jones sets out some simple sums, and the answers which he himself gives would get any sixth-standard schoolboy "ploughed" in an examination in elementary arithmetic.

On page 17 of *The Coal Scuttle* he gives correctly the annual output of each wage earner in the industry at 280 tons (Ministry of Mines Report, 1934). Then on page 120 he says that at present the hydrogenation plant at Billingham uses 180,000 tons of coal in producing 15 million gallons of petrol, adding: "At the present rate of production in the coal industry this gives employment to about 800 miners." The schoolboy's sum is: Divide 180,000 by 280. His answer is

$$\frac{180{,}000}{280} = 642 \cdot 85$$

A discrepancy of 25 per cent may mean little in the author's method of calculation, but it seriously affects his arguments as to increased employment, and, indeed, does so in the figures he derives immediately afterwards from the result of his little sum. He goes on to add: "If, therefore, the 1,240 million gallons of petrol now imported every year were obtained from coal by the hydrogenation process, direct employment would be given to over 70,000 mineworkers. Here our schoolboy has two sums. (1) "If 180,000 tons of coal are required to produce 15 million gallons, how many tons will be required to produce 1,240 millions?" His answer is 14,868,000 tons. The second sum is: "If one miner produces in one year 280 tons, how many miners will be required to produce 14,868,000 tons?" His answer is 53,000.

Mr. Jones's figure is "over 70,000", a difference of 20,000, or 36 per cent above the correct answer.

On the following page (p. 121) another of these crude calculations appears. In this case the figure is 19 million tons. "This would give direct employment to about 75,000 mineworkers." The correct number, using his own basic figure, is 67,857, not so gross an error as the other, but misleading enough.

In addition, the 280 tons per person employed per annum is produced by miners working only 4·84 days per week. They provide 1·2 tons per shift, so that if the 180,000 tons is to give work to 800 miners they will be employed not even for 4·84 days, but for 3½ only, and their annual output will be not 280 tons, but 225. On the basis of 1·2 tons per shift and 6 shifts per week, with 12 days for holidays, the miner's output for full-time employment would be 360 tons per annum. The 180,000 tons would therefore give full-time employment to 500 and not to 800, as so irresponsibly suggested by one who ought to know better.

This admixture of unsound theory and bad arithmetic can result only in misleading the average citizen and inspiring false hopes in the minds and hearts of the workers in the mines. It is difficult to write with patience of those who misuse figures in this fashion for purely propagandist purposes. The simple facts are as I have given them and they cannot be disputed. It is time for the public to understand and appreciate them, and as truth is always the strongest argument, the Mineworkers' Federation would be well advised to do so also, and cease deceiving the people by issuing inaccurate and therefore useless figures regarding potential employment, for which, in their case, there is neither justification nor excuse.

Wages: In *The Coal Scuttle* the chapter on wages, and, indeed, all references to wages, are frankly propagandist in character and not designed to give the reader a clear-cut picture of the wages position of the 750,000 workers in the industry. Throughout, attention is focused on the lowest wages paid, in order to create the impression that the general level of wages in the industry is "abnormally low". This is not the case. The number of workers engaged in the industry whose wages are too low is too great. The low-paid wage earner is the crux of the problem. It is on his case that the whole of the effort to raise wages should have been centred, especially the workers in the poorer districts and particularly in the exporting districts. Instead of that the demand made, and the concession granted in 1935, was for an increase for all wage earners. There are thousands of miners, in particular the piece workers, who earn, regularly, wages which will bear comparison with those paid in any industry. They could earn more, and the lower-paid workers receive also a substantial increase, were it not for the artificial restrictions imposed on the industry by the legislature. In modern times no industry can pay high wages if it is expressly debarred from working at full capacity. A modern, well-equipped colliery, restricted by the quota, and thereby compelled to work short time, has to carry all its "overheads" on an output of only two-thirds of its potential output capacity, and the men on piece work have to exert themselves to the utmost to earn what they can in the four days, while the datal hands have no remedy at all. The real road to higher wages is the road to higher efficiency. The effect of rationalization is dealt with elsewhere. Higher prices can and ought to be obtained from some of the consumers in the home market, and this will assist in securing the additional revenue needed for the payment of higher wages. There is a limit, however, to the extent to which prices can be raised without reducing demand, so that this alone will not suffice.

There must be, in addition, concentration on the more modern collieries in order to reduce the cost of production, and the two combined ought to enable the industry to increase the wages of the lower-paid workers to a level which will leave no cause for complaint.

When it is generally acknowledged that the wages of the lower-paid workers are too low, it is not much use trying to show the real position by averages. Everyone is agreed that such a method does not give a true picture. But if we *are* to use averages, let us use the right ones. Mr. Jones says: "The earnings in every district averaged little more than £2 per person per week." The true figure is given on page 120. With the allowances in kind the figure for adult workers in all the coalfields is just over £2 10s. This does not excuse or justify the extremely low cash earnings in some cases and it is not enough, even expressed as an average, for the service rendered. No useful purpose is served, however, by seeking to make the case appear worse than it actually is. The figures given in Appendix VI are the average weekly wages received and to these 4½d. per shift must be added for allowances in kind. There is nothing hypothetical about them; they have nothing to do with average earnings per man shift, or with short time; they represent the average amount paid to the worker in the weekly pay packet.

The attempt to show that wages in general are "abnormally low" is buttressed by the use of miners' pay notes in the appendix of *The Coal Scuttle*. It is very doubtful whether these should be accepted as evidence, for they bear no name of either workman or employer. A claim was made by the Miners' Federation before the Sankey Commission to submit similar notes. The owners at once demanded that if they were to be submitted as evidence, all details should be disclosed and an opportunity given to test their authenticity. The Court upheld this claim, the pay notes were withdrawn and nothing more was heard of them.

Mr. Jones says of the pay notes he uses to support his case: "These are all recent examples, taken at random. . . . None of them is exceptional." Yet, strangely enough, with one exception, they show remarkably low earnings, without any attempt to explain the causes. Certainly, no one with any knowledge of the industry will accept pay notes showing gross earnings of 18s. 4½d. for six days' work, or even £1 11s. 4d. for five, as being typical cases of the normal wages received. I am here ignoring "offtakes".

The one pay note which does show good wages is also one requiring some explanation and is evidently utilized for the purpose of calling attention to the deductions.

As has been explained in the chapter on "offtakes", these are deductions made weekly from the worker's earnings, always with his consent and for his benefit. In this particular pay note the gross earnings of two men were given at £6 8s. 4d., or £3 4s. 2d. each.

The deductions, however, total £1 4s. 6d., or 12s. 3d. each. The details are:

	£	s.	d.
Health Insurance		4	6
Unemployment Insurance ..		5	0
Welfare			6
Death Fund		3	0
Pit Head Baths		3	0
Coal		4	0
Coal Leading		4	6
	£1	4	6

The worker's weekly contribution for Health Insurance is 9d. For Unemployment, 10d. A fair figure for the Death Fund would be 6d., and the same for the baths. Coal and leading should be spread over a month or more, making the figure just over 2s. for each worker. With 3d. each for Welfare this makes a total of 4s. 11d. each. All voluntary, and for all which he gets something in return. But on this one week's pay note there are charged three weeks' health and unemployment insurance, and other charges which ought legitimately to be divided over three or four weeks. The result is, of course, to make the "offtakes" for that week unduly high at 12s. 3d. each and each man's wages to appear in what is, presumably, a normal week not what they actually are in any fair method of calculation, £2 19s. 3d., but £2 11s. 11d., both after deductions—a difference of 7s. 4d. each per week.

It is difficult to understand how or why these deductions should all be made from one week's earnings, and equally difficult to understand what purpose Mr. Jones thinks can be served by using a pay note so open to criticism and so calculated to give false impressions to those who do not look beneath the surface. There is certainly something "exceptional" in this pay note. Incidentally, it shows that some miners do not do so badly. The coalfield in this case is Yorkshire.

For purposes of contrast the author of *The Coal Scuttle* gives also particulars of the balance sheets of certain selected companies, all of them composite undertakings, apparently with the idea of showing that while wages are "abnormally low" profits are abnormally high. He must have had a difficult task, for even in these selected undertakings he has had to show that in some of them the ordinary shareholders have had to go for years without any dividend, whilst in the others, with the exception of two (one making bricks and the other pipes), the dividends are quite modest, the lowest being 2 per cent and the highest 8 per cent.

Not a word is said of the dozens of companies who have had to write down their capital (a loss of millions to the shareholders), of those who have spent millions both from revenue and in new capital in modernizing their plant, of those forced out of business by economic factors over which they had no control, with the loss of all their money, or the very large number of concerns which have kept going for years under exceptional difficulties, providing employment for thousands of workers, but no return to the investor.

The contrast is valueless and its propagandist character so obvious that it defeats itself.

Output: In his references to individual output, Mr. Jones is really too disingenuous. He says: "The individual output of coal has not diminished." By calmly stepping from 1914 to 1934 he proves his case, for it is quite true that the output per person employed is now higher than in 1914. The figures are given in Appendix IV. The President of the Federation ignores completely the heavy decline in individual output between 1913 and 1926, one of the main reasons for the plight of the industry, for the 1925 subsidy, and the subsequent seven months' stoppage. The figure fell from 260 tons in 1913 to 187 tons in 1920, only reached 221 tons in 1925, and did not exceed the 1913 figure until 1929. Output per man shift fell from 20·32 cwt. in 1914 to 14·46 cwt. in 1921, and did not reach the 1914 level again until 1927.

The increase in individual output is mainly due to mechanization. In the last ten or twelve years the owners have put an enormous amount of new capital into the industry, a point Mr. Jones never even mentioned. The money has been mainly spent in installing machinery, with the result that whereas in 1913 only 8·5 per cent of the output was machine won, it is now exactly 51 per cent. This is a process which will continue, and the resultant displacement of human labour is one of the vital factors which must be reckoned with.

Exports: This has already been dealt with in the chapter on exports. There is almost general agreement as to the causes of the decline, except on the very controversial issue of the effect of the 1930 Act. The only additional comment that need be made, so far as the views in *The Coal Scuttle* are concerned, is that the President of the Mineworkers' Federation should appear to attach so little importance to the injury suffered by the export trade through the 1926 stoppage, for the prolongation of which, at least, his organization was entirely responsible. Mr. Jones says: "I claim that the record of the miners' organization, the Mineworkers' Federation, is one of which any body of men may well feel proud." The sorry record of the Federation in the 1921 and 1926 disputes does not confirm that view, and it was in the export section of the industry that the effects of their misguided policy was most severely felt, for we lost in 1926 markets we had held for many years, and have probably lost them for ever.

Coal and Politics: Like all his colleagues, Mr. Jones waxes indignant at the suggestion that the continual agitation carried on by his organization is inspired in any way by political motives. Yet it is undeniable that in no other of our staple industries have politics and industry been so intermixed. The Mineworkers' Federation has been dominated by politics for the last thirty years. One result has been that coal has never been out of the House of Commons and if our other staple industries made as much demand on the time of Parliament as the mining industry, it would cease to function as a legislative machine and we should really need the Industrial Parliament advocated in some quarters.

Political activity has made the miners a powerful

force in the counsels of the Socialist Party; it has enhanced the prestige of the Federation; it has given seats in the House of Commons to miners simply because they are miners; but it has done nothing for the rank and file of the workers in the pits which could not have been done by other means just as effectively, and without one-tenth of the bitterness engendered by the introduction of the political element.

In the House of Commons the narrow outlook of the "miners' member" has led them to the firm belief that no one, even if elected by miners' votes, has the right to speak for the miner except those attached to the Mineworkers' Federation and the Socialist Party. As a result, any effort made by others to help in improving the lot of the miner is looked upon with distrust and receives little support or encouragement from that quarter.

In the last Parliament, Mr. Godfrey Nicholson, National Conservative, the member for Morpeth, introduced a private member's Bill for ensuring that miners awarded compensation for injuries received in the pits should be certain of receiving it for life, or as long as disablement lasted, irrespective of what happened to the colliery company concerned—whether it closed down or went bankrupt or sought to repudiate liability. He succeeded in inducing the Government to give facilities for it, piloted it safely to the Statute Book, and as a result of his efforts the disabled miner is to-day safe for life. When he did this Mr. Nicholson did more for the disabled miners than any individual miners' member has ever done. Yet he received little help from the Socialists during the passage of the measure, and at the election the miners showed their gratitude by turning him out. He was not a Socialist.

When the writer, in collaboration with several other Liberal members, introduced into the House a modest measure to provide pensions for aged miners, we received neither encouragement nor support from Socialists representing mining constituencies. They were our political opponents; politics came first, and outweighed any other consideration such as the usefulness of the measure or the benefit it might confer on a very deserving class of workers. We were not Socialists.

It is idle for Mr. Jones to pretend that politics does not play a big part in the Federation policy. He could not prevent it now if he would. Mining is a localized business. The miners and their wives, sons, and daughters far outnumber the other members of the community. With a wide franchise and an alliance with the Socialist Party, the mining divisions provide for a miner the easiest road to the House of Commons since the days of the old pocket boroughs. He need only keep his lamp shining a little in front of those of his fellows and he is there for life. In nine cases out of ten the "miners' member" is also an official of the Federation. It is "politics" that got him into the House and he is not allowed to forget it. In the coalfields there is no room for the spirit of political compromise. He has won his way by denouncing the whole capitalist system, with the colliery owner as the epitome of all its evils, so that every problem arising in the industry is given a political colouring and the rank and file taught to look to political action for a solution. The miners' lodges are always discussing politics, and in their counsels there is no room for any but Socialists. The perpetual insistence on "politics in industry" has poisoned the wells of social intercourse in every mining village, and in many cases led to family bitterness and strife. The leaders are subject to continual criticism and their Members of Parliament to perpetual pressure by their followers. They themselves have "blazed the trail" of political activity, and if the responsibilities of leadership or experience in the House should exercise a mellowing influence and tempt them to abandon it for the calmer atmosphere of the council chamber, they are speedily reminded that there must be no truckling with the "enemy"; that "youth is knocking at the door"; that the movement is at least as much political as industrial; and that others are waiting to slip into their shoes and to march to the tune of the *Red Flag* on the slightest sign of wavering in their zeal for political action.

The never-ending intrusion of political element is common knowledge to all connected with the industry and Mr. Jones's protest will not be taken seriously by anyone familiar with the facts; least of all by those who have had experience of it in the House of Commons. The curse of the industry is now and has for years past been "politics", and the never-ceasing demands by the workers' representatives, both in Parliament and out of it, for more and more Government intervention and Government control.

Even the miners' leaders have occasionally been frank enough to acknowledge the danger of political influences in the conduct of industry. For example, in *Coal and Commonsense,* "Labour's Scheme for the Future of the Coal Industry", we find this significant passage:

"With a nationalized industry, however, this method (negotiations between employers and employees concerning wages) is unsuitable, as it would involve negotiations between the State as owner and the employees' representatives, and the discussion would immediately be fought out in the cockpit of politics—a course which we deem to be undesirable from the point of view of both the industry and the State" (*Coal and Commonsense*, by Herbert Smith and A. J. Cook).

It is little wonder that statesmen, colliery owners, and many public-spirited men and women unconnected with the industry should now hold that it is time to call a halt, that, subject to the safeguards already existing, employers and employed should work out their own salvation in an economic and industrial atmosphere, enjoying, no more and no less, the same immunity from political influences as is accorded to other great industries, instead of being made the shuttlecock of perpetual political agitation. This matter is dealt with further in the chapter on the Mineworkers' Federation.

Other points in the re-organization policy of the Federation on which there is room for legitimate criticism and difference of opinion are dealt with in other parts of this volume as matters affecting the general conduct of the industry. Enough has been said here to show that this latest scheme is thoroughly impracticable and offers no solution for the problems of the industry. The world owes much to its visionaries; it owes more to its practical reformers. Mr. Jones's "vision" is indeed "Such stuff as dreams are made on". And a very bad dream too. If it were possible to translate it into reality, it would mean: Complete bureaucratic control not only of the production of coal, but also of all the complex processes in the coal-using industries; the creation of thousands of jobs for well-paid State officials only remotely connected with the industry and contributing nothing to it; a decline in efficiency similar to that which has characterized nationalization of industry in every part of the world where it has been tried; a heavy increase in the cost of production with a rise in price to all the coal-consuming industries; a further fall in our already greatly reduced export trade in coal; increased costs of production in other exporting trades, such as iron and steel, already struggling against fierce world competition to hold their places in overseas markets, and without retaining which this country cannot prosper; the stifling of that individual initiative which is vital to progress in any industry under modern conditions, and its replacement by the enervating spirit of bureaucratic control; and in the end, the same heavy loss, industrial unrest, and economic confusion which have marked attempts to nationalize competitive industry in other parts of the world, and which we ourselves experienced through State Control in 1920–21, and paid for so dearly in subsequent years.

There is need for a wider and more enlightened outlook for the future of the industry. There is ample scope for progress and development along modern scientific lines in this industry, and room for improvement in the wages and working conditions of those engaged in it. Utopian dreams such as that envisaged by the President of the Mineworkers' Federation are all very well in their place, the "land of make-believe". What is required to-day, however, and what is very much more useful, is a realistic grasp of those world conditions, the changes in which threaten that industrial supremacy which we have for so long enjoyed and in which coal plays so vital a part, with a fixed determination on the part of both owners and men to join forces in a spirit of co-operation and good will to get the best out of the industry for the mutual benefit of all who render service in it, and for the enrichment of the nation as a whole.

Our position as one of the chief manufacturing nations and the leading export nation of the world, both resting on the foundation of a cheap and abundant supply of coal, and both vital for the maintenance of our growing population, is very much more likely to be maintained by that spirit of private enterprise which made it possible and has retained it in the face of declining world trade and fierce competition, than it is ever likely to by the enthronement of bureaucracy envisaged by the imaginative author of *The Coal Scuttle*, whose idealism does more credit to his heart than to his head, and who would be well advised to harness that idealism to the chariot of reality if he desires to see, in his own lifetime, that advance in the workers' standard of life for which he so eloquently pleads.

CHAPTER XXVI

THE MINEWORKERS' FEDERATION AND AVERAGE WAGES

MR. JONES is not alone in handling so loosely the figures of the industry in pleading the cause of the miner, and in such fashion as would be amusing were it not concerned with such a serious subject.

His colleague, Mr. Ebby Edwards, the Secretary of the Mineworkers' Federation, shares his apparent simplicity and real ingenuity, and with all the appearance of injured righteousness presents his case on wages in even more disingenuous terms than Mr. Jones on the volume of employment. Like Bret Harte's Chinaman, "childlike and bland", he handles figures in a manner which turns the actuary's hair grey; and greyer still when he sees that this sort of presentation of the case carries more weight with the average citizen than that of the economist.

On December 10, 1935, Mr. Edwards replied to the owners' statement of their case against the demand for a flat-rate increase of 2s. per shift for men and 1s. for youths. I am not here concerned with whether wages are low, or too low, or whether some are too low and none too high. I am concerned only with the manner in which the Secretary of the Mineworkers' Federation uses the figures of a Government department to prove his case on average earnings.

The reply is a long one, but the relevant passage is the most important part of it, and if it is to be examined it ought to be quoted in full. Here it is, as reported in *The Times* of December 10, 1935:

"In the first six months of this year, the total shifts worked were 91,727,983, of which 35,594,753 were worked at the coal face. The gross wages paid for the total shifts worked were £42,329,063. The coal-face workers, on the owners' own figure, took £20,057,643 for 38·8 per cent of the workers. This only leaves £22,271,419 to cover 61·2 per cent of the miners, or a wage of 7s. 11¼d. a shift for all classes other than coal-face workers. As the average days worked for the period was 4·84 per week, this means that 61·2 per cent of the miners earn on the average a gross wage of 38s. 5d. per week."

Now, for the reader who knows nothing of the industry, what do all these figures mean?

In trying to explain them let me put, first of all, the meaning Mr. Edwards gives them. Just before this quotation he accepts "for argument" the owners' figure, for the earnings of the workers at the coal face, at 11s. 3¼d. per shift. They numbered 38·8 per cent (say 39 per cent).

He then takes the combined earnings of the 39 per cent, deducts them from the total wages paid, and points out that the balance must be divided between the 61 per cent. He is quite right so far. He takes the direct and simple route. He divides the £22,271,419 by 444,067, representing the 61 per cent, and, getting 38s. 5d. as his answer, says that is the average earnings of the miners in the 61 per cent total. That is his case. But, as it is stated, it is not the whole case.

Now for a look at it. The whole of the 39 per cent are adult workers. They are the better-paid workers (mostly paid by results, i.e. piece workers). Mr. Edwards accepts the figures of the owners, and makes no complaint that their earnings are inadequate. The average number of workers in the six months under review was

727,978 (Mines Department Summaries). 39 per cent of that is 283,911. The total wages bill was £42,329,063, of which the 39 per cent took £20,057,643. This left £22,271,420 for the remaining 61 per cent. They numbered 444,067. Who were they, and what did each receive as earnings? It is not possible to say with any degree of accuracy, for the official method of showing occupation and earnings in the industry is incomplete and entirely out of date.

The official returns group all workers together—old and young, skilled and unskilled, piece workers and day workers, underground and surface workers, well paid and badly paid, are all grouped together and their earnings expressed as an "average". The returns do, however, make one important distinction. They give the number of boys and youths under twenty who are employed as wage earners.

The Annual Report of the Mines Department (1934) shows that in that year 3·75 per cent of the workers were under sixteen years of age and 10·67 per cent between sixteen and twenty. The figures were:

Under 16 years of age	28,826
Over 16 and under 20	82,078
Total of young persons ..	110,904[1]

Included in this figure are 1,069 females.

The total represents 14·4 per cent of the wage earners, and the inclusion of the wages of this large percentage of young people in the calculation which determines "average earnings" unduly depresses the figures showing the weekly wages received by the adult workers and results in a misleading average figure. The

[1] For 1935 figures see App. VII.

boys and youths do not receive, and cannot expect to receive, the "average" arrived at by Mr. Edwards, and their earnings ought to be shown separately. This is not at all a question of whether wages are too low. The point is, quite simply, that if "averages" are to be used they should be averages which give at least a tolerably true picture of the situation. The method employed is unsound, but one of its defects can be overcome by separating the young persons from the adults.

The fact that there are 110,904 young persons employed in the industry does at least enable us to get correctly the number of adult workers. As the ages of the young people are taken only at the end of the year, the figures apply strictly only to that date, but they are sufficiently accurate to give a clear picture of the effect of their earnings in the "average" earnings. Apply these figures of December 1934 to January–June 1935.

None of this 110,904 is included in the 283,911 coal-face workers, who are all adults, or if a few of the older youths are included it does not seriously affect the figures, as they are in one or other of these categories. The 61 per cent consists of the total less the coal-face workers, i.e. 727,978 less 283,911, or 444,067. None of the young persons being included with the coal-face workers, they must all be grouped with the balance. The number of adult workers, therefore, in that group must be 444,067 less 110,904, that is 333,163.

What do the young persons earn? A fair figure for those under sixteen is 15s. per week, and for those between sixteen and twenty years of age a similar figure is about 25s. per week. 28,826 persons under sixteen at 15s. per week gives a wage bill for the six months of £562,107. The wage bill for the 82,078 at

25s. per week for the six months is £2,667,535. Added together they give a total of £3,229,642, wages paid to all young persons for the six months.

The wages paid to the 61 per cent totalled £22,271,420. Of this the young persons took £3,229,642, leaving £19,041,778 for the adult workers, who numbered 333,163. This gives an average weekly wage of exactly 44s., and not 38s. 5d. as stated by Mr. Edwards, a very substantial difference of 5s. 7d. per week. As shown elsewhere, this calculation is not affected by the fact that some of the under officials' wages are included in the figures giving the total wages paid.

This analysis reveals two things. Firstly, the utter unreliability of "average" figures as a guide to the wages paid in the industry. The boys and youths would be very glad indeed if they received 38s. 5d. weekly.

Secondly, they show once again that the real grievance is that of the lower-paid adult worker, those receiving wages below this figure of 44s., who ought not only to receive the first consideration when wages are increased as the result of the selling schemes, but also to have a larger share of the increased revenue falling to the wages fund than their more highly paid fellow workers.

This is the first readjustment which ought to be made. It would not be too popular with some of the workers and might possibly lead to political repercussions, but it is common justice, and no consideration of the kind should prevent the Federation officials from insisting on it. They put the low-paid worker first on the list in all their propaganda. He should be first on the list at the Council table whenever any increase in wages is under discussion.

CHAPTER XXVII

ALTERNATIVE POLICIES

NOTE.—The reader will observe that in the making of the calculations he will find in this chapter and elsewhere the output for 1935 is given sometimes at 222 million tons and sometimes at 215, and the number of wage earners sometimes at 754,000 and sometimes at 720,000. The explanation is that the Annual Statistical Summary issued by the Mines Department, which gives the figures for output and wages, deals only with 96 or 97 per cent of the output, while the Annual Report of the Department gives the totals of output and number employed for all coal mines. It should also be noted that in addition to the "wage earners" there is an average of 15,000 "clerks and salaried persons" carried on the pay roll of the industry.

IN these pages I have endeavoured to give a picture of the coal-mining industry which will enable the reader unacquainted with its history or its technicalities to understand and appreciate something of its difficulties and its complexities. I have throughout dealt only with the historic, political, economic, and financial aspects of the industry and have deliberately excluded the sentimental.

I have not done so because of any lack of sympathy with the miners, and particularly with the lower-paid workers in the industry, but because the question of ensuring for them a greater reward for the service they render in their arduous and hazardous occupation is an economic one, and all the sentiment in the world will not alter that fundamental fact.

U

For those who desire it there are reams of sentiment to be found in the propaganda leaflets and pamphlets of the Mineworkers' Federation, in the articles written for the popular Press by journalists who learn all about the industry in a flying visit to a distressed area, in the biographies of miners who have become Members of Parliament, in their speeches in the House of Commons, and in the writings of popular novelists, who seem to delight in painting a lurid picture of the most sordid side of life in a mining community—pictures which are not only grossly exaggerated in many respects, but are in others a grave reflection on one of the most hard-working and most respectable sections of our industrial population.

I know the coalfields well. I have been down the pits dozens of times. I know the miners both in their work and in their play. I know them in their homes and in their clubs. I know the miners' wives and how cheerfully and how uncomplainingly they contribute their share to a partnership in which it may truthfully be said that "woman's work is never done".

I know them to be not only a hard-working and clean-living people, but also a proud and self-reliant one. They have no desire to be slobbered over by sentimental idealists who do not understand them or their job and who can contribute nothing to the improvement of their economic situation but a patronizing sympathy. The workers in the industry do not want charity, and they resent excessive sentimentalism in the presentation of their case for a share in that higher standard of life which the onward march of science and civilization and progress is bringing to the workers in all industries in this country to a greater degree than in any other of the older countries of the world. They have been up against the cold, hard, economic facts of a changing world since the end of the war, and in a few short years have seen the number of workers employed in their industry reduced by no fewer than 400,000. In those years the number of work-people engaged in "productive" industries has steadily declined, while the number engaged in "service" occupations has steadily increased, and in this change the coal-mining industry has suffered more than any other.

The causes have already been dealt with.

The altered conditions of international trading and its effect on the coal-mining industry have not only created this vast army of the workless, but have also been the principal factors in the creation of what are known as the distressed or "special" areas, for these areas are, in the main, the coal-producing areas. The problem of the "special areas" is not one for the solution of which the mining industry can be responsible. That responsibility rests with the Government, and of the seven post-war Governments—Coalition, Conservative, Socialist, and National—none has produced any measures for dealing with the problem commensurate with either its magnitude or its gravity.

In order, however, that the position of the mining industry in the matter should be clearly understood, it is important that the essential facts should be stated with brutal candour, no matter how unpleasant they may be or how distasteful to the sentimentalist.

The simple truth is that, under existing conditions, the output capacity of the industry (260 million tons) is just enough to enable it to supply its available market, with a reasonable margin of productive capacity in reserve to meet any increase in the demand. It is compelled by Act of Parliament to employ too many workpeople for its efficient management, with the result that many thousands of them have to work short time, and production costs are unnecessarily increased. In addition, there are registered as miners hundreds of thousands on unemployment benefit or transitional payments who will never again find employment in the pits.

This pathetic army of the workless will never again be an army of occupation so far as the mines are concerned. Its numbers will grow less only as they die or find employment in other industries. And as they drop out their places in the ranks will be taken by others compulsorily enlisted by recruiting sergeants, Mechanization and Economic Nationalism. There is no hope whatever that this industry will ever again employ the million of workers engaged in it ten years ago. From time to time, as there is a little spurt in one of the coalfields, some of the unemployed will be temporarily absorbed for a few weeks, and at the end of it find themselves "on the dole" once more, for almost all the influences affecting the economic operation of the industry are to-day tending to reduce the volume of employment which it provides.

The remedies propounded by the idealists outside the industry, and by some of the visionaries within it, afford but small grounds or any hope of increased employment. I have already shown that rationalization means a reduction in the number of workers of about 134,000 (page 130). I have shown also that the expectations based on "oil from coal" plants are grossly exaggerated so far as they will affect employment in the winning of coal. I have shown that pensions for the older men and raising the age of entry will not increase the volume of employment, however desirable they may be. I have shown that international agreements such as that recently concluded with Poland will merely assist in reducing competition abroad at fair prices, without any substantial expansion in the severely diminished export trade. I have shown that mechanization has reduced, and is still steadily reducing, the number of workers in and about the mines. In one of our coalfields 84 per cent of the coal is now machine won, while others are daily enlarging the field of mechanical operation in winning, conveying, screening, grading, and sizing of coal.

What then remains? Nothing but a reduction of hours, either "on our own" or by international agreement with other coal-producing countries. Will this, if effected in the present condition of world trade and with modern methods of mining, increase the sum total of available employment in British coal mines? The stumbling-blocks at Geneva to an all-round reduction in hours have been the difficulties of securing simultaneous ratification to the convention, of raising the wages of miners in continental countries to the higher level of the British miner, and of defining, in generally comparable terms, the meaning of that ambiguous phrase "the standard of life".

But if we leave aside the international complications, ignore for a moment all the other grave economic implications, and assume that in this country we adopted the policy of substantially reducing the hours of labour, what would be the effect on the volume of employment in the industry and on the number of workers who can earn a livelihood in it? In considering the matter it should be noted that the chief argument advanced for a reduction of hours is that it would greatly help to reduce unemployment. The President of the Mineworkers' Federation says: "But whether it be affected [effected?] by international agreement or not, the miners are convinced that a reduction of hours is one of the ways in which unemployment can best be dealt with" (*The Coal Scuttle*, page 111). And on the previous page (page 110) Mr. Jones commits himself definitely to the statement that "it" (reduction of hours) "would necessitate the employment of more men in the industry".

I desire, as he desires, and as the reader undoubtedly desires, to see more men working in the industry, but I am not going to allow my heart to run away with my head and lead me to a belief that it can be accomplished or that this is a royal road to it. Let us therefore look at it.

The proposal most frequently and most strenuously advocated is that of the 6 hours day. The present hours are 7½ per shift. Through the operation of the schemes imposed on the industry by the Act of 1930, a policy of spreading the work available is actually in practice on a national basis. In some districts it has been spread further by the "rota" system, under which all the men voluntarily lay off for one week in three or four in order that all may share in the employment available. And the effect of the control is liable to variation by the fluctuations in demand for different classes of coal, which may create a rush in one district and a slump in another. The policy has been in operation since 1931—long enough to enable one to arrive at a reasoned judgement on what it has achieved. The Annual Report of the Mines Department shows exactly the extent to which each district is affected by giving the output, the number of men employed, and the number of shifts worked.

I am, however, dealing with the *total* volume of employment, which is also dealt with in the report.

In 1935 the total output was 222 million tons, produced by 754,000 workers, who each worked on the average 256 shifts in that year, or 4·92 shifts of $7\frac{1}{2}$ hours per week. This gives an average of 36·9 hours per person employed per week. A full week of 6 shifts of 6 hours each is 36 hours, and a simple calculation will show that if these 754,000 workers had worked this, instead of a $7\frac{1}{2}$ hours shift with short time, the output would have been almost exactly the same. In both cases the "one-winding time", additional, is ignored (see note on page 296).

But the advocates of a shorter working day demand not only a 6 hours shift. They advocate concentration of production on the best pits and the closing down of the uneconomic mines. The President of the Mineworkers' Federation is emphatic on this. After condemning the quota system as "indefensible", he adds: "This failure to concentrate output, with its short-time working, is, in fact, just as destructive to wages as competition within the industry."

I have shown (page 130) that concentration on the bigger and better-equipped collieries would result in throwing out of work at least 134,000 men. But if this concentration is to be accompanied by the adoption of a 6 hours day in all the coalfields the combined effect of the two must be examined.

Rationalization, by reducing the total number of workers from 754,000 by 134,000, would leave in the industry 620,000 men fully employed for $5\frac{3}{4}$ shifts of $7\frac{1}{2}$ hours per week, and producing each 360 tons per annum against an average of 294 in 1935.[1]

[1] Wage earners only. Figure "per person employed" for 1935 was 289.

A reduction of working hours from $7\frac{1}{2}$ to 6 would reduce the individual output approximately by one-fifth, and thus necessitate an increase in the number of workers to approximately the same extent.[1] One-fifth of 620,000 is 124,000, making the new total under rationalization and a general 6 hours day 744,000, or 10,000 less than in 1935.

Thus the effect of a reduction of hours to 6 per shift, while retaining the principle of spreading the employment by means of quotas which keep alive the uneconomic units, is merely to regularize hours, and by spreading the production over $5\frac{3}{4}$ shifts, instead of 4·92, to give the workers nominal full-time employment without finding work for any of the unemployed at all. The combined effect of rationalization and a reduction of hours, as shown above, would be, not the absorption of some of the unemployed miners, but an addition to their number.

In a varied and complex industry like the mining industry it would be idle to pretend that in making these calculations an application of the elementary rules of simple proportion to the problem of output and man power will give a mathematically accurate result. But in these figures there is room for a wide margin of error, and they would still show clearly that there is no prospect of finding in the industry employment for any more men than are now engaged in it, either by rationalization or by reduction of hours or by a combination of both. This is not sentimentalism. It is not pessimism. It is realism. And it is time the inescapable truth was realized by all connected with the industry, as well as by the Government and the

[1] Not strictly accurate, as the time spent at the coal face would be proportionately less.

dreamers who inspire false hopes in the breasts of the helpless victims of changes brought about by the relentless operation of economic forces over which they have no control.

Up to this point I have confined consideration of the economic possibilities of the industry to the question of the man power required to maintain an output stabilized at the 1935 figure of 222 million tons. There is, however, another factor, the cost of the man power, i.e. wages, of vital importance to all concerned.

POLICY NO. 1.—If the policy for the future is to be an extension of the existing system of "spreading the work" by reducing the hours of labour to 6 with all pits now working still receiving their "quota" and paying wages on the same basis rates, then a heavy increase in the wages costs is inevitable. On the nominal full-time basis the wage earners in the same numbers would receive payment for $5\frac{3}{4}$ shifts per week instead of for 4·92, and the piece worker would naturally demand that, as his hours had been stabilized on the same short-time basis as the datal workers, his method of payment should be readjusted by an increase on his percentage or yardage basis so as to permit of a corresponding increase in his earnings. The total addition to the wages bill of the adoption of this policy is extremely difficult to forecast, but after working it out in several ways, I have come to the conclusion that it would not be less than £20,000,000, entailing an increase in wages costs of 2s. per ton on all coal commercially disposable and an average increase in wages to all workers of 10s. per week by raising the average cash earnings from £118, the 1935 figure, to £144 on the 1935 output.

POLICY NO. 2.—If the policy were one of concentration on the best pits, with a $7\frac{1}{2}$ hours shift and $5\frac{3}{4}$ shifts per week, the average cash earnings would be substantially the same as in No. 1, but there would be fewer workers employed. With full-time working, the individual output would rise from 298 tons per annum to 360 tons, without adding anything for increased efficiency, and the 215 million tons of 1935 (96 per cent of output), produced by 720,000 workers, would be produced by 600,000. The wages bill for the 720,000 was £85,000,000. The reduction in the numbers sharing this wages fund would automatically raise the average cash earnings of those still employed by £22 per annum, giving almost the same result as the other policy in this respect, without any addition to the wages cost of the coal commercially disposable. If concentration increased the individual output by only 8 per cent, the number of workers would fall to 550,000.

POLICY NO. 3.—Under a policy of rationalization combined with a reduction of hours to 6, the results would be different from either of these two. If the number of workers required under rationalization to produce the 215 million tons of 1935 with the same number of hours is reduced from 720,000 to 600,000, then obviously the number of workers must be increased if the hours are reduced from 7½ to 6 per shift. Whilst it is not possible to assert with mathematical precision that it would be exactly so, it is sufficiently accurate for my purpose to assume that if the time available for the winning and drawing of coal is reduced by 20 per cent the number of workpeople needed to produce the 215 million tons of coal will increase roughly in the same proportion. It would not be always so, but on broad lines the assumption is justified in an endeavour to estimate the probable effect of this combined policy. There would, then, be an addition of 20 per cent or 120,000 to the 600,000 required under rationalization with the 7½ hours shift (Policy No. 2), making the total 720,000 on a full-time 6 hours basis, exactly the same number actually employed in 1935 to produce 215 million tons without rationalization and with a 7½ hours shift. (Yet in the House of Commons on July 29, 1936, Mr. Shinwell, an ex-Minister of Mines in a Socialist Government, said that a 6 hours day would give employment to an additional 125,000 to 150,000 men, which would mean a total of 875,000 to 900,000.) The output per wage earner employed would remain at nearly 300 tons per annum, but would not reach the 360 tons of Policy No. 2. These 720,000 workers would, however, be on a full-time basis of $5\frac{3}{4}$ shifts of 6 hours each per week. Output per man shift would fall from 24 cwt. to 20 cwt. If concentration on the best pits increased the output by, say, 10 per cent, there would be a corresponding reduction in the numbers employed from 720,000 to, say, 650,000 fully employed on a 6 hours shift basis. The advocates of the 6 hours day hold that there must be no reduction of wages when hours are reduced, so that the result of this policy of concentrating on the best pits, if accompanied by a 6 hours day, would be that all the day workers would receive payment for $5\frac{3}{4}$ shifts instead of 4·92, the piece workers would demand a corresponding rise in their rates, and there would be an increase in the wages cost for the same output of just a little less than the 2s. per ton under Policy No. 1, with a similar increase in average earnings.

Policy No. 4.—There is another policy possible. That is to let the mines go on working as they are, keeping the uneconomic units alive in order to prevent any great increase in the number of the unemployed, leaving the actual hours of labour per shift as they are, but with every district except Scotland working short time, and as no great economies can be effected in "other costs" under this system, to find the money required to pay increased wages by raising the price to the consumer, the amount of the increase being dependent on the extent to which the consumer can be squeezed.

Of these policies, the one which has most to recommend it in the purely economic sense is No. 2, that of rationalization or direct concentration on the best pits, closing down the uneconomic mines, and retaining the $7\frac{1}{2}$ hours shift. This would enable higher wages to be paid at once on the prices now being obtained, permit substantial economies to be effected in "other costs", and allow the financial advantages derived from this and the increase in prices which consumers in the home market have shown themselves willing to pay to be shared between capital and labour in the agreed proportions, thereby further increasing wages and giving a better return to the investor. Its great disadvantage is that it throws another 120,000 to 130,000 workers on the industrial scrap-heap. This could only be avoided by reducing the hours and increasing the man power required, thereby minimizing the adverse effect of rationalization on the volume of labour required. In any scheme of rationalization fewer workers will be needed, a feature which will progressively grow more pronounced as efficiency increases and the older pits close down. It is inevitable, though regrettable, and it is a problem which should be boldly faced, for concentration on the best mines is the only means whereby the industry can be placed on a sound, secure, and lasting foundation.

Policies No. 1 and No. 4 may be dismissed at once, for they are economically thoroughly unsound, and in the evolution of the industry we have arrived at the stage when there is almost universal agreement on the need for some form of rationalization. Both of them involve a very substantial addition to the wages bill, roughly £18,500,000 to £20,000,000, the former being the estimated cost of the 2s. per shift flat-rate increase demanded by the men in 1935. Both would involve a substantial increase in the selling prices, somewhere about 2s. per ton on the total "commercially disposable". It is utterly impossible, however, to obtain such an increase on the total output. Of the total output of 222 million tons in 1935, 15½ millions was used by the collieries themselves or supplied to the miners for domestic purposes. The tonnage "commercially disposable" was therefore 206½ million tons. Of this, 55½ million tons went for exports and bunker coal for vessels engaged in the foreign trade; 1¼ million tons were used as bunkers by vessels engaged in the coasting trade; 18 millions were used by the iron and steel industry in their works; 12 millions were supplied to the railway companies for locomotive fuel.

An increase of 2s. per ton on export or bunker coal is to-day unobtainable, except on a very limited scale, and any attempt to secure it all round would result immediately in a loss of orders. In the home market there is a limit to what could be obtained from the iron and steel industry without seriously increasing its production costs. If an effort were made to advance prices by 2s. per ton to the railway companies it would merely encourage them to turn still more to electricity, to the Diesel or semi-Diesel drive, or to the oil-fired locomotive.

The full increase being unobtainable on this total of nearly 90 million tons, and any increase in price tending to diminish consumption, the 2s. per ton could only be secured on the sale of about 100 million tons. This, however, would only yield £10,000,000, and as £20,000,000 would be required the increase would have to be not 2s. but 4s. per ton on this quantity. The buyers affected would be the domestic consumer, the public utility undertakings, and the general manufacturing industries. There would be a storm of protest, the colliery owners would be accused of exploiting the consumer, and when it was realized that the nation was getting nothing in return, but merely perpetuating the existing system and stabilizing the coal-mining industry on an uneconomic basis at the public expense, there would be still another call for Government intervention, and in this case a thoroughly justifiable one.

Policy No. 3, that of rationalization and reduced hours, is rendered attractive by reason of the fact that it would permit of concentration on the larger and better-equipped collieries with a less disturbing effect on the total volume of labour than any other. As already shown, it would involve an addition to the wages bill of £20,000,000 on the basis of a 10s. per week increase in wages to all the workers. This sum, for the first year or two at all events, would have to be paid by the consumers of coal in the home market, for the money is not in the industry to do it now, and even part of it would not be there until the advantages of rationalization and the selling agencies made themselves felt. The rise in wages could, of course, be made progressive, and, instead of the stupid method of a flat-rate increase, be adjusted so that the first additions and the largest additions would be given to those most in need of them, the low-paid datal workers and those on the subsistence wage level. Thus applied, the cost would not be so great, the scandal of shamefully low wages would be eliminated, and the industry given time to adapt itself to the new conditions.

There is still another policy (there may be more), that is the policy of subsidizing the industry, either directly or indirectly, or both. Other nations not nearly so dependent as Great Britain on coal, to us "the life-blood of the nation", have deliberately adopted this method of retaining their own trade and meeting competition in the foreign market. It is an artificial and uneconomic means of bolstering up an industry at the expense of the general taxpayer, repugnant to every sound economist, and, with economic nationalism, is one of the chief obstacles to freeing the channels of international commerce, as well as one of the principal causes of the decline in world trade in recent years. The principle is a wrong one, but, apart altogether from that, no one who has any knowledge of the coal industry and remembers the subsidies of 1921 and 1925 has any desire to see repeated the experiences of those years.

Other nations, however, have no regard for the rigid tenets of the economic textbook when it is a question of their own immediate interests, and as self-preservation is the first law of nature we may, in the future, be driven to fight them with their own weapons, just as we were compelled to do when we had to abandon Free Trade in 1931, and as we have since had to do by subsidizing the tramp shipping industry to save it from being ruined by this illegitimate form of competition. And as we shall be compelled to do for our passenger vessels, if indeed it is not too late, in such a case, for example, as in the Pacific.

I am one of those who had to throw overboard the beliefs of a political lifetime when we were forced to adopt tariffs. I agreed with the greatest reluctance, and only because no other course was open to us. I dislike subsidies, and I trust we shall never find it necessary to have to resort to them. I should consent to a subsidy for the coal trade only as a last resource, and with both regret and reluctance. If we are ever driven to it, I should regard it as imperative that it should be applied on a scientific, well-considered, and carefully thought-out plan, and not in the slipshod, haphazard, and wasteful fashion in which the nation's money was dissipated in 1921, and even more so in 1925.

Consideration of these or any other policies for the

reorganization of the mining industry reveal the paramount importance of the economic aspect of the problem, for without an improvement in the economic position of the industry there can be none in the social condition of the workers employed in it. It is unfortunate that it should be necessary to voice such a platitude, but it must be pointed out that, in their zeal for reform and their ignorance of the industry, this simple but vital fact is overlooked or ignored by many of the sentimentalists, whose intentions may be of the best but whose criticism is rarely of a helpful character.

The folly of interference by outsiders, ignorant even of the elementary facts of the industry, is being illustrated further as I write (June 1936) by the intervention, once again, of the Church in the controversies raging around it. One would have thought that the bishops would have been warned by their experience of 1926, when their proposals were rejected by all three parties to the dispute and they were rebuked by the Prime Minister for intervening in a bitter controversy on a subject outside their legitimate sphere. Or, if not by that collective experience, by the individual experience of the Bishop of Durham, who was almost thrown into the River Wear because he had the temerity to tell the miners some unpalatable truths about their own industry.

This time it is the Bishop of London who is taking the lead.

At a meeting of the Church Assembly he spoke of coal of the value of 13s. 6d. at the pithead selling at 50s. in London. The average price at the pithead for this class of coal is just about twice 13s. 6d.

The Church Assembly report speaks of "a deplorable

drop in wages" in the last ten years. There has been no such drop. The "average earnings" figure is the same as that of 1929 and the highest of any year since 1927. In the meantime the cost of living has fallen substantially, so that "real wages" are higher than at any time since 1926.

The report makes the inexcusable error of using the year 1920 as a basis for comparison in the export trade (see page 26).

So unrelated to real values was the situation in 1920 that the 25 million tons exported in 1920 realized £100,000,000, while the same quantity exported in 1921 realized only £43,000,000.

This report gives its support to "amalgamations", "improving efficiency", and "economy of production", but fails to recognize that these things all mean fewer workers in the industry.

At the meeting referred to there seemed to be some misgiving as to the wisdom of the Assembly intervening in a mundane controversy of such a highly complex character, and it is little wonder that the Archbishop of Canterbury was careful to say that he assented to and supported the motion to commend the report "as an individual".

This report contains no evidence of the competence of the signatories to pass judgement or make recommendations on the conduct of this difficult and complex industry, and of the two Members of Parliament on the Commission, one objected to its findings and requested that his name should not be associated with it.

Resolutions and reports based on such imperfect knowledge as is revealed here can only do harm instead of good, however well intentioned those behind them may be.

CHAPTER XXVIII

STATE CONTROL

THE objective of the Miners' Federation and the Socialist Party which they support in the House of Commons is nationalization of the mines, in the full sense that the mines of the country shall be owned, managed, and worked by the State, and private enterprise, private control, and private profit completely eliminated.

They believe that only by State ownership, with the Government running the industry as a public service, can they secure for the miners the conditions of labour and the wages to which they consider them entitled for the work they have to do.

It is not at all a difficult matter for the State to give to any industry both high wages and favourable conditions of service at the expense of the taxpayer. The principle, however, is one which if applied to one industry must assuredly spread to others, and that way lies inevitable disaster. Where a demand for State management and control comes from the workers in an industry but little consideration is given to the economic factors governing the success or the failure of the industry. When any industry is nationalized and the workers powerfully organized the level of wages must never be reduced, no matter what may be the economic position of the industry or what changes may take place in its structure or relative position in the national economy. There is always the taxpayer to foot the bill. This is particularly so in cases where nationalization takes the form it took in the Nationalization of Mines Bill, introduced by a Socialist member in the Parliament of 1924 and supported by the Socialist Government of the day, and which provided that profits, if any, should go back into the industry to raise wages, and losses, if any, should be made good by money provided by Parliament, i.e. by the taxpayer.

Despite the tenacity with which the Mineworkers' Federation adheres to the policy of nationalization, all the evidence indicates that such a policy is one which, if adopted, would in the end make things worse for all concerned. Where the national interest is placed last instead of first, no matter what the industry, there is almost certain failure in the end.

Experiments in nationalization have been tried all over the world. The idea is not new. The experiments have been numerous, yet it would be difficult for any advocate of nationalization to point to any successful attempt to nationalize a competitive industry in any part of the world at any period in the world's history. Where a monopoly exists, success is easy, but Britain has no monopoly of coal and still less any monopoly of other forms of power production. All the illustrations of the failure of national control of industry have completely failed to convince its adherents of its weaknesses. The colossal losses incurred in shipping by the United States of America and Australia are lightly dismissed as being due to "abnormal circumstances", the heavy losses on nationalized railways are just ignored, the ghastly failures of the Queensland experiments in State control of the sheep stations, fisheries, etc., convey no lesson to them. Unlike the Bourbons, they learn nothing and forget everything.

The average citizen, however, may be forgiven if he thinks that the leaders of the miners, even if refusing to have their belief in their pet theory shaken by examples from other parts of the world, would have been convinced by the experience of their own industry under State control.

Most people outside the industry are apt to forget that the mines of this country were under complete State control for over four years—from 1917 to 1921. For all practical purposes the mines were nationalized, and the results of that period of State control should be sufficient to convince any unbiased student of the utter hopelessness of the industry ever attaining either efficiency or prosperity under the system. It would be unfair to attribute the whole of the decline in efficient working to this one cause. The period was one which was, in part, a period of war, and the remainder a period of transition from war to peace. The lapse, however, was so great that there can be no doubt whatever that it was due in a very large measure to that inefficiency, extravagance, and waste which has characterized State management of industry in every part of the world where it has been tried.

The contrast between the last year of management under private enterprise and the last year of State management speaks for itself.

The amount of coal produced in British mines in 1913 was 287 million tons. In 1920 that had fallen to 229 million tons. At the same time the number of persons employed in producing the coal had increased from 1,104,000 to 1,226,000.

The quantity of coal produced per annum per person employed had fallen from 260 tons in 1913 to 187 tons in 1920.

The quantity produced per man shift worked had decreased from 20·32 cwt. in 1913 to 14·54 cwt. in 1920.

The wages costs per ton commercially disposable had increased from 6s. 10½d. per ton in 1913 to 25s. 9½d. per ton in 1920. "Other costs" had risen from 2s. 7d. per ton in 1913 to 8s. 5¼d. per ton in 1920.

Total cost per ton commercially disposable was 9s. 5½d. in 1913, 34s. 2¾d. in 1920, and 39s. 1d. in March 1921.

Hours had been reduced in 1919 from 8 to 7 per day, and wages per man shift worked had increased from 6s. 5¾d. in 1913 to 16s. 10d. in 1920 and 19s. 2d. in March 1921.

Towards the end of the period, as related elsewhere, the industry was in a state of complete chaos, the burden the taxpayer was being called upon to shoulder became insupportable, and the Government of the day found itself compelled to put an end to a state of things which, had it continued, would not only have ruined the industry itself, but would have involved the nation in enormous losses and imposed on other industries an altogether unjust burden of taxation for the benefit of one section of the community alone.

The ultimate result of these years of State activity in the mining industry could not be better expressed than it was by the then Chancellor of the Exchequer, who said, in dealing with the Government proposal to decontrol the industry in 1921:

"I find that we lost £5,259,209 in the month's (March 1921) working. That was a dead loss. In arriving at that result nothing is allowed for any profits to owners, nothing for depreciation, nothing for the interest on the loan of money. Estimated per ton, the loss amounts to 6s. 10d. The wage cost per ton was 27s. 9d., while the amount of money received per ton for the coal disposed of was 32s. 1d. The whole cost per ton amounted to 39s. 1d. I think it is very obvious upon these figures why we are in such difficulties to-day. No system, nationalized or otherwise, could carry on upon that basis. No system of a pool or otherwise could meet these costs with the proceeds of the industry, and I think it is certain from such investigations as I have made that a considerable number of collieries were being operated at losses which could not be faced upon any proper economic system, whether the industry was being conducted by a Wages Board, by a Government department, or by private enterprise" (Board of Trade Conference, April 26, 1921).

This authoritative statement makes it perfectly clear that all the ordinary economic considerations which govern the carrying on of any great industry were being completely ignored, and it is equally clear that this was mainly due to the effect of State control. No form of private enterprise could have borne these colossal losses without bringing about a financial crash, with enormous loss to those who had invested their capital in the industry, the closing down of hundreds of pits, and privation, suffering, and hardship to thousands of workpeople engaged in it and their wives and families.

It was only made possible for it to continue so long on such an unsound basis by the fact that the general taxpayer was being relied on to make good the deficiencies, and even after making the fullest allowance for the difficulties inherent in the transition from wartime conditions to those of peace there cannot be the slightest doubt that the disastrous results were, in the main, directly attributable to State control.

However necessary it may have been in time of war, the experience indicates beyond question that such a system is quite unsuited for the normal conditions of peaceful trading, either at home or abroad. It was terminated hastily, it is true, but hastily lest worse should befall. In addition to the heavy financial burden it imposed on the country it brought in its train very serious labour troubles, comment on which will be found elsewhere.

These years of experience of the State control of a great industry contain a valuable lesson for us all. Having escaped from it with consequences less serious than at one time seemed probable, the country should firmly resolve that it was an experiment which in the interests of the nation as a whole, and not less in the interests of the miners, ought never to be repeated in any circumstances whatsoever.

CHAPTER XXIX

THE NATIONALIZATION OF MINES BILL

THIS measure, drafted in 1923, was introduced into the House of Commons on January 18, 1924, as a private member's Bill, and a debate took place on the second reading on Friday, May 16th.

Although a private member's Bill, its promoters had had the advantage, in drafting it, of the assistance of the law officers of the Crown; it was introduced in the lifetime of a Socialist Government, and was supported by members of the Government. It may, therefore, be regarded, without injustice, as being exactly in the form a Nationalization of Mines Bill would take if a Socialist Government were in office with a majority and in a position to enforce its passage through the House of Commons.

The Bill provided for the setting up of a National Mining Council consisting of ten members appointed by the Government and ten members appointed by the Miners' Federation, with the Minister of Mines as President and responsible to Parliament with his Parliamentary Secretary for the acts of the Mining Council. The Council was charged with the sole and complete responsibility for winning, distributing, selling, and searching for coal and other minerals. Provision was made for the appointment of a Permanent Secretary and other officials of the Mining Council.

District Councils of ten members were to be established in each mining area and various powers delegated to them by the Central Council. Each district was to have its pit committees composed of ten members and similarly appointed. All members of these various councils were to be paid officials and remunerated by moneys "provided by Parliament".

Under the Bill, the Mining Council would have power to purchase, compulsorily, all collieries, mines, and minerals (including ironstone, shale, lignite, limestone, and others), and for this purpose a Mines Purchase Commission was to be appointed of ten members, three of whom would be the nominees of the Miners' Federation, three of the Mining Association, and the remainder appointed by the Government.

Provision was made for the valuation of the coal mines, and the Bill limited the purchase price to a capital sum equal to one year's output at 12s. per ton in the case of the smaller mines and 10s. per ton in the case of the larger.

For payment of the purchase price, the Treasury was to be authorized to create a new capital stock (Guaranteed States Mine Stock) bearing interest equal to the nearest equivalent Government stock. There was to be a right of appeal to the High Court on the question of title, but for no other purpose.

Mining royalties were to be taken over by the Mining Council without compensation, no payment of any kind being proposed.

A Fuel Consumers' Council was to be established with its expenses paid by the Mining Council. Its functions, however, were to be purely advisory and not executive.

Finally, the Bill provided that all arrangements under the Act were to be completed by the first day of the third year after the coming into operation of the Act.

In the debate the Bill was riddled with criticism and shown to be a thoroughly impracticable and unworkable measure. The mover made only a very inadequate attempt to explain the measure to the House, and the seconder made scarcely any reference to it beyond attacking the royalty owners, and the Secretary for Mines (Mr. Shinwell), whilst accepting the principle of the measure, made no effort to examine it, to explain its details, or to show the House what its manifold and far-reaching proposals would really mean to the industry and the State.

The closing speech for the promoters of the Bill was made by Mr. R. Smillie. Like his fellow Socialists, he had little to say about the measure itself, and in one respect showed the most extraordinary inconsistency.

He was replying to Mr. Lloyd George and in the course of a speech which dealt only in the vaguest terms with the proposals before the House, he referred to the provisions in the Bill for giving the miners a share in the management of the industry and said: "I plead that the miners are entitled to have a say in the management of the concern in which they invest their lives."

He had apparently quite forgotten the reply which he made to Mr. Lloyd George on October 10, 1919, when he was offered the very thing which he was now asking for, and which will be found on page 19.

The debate brought out all the weaknesses of the Bill. They were so numerous that it is not possible here to deal with them all at any length, but they may be briefly summarized.

In the first place it was shown that it was not a "Nationalization of Mines" Bill at all. The Federation was to have half the representation on the councils, but as the Federation represented only two-thirds of the workers in the industry, provision was to be made for the representation of the other third. The workers in the industry would thus be in a permanent majority on the National Council and other councils and committees. There was no room for any independence of outlook, for power was given to the Federation and the Government to remove any member at will, although appointments were made for five years.

The National Council was vested with enormous powers. In addition to the powers of purchase, which did not err on the side of generosity, it had the power to fix wages and prices, to control distribution, marketing, export, and selling, with special powers for dealing with the railway companies and shipping companies in respect to the transport of coal, and control over by-product industries, extending even to iron and steel.

Although the Federation, being in a majority on the council, would have the power to fix wages, the miners were not bound to accept their decision, for they retained the right to strike. Not only so, but there was nothing to prevent the members of the councils from participating in a strike, or indeed from fostering or promoting one against the decisions of the councils of which they were members. The community was bound to accept the prices, but the miners were not bound to accept the wages offered.

The proposal to take over the mining royalties without payment was merely confiscation for which there was no more justification than for the State confiscating any other form of property, possession of which has been recognized by the State as legal, and which by law has been bought and sold, transferred or mortgaged for hundreds of years.

Another provision of the Bill was that in the event of the industry being run at a loss by the Mining Council, any such losses were to be made good by the taxpayer. On the other hand, any profits were not to benefit the taxpayer, but to go back into the industry. The Federation was to have complete and absolute authority over the entire industry, and the taxpayer was to foot the bill and get nothing in return, for there was no real protection for the consumer. He would have no voice in the control of the industry, be compelled to meet the cost of any experiments of the Mining Council, any inefficiency, extravagance, or waste, and pay any price asked for the coal he required, as the Fuel Council to be established was purely advisory without any power or any authority, and therefore powerless to protect him.

The debate revealed the enormous difficulties in the way of producing a measure for the complete nationalization of a great competitive industry without gravely impairing its efficiency and threatening it with ruin, as well as doing serious injury to other industries, and, in the case of the British coal industry, so undermining the fabric of our industrial life as to endanger the whole economic system and imperil the standard of life of the whole community.

This attempt was not an effort to nationalize the mines. It was an effort to syndicalize them in the interests of the Miners' Federation, to make effective the slogan so often heard on Socialist platforms in the coalfields—"The Mines for the Miners", *not* "The Mines for the Nation".

The avalanche of destructive criticism to which it

was subjected completely destroyed it. It never reached a third reading; in fact, it was never heard of again. It was buried, and all who have the welfare of the industry and the miner really at heart may fervently pray that it may never be disinterred.

Should the time come when public opinion decides that this great industry should be nationalized, it is to be hoped that we shall see a more practical, sounder, and more carefully considered scheme, one which will not only have regard for the miner, but one which, while seeing that he receives adequate remuneration and fair conditions of labour in his arduous toil, will also give full weight to all the other interests involved, and above all, place first the welfare of the nation as a whole, and not permit our greatest asset to be used for the benefit of any section of the community at the expense of the rest.

CHAPTER XXX

THE FUTURE

As indicated in the Introduction, this little volume has been written with the object of giving the average man an insight into the present position of the mining industry by recounting the principal events in its recent history, and giving the causes of the frequent disputes, along with the essential figures as to production, wages, etc.

In order, however, to show that the writer is not concerned only with the past it may be permissible to conclude with a brief review of the future prospects and possibilities of the industry; not as an attempt to show how the problems of the industry can be solved, or should be solved, for which this is not the place. Rather in the hope that it will stimulate thought on the part of the reader unacquainted with the industry.

In the first place the pessimist should be heavily discounted, if not disregarded altogether. Coal is the basis on which rests the whole structure of our industrial life. Coal made Britain the "workshop of the world". Without coal Britain would sink to the level of a third-rate Power. The pessimist has been foretelling the dethronement of King Coal for years, but unless natural oil should be discovered here in quantities comparable with those produced in other oil fields, his supremacy will remain unchallenged.

Coal is by far the most important of all our industries except agriculture. Till recently, it has developed along individualistic and competitive lines, adjusting itself to the normal operation of ordinary economic forces, a steadily expanding industry until the outbreak of war in 1914. In one generation production had doubled, and reached its peak in 1913 at 287 million tons.

The end of the war brought great changes, changes to which the industry had great difficulty in adapting itself, in both the home and the export market, as has been already related. In 1930 the first effort was made at general regulation and control, and now a further step has been taken in this direction by the establishment of selling agencies. These will doubtless lead to closer co-operation between the separate concerns in each district, and to some form of co-ordination between the districts themselves. They may lead also to further voluntary amalgamations where these are desirable in the interests of efficiency and economy, a process which may also be accelerated by the Unification of Mining Royalties Bill which the Government has promised to pass through the legislature in this session of Parliament (1936).

If the industry is to become completely modernized and 100 per cent efficient it seems inevitable that production must be centred on the more efficient and more up-to-date collieries with thick seams, modern equipment, and lower costs of production. The keeping alive of uneconomic units by spreading production over all the pits under the 1930 Act can only reduce the efficiency of the industry as a whole, and even the President of the Mineworkers' Federation now admits that it is "indefensible". It is doubtful, however, whether even he has realized the extent to which employment would be affected as shown on page 265.

These matters may be supposed to come within the

purview of the new Joint Standing Consultative Committee along with others of "common interest and of general application to the industry" as the process of reorganization goes on. The latter may include such things as the pooling of railway waggons, the position of the exporting districts in relation to the inland districts, the position of the composite concern, the methods of ascertainments, hours of labour, age of entry into the industry, and other relevant matters coming within the definition of the powers of the Committee.

There are signs that the world is awaking to the folly of economic nationalism and when this occurs, there should be a moderate increase in the export trade. In the home market our own people are becoming more "coal minded", a process in promoting which the Coal Utilization Council is doing admirable work. The scope for increased employment in the industry itself, however, is limited, as has been shown. The hope for the future lies in the scientific utilization of coal and in this direction the next few years should see a great advance with a large volume of employment in the new industries.

Oil from coal plants would help to solve the problem of the special areas, Jarrow, for example, being an ideal site, with large measures of suitable coal on the doorstep, and road, rail, and water transport facilities already available. If the Government is to help, there must be a greater willingness to take risks, a less rigidly orthodox financial outlook, and greater freedom for the officials entrusted with administration. There is already a wealth of knowledge and experience and the time is ripe for a big advance.

CHAPTER XXXI

The By-Product Industries (Oil From Coal)—The Various Processes—Other Uses for Coal

THE BY-PRODUCT INDUSTRIES (OIL FROM COAL)

THIS question of the by-product industries, and particularly "oil from coal", is of vital importance, not only to the mining industry, but to the nation as a whole. The transition from the field of laboratory experiment to that of commercial exploitation has been one requiring infinite patience, bringing many disappointments and involving both loss of capital and heavy expenditure with no certainty of return. As in other fields, however, scientific research work has been crowned with success and brought its reward in the establishment, on a commercial scale, of at least two processes—low-temperature carbonization and hydrogenation. The former gives smokeless fuel, fuel oil, creosote, petrol, and gas, while the latter is a process devoted entirely to the production of oil. The quantity of petrol obtained by the low-temperature carbonization system is comparatively small, but the quality excellent. The expansion of the process is limited by the necessity for finding a market for the other by-products, particularly the coke. This difficulty should be overcome in time, for smokeless fuels have many advantages over raw coal for domestic use, and if produced in greater quantities and on sale at a lower figure, would doubtless command a ready market for increased sales.

Having regard, however, to the fact that in hydrogenation there are few or no residuals, it is probably to this process that the nation must look for any really big expansion in the extraction of oil from coal. The Billingham plant is in production and is yielding already some 14 or 15 million gallons of petrol. Once it is firmly established there is no reason worth considering why it should not be enormously expanded. The economic advantages which would follow from home production on a vast scale, plus the strategic advantage which would accrue in time of war, or danger of war, would far outweigh the disadvantages arising from the reduced importation of oil from overseas, such as less employment for British tankers, reduced employment at the docks, or a possible loss on investments in oil-producing concerns in other countries. This is a development which the Government could encourage. The benefit derived from the preference of 4d. per gallon under the Hydrocarbon Oil Production Bill may not be sufficient to bring about results on the larger scale as quickly as are desired, and it may be necessary to offer some further inducement in the form of cheap capital or additional exemption from taxation in order to accelerate production.

The question of the expansion of "oil from coal" processes is one of vital national importance, and the two methods referred to are full of hope for the future. At the same time the measure of success achieved ought not to blind us to the difficulties in the way of expanding them on the enormous scale required in order to produce a reasonable proportion of our own oil and petrol.

The technical difficulties in the way of large-scale production on an economic basis hold no terrors for the journalist called in to write a brief article on its possibilities, or the newspaper correspondent who regards coal as being simply coal, and knowing we are actually producing oil from coal demand that those responsible should get on with it.

The Mines Department, the Fuel Research Board, the colliery owners, the oil-producing companies, and the inventors of the various processes know too well, however, that it is not quite so simple as that. There are many other processes, some of them still in the laboratory stage, some which have reached the stage of the erection of small-scale plants, and two at least, one in the North and one in the Midlands, which have reached the stage of commercial production. The large extent to which experimental work is being carried on shows clearly that we are as yet only in the early stages of development.

All the indications are that the vast and costly experiment embarked upon by Imperial Chemical Industries Ltd., at Billingham, will prove successful technically, and with the preference granted by the Government of not less than 4d. per gallon for nine years, it bids fair to succeed in the economic sense also. The process, though costly, enjoys one great advantage over the other processes in not having to find a market for residuals, for it is an entirely oil-producing one.

The other processes give oil only as a secondary product, their main output being smokeless fuel with coal-tar as a residual. The latter being highly suitable for hydrogenation, the progress made in the two processes has resulted in it being found that they are not opposed to each other (except in so far as the marketing of a relatively small proportion of low-temperature-produced petrol is concerned) as was the case originally, but really complementary to each other. Billingham is now using tar and creosote from these plants as well as from coke-ovens and gas-works.

The success of all or any of these methods of oil production depends on the capital cost of the plant, the suitability of the coal selected for the particular process, the extent of the market for its products, the cost of production, and most important of all the perfection of the processes by the skilled technicians who are every day making fresh advances in this direction.

The layman, even with some knowledge of the coal industry, is not competent to speak with authority on these matters. One broad consideration, however, does emerge. This is that having regard to the progress made encouragement should be given to the undertakings operating the two systems to come to a working agreement whereby a low-temperature carbonization plant could be put down in every district where coal is of the right quality, and alongside it a hydrogenation plant for utilizing the coal-tar and creosote from the former in addition to the direct hydrogenation of coal. Such large-scale operations if successful would be of enormous national advantage and help considerably to solve the problem of the long-neglected "special areas". There may be risks attached to this course, but they are risks worth incurring, and the Government ought not to be deterred from embarking on it either by the risk of failure or by the prospect of finding natural oil as a result of the extensive borings now taking place.

On every ground of public policy something of this kind should be undertaken, for the last consideration is much too uncertain to be allowed to count as a factor in the situation at all.

The colliery owners themselves should take the lead and in conjunction with the Government attack the problem afresh with a view to eliminating the useless processes and concentrating on those which give promise of bringing a successful result. A levy of ½d. per ton on output would yield £450,000 per annum, a sum which, wisely used in research work on commercial lines with the aid of the Department of Scientific and Industrial Research, should speedily find the solution if modern science can find one at all.

There would then be no need to talk of spending millions on constructing storage depots for imported oil, and the colliery owners in their own industry would reap the reward of their own enterprise.

THE VARIOUS PROCESSES

The layman is not unnaturally puzzled by the descriptions he reads of the methods adopted or proposed to be adopted for extracting "oil" from coal. The processes are all so highly technical that it is only with great diffidence that anyone who is neither a chemist nor a fuel expert dare venture on the attempt to explain them. This chapter, however, would not be complete without some explanation of the differences between them. No attempt is made to enter into the details of the processes, which for complete understanding require both engineering and chemical knowledge of a highly scientific character. All that is possible here is to endeavour to give in non-technical language a brief description of the more important, and refer the reader who desires fuller information to the numerous scientific publications which are continually dealing with the problem in its various aspects, to the literature of the Fuel Research Board, and to the pamphlets of the companies operating the processes.

In dealing with coal derivatives the term "oil" is very widely and very loosely used. It is applied to almost everything of a liquid or semi-liquid nature which is a product or a by-product of the distillation, carbonization, or hydrogenation of coal, or of a mixture containing a proportion of coal. The lightest of the spirits, the heaviest of the tars, and everything in between the two, are all grouped together under the one generic term of "oil". None of the processes now in commercial production yield an "oil" direct from coal in any appreciable quantity. The coal is either mixed with some other material before processing, or during the process enters into combination with some other body to form the final product. This is not to say that science will not evolve a method of producing "oil" from coal by direct distillation on a commercial scale. All the evidence is in the other direction. Great progress has been made in recent years, and research work is going on continuously in every coal-producing country. But up to the present time there is no process in actual operation on a commercial scale which is producing a "true oil" from coal alone, in large quantities, and as the principal derivative of the coal.

For 95 per cent of the various commodities coming under the heading of oil we are dependent on supplies from overseas. When classified, the "oils" come under a large number of headings—crude mineral oil, fuel oil, Diesel oil, kerosene, naphtha, petrol, benzol, lubricating oils—all of which play a very important part in industry and transport. The major portion of these oils come into this country ready for use, but substantial quantities of crude petroleum are imported for refining, and in 1934 about one-sixth of the total consumption was refined here. This is not, of course, home production of oil.

The home sources of supply of oils are the gas-works and coke-ovens by the high-temperature carbonization of coal and the recovery of the volatiles in the form of benzol; the smokeless-fuel plants in which tar oils and a small percentage of spirit are obtained as by-products; the distillation of tar oils, and the hydrogenation of coal, crude petroleum, tar oils, or creosote, either separately or mixed in varying proportions before processing. As yet, natural oil is not available in commercial quantities.

In the high-temperature processes the oils are essentially by-products. The gas undertakings are mainly concerned with the production of gas for domestic and industrial use, whilst the coke-oven proprietors concentrate principally on the production of metallurgical coke for use in iron and steelworks. In both cases the production of oil is subsidiary to the principal operation, and the output limited, in the first case by the demand for domestic coke, and in the second by the demand for high-temperature coke by the metallurgical industries.

As indicated by the term "high-temperature carbonization" the method employed is similar in the two cases. The coal is carbonized at a temperature of 1,000° C. or over, a large volume of gas is obtained, and as a high percentage of the volatile content of the coal is driven off a strong coke is left behind. The gas is passed through a scrubbing plant and the benzol recovered in the process. The spirit is excellent in quality, but as it is essentially a by-product the output can never be large enough to become a real factor in the oil supply of the nation.

In the low-temperature process the coal is carbonized at a much lower temperature, usually about 600° C. A lesser quantity of the volatiles being driven off in the process the coke or semi-coke is more readily ignited, though practically smokeless and therefore more suitable for domestic use.

The chief purpose in the process is the production of a high-grade smokeless fuel, the use of which in the household grate in place of raw coal would very materially assist in the abatement of the smoke nuisance. In obtaining the solid fuel, large quantities of coal-tar are deposited, and from this, by various methods, the heavier oils may be produced. In addition this crude coal oil is eminently suitable for obtaining petrol by the hydrogenation process, and is being extensively used at Billingham for this purpose. From the gas, which is mostly used up in the process for heating purposes, a quantity of petrol (relatively small, but excellent in quality) is obtained by scrubbing, and the spirit so produced is now in daily use, a large proportion of it in aeroplane work. The technical term "scrubbing" means passing the gas through oil in which the uncondensed vapours are dissolved and recovered again by a process of distillation in the form of the spirit.

The hydrogenation process is essentially an oil process in that its main objective is the production of oil by mixing hydrogen with carbon in some form under very great pressure and at a very high temperature in the presence of a catalyst. A catalyst is a body which in the presence of other bodies effects a change in the composition of the latter, while remaining itself unchanged. The only hydrogenation plant in operation in this country is at Billingham. It is designed to produce per annum 45 million gallons of petrol, 30 millions from coal and 15 millions from tar oils or creosote oils, and to consume 600,000 tons of coal per annum overall in the process.

In actual operation the coal is pulverized and mixed with the oil to form a paste. The paste is then subjected to great heat at high pressure in the presence of the catalyst. In the retort changes take place in the chemical composition of the coal, the results of which are to break down the hydrocarbons in the coal and combine them with the hydrogen which is forced into the retort, and thus to form hydrocarbon oils. The oils are fractionated by a distillation process, the lighter oils being further refined to produce the petrol which is the principal product of the whole series of operations. The heavier oils resulting from distillation are themselves hydrogenated to yield petrol, and as the gases given off are also utilized, the process is a self-contained petrol-producing one, using up its own by-products and leaving only as a residual a quantity of ammoniated liquor.

At the Billingham plant production of petrol from creosote oil commenced in February 1935. The first of the coal units was started up in June 1935. At the end of May 1936, 33 million gallons (110,000 tons) of motor spirit had been obtained, the total quantity of coal used at the plant in every phase of the process being 411,500 tons (Secretary for Mines Department, House of Commons, May 26, 1936).

The total home production of light hydrocarbon oils in 1935 from coal, coal-tar, and tar oils was

79 million gallons. Of this 66 millions was refined motor spirit, and the balance naphtha, etc.

The Scottish shale-oil industry produced 10 million gallons of motor spirit.

The total of home-produced motor spirit in 1935 was thus 76 million gallons compared with 54½ millions in 1934. The sources of supply were:

	Million gallons
Coke-ovens	26¼
Hydrogenation	20¾
Tar distillation	10½
Gas-works	8½
Scottish shale	10
Total	76

In addition to the light oils 93 million gallons of creosote and heavy oils were produced at home from coal-tars obtained from the carbonization of coal or from the distillation of shale. The 1934 figure was 90 millions.

It is possible that the next few years may see not only a big expansion in the production of oil from coal, but also a change in the nature of the oil most in demand. Hitherto the main object aimed at has been the production of motor spirit, but the improvements made recently in the development of the Diesel type of engine is rapidly threatening the supremacy of the lighter oil for use in the internal-combustion engine.

Diesel engines are already extensively used on land both in transport and for the generation of power in the mercantile marine and in the world's navies both on the sea and under the sea, and now this type is being used in aeroplane work. It is not inconceivable that this type of engine may supplant the petrol engine and provide a market for the heavier oil. As yet no suitable Diesel oil has been produced from coal by any of the processes in commercial quantities. It is, however, being produced from shale.

Leaving aside the gas undertakings and the metallurgical coke manufacturers there is only a small number of firms engaged in the production of oil from coal on a commercial scale.

In the hydrogenation process the only firm which has commercialized it is the Imperial Chemical Industries Ltd., and their plant at Billingham is the only one in production. The petrol is produced by a series of operations covered by patents for which they have the sole rights. The question whether any other plants similar to that at Billingham will be established depends on the results there, and enough information as to the costs of the process will soon be available for guidance on this point.

There are several firms operating on the low-temperature carbonization system. Chief of these is Low-Temperature Carbonization Ltd., the manufacturers of the well-known smokeless fuel "Coalite". They have two plants in operation and are putting down a third. The demand for their smokeless fuels exceeds the supply, and there is a ready market for their tar oils and motor spirit.

The National Coke and Oil Co. Ltd. employ a low-temperature process also, the mixture used being 50 per cent pulverized coal, 3½ per cent creosote, and the remainder residual coal oil. The Company has three plants in production on a small scale and markets a smokeless fuel called "Naco" as well as a motor spirit named "Napet". In the summer of 1936 this firm launched an ambitious scheme for establishing a chain of twenty plants in different parts of the country. A public appeal for fresh capital met with failure however, mainly, it is believed, because the process had not been tested and approved by the Fuel Research Board.

Another large-scale plant has been laid down by Coal and Allied Industries Ltd., but is not yet in commercial production. At the time of writing the process employed has not had the approval of the Fuel Research Board.

There are many other processes but as yet no others in commercial production. Two which have attracted a good deal of attention, though not yet commercialized, are those of the hydrogenation of cannel coal on the lines of the experiments carried out by the chief engineer of the Edinburgh Corporation Gas Department and the Freeman Process of direct distillation of coal. Both of these, it is understood, have been unofficially tested by the Fuel Research Board, but as the Board is debarred by the rules governing its procedure from giving a written report on any process except those in actual commercial production, no official report on the results is available to the public.

The cannel-coal proposal depends very largely on the use of cannel by the gas industry and the hydrogenation of the residual tar oils. No information is available as to whether any patent rights are involved, and a reply to a question in the House of Commons on July 29, 1936, failed to elicit any information as to the possibilities of the process.

The Freeman Process is different from any now in operation. It depends for its results on rigidly controlled temperatures and rigidly controlled times in the passage of the raw material through a series of eight chambers. Both time and temperature control are automatic, and as both can be predetermined it is claimed that the gravity and nature of the yield can be regulated at will. The process is a "true oil" distillation process, coal alone being used with no other material added either before or during the process.

Except in the hydrogenation process the oil is not the main product and in that process the cost is so high as to be uneconomic. Science will undoubtedly solve the problem of "true oil" from coal, and while it is too early yet to say that the Freeman Process has done so on a commercial scale it is undoubtedly along this line that future progress must be made until we arrive at a final solution which will not only make this country independent of foreign supplies, but by establishing a *real* oil-from-coal era will give largely increased employment to those working in the mines.

The enormous importance of the matter may be gauged by the fact that in 1935 the total quantity of "petroleum products" available for consumption in Great Britain and Northern Ireland was 2,460 million gallons, of which 1,245 million gallons was motor spirit.

Against this vast total, only 76 million gallons of motor spirit are officially recorded as being "home produced". The figure of 93 million gallons of heavy oil given on page 330 is an estimate prepared by the Mines Department from information voluntarily supplied. Of this 93 millions the quantity produced from coal and used as fuel oil is described as "comparatively small".

The nation is thus, for all practical purposes, entirely dependent on imported oil in various forms.

If one-hundredth part of the money wasted on futile strikes and useless subsidies during the post-war period had been devoted to large-scale research—research work on a scale commensurate with the importance of the problem—we should, in all probability, have been well on the way towards independence, and certainly be to-day in an infinitely better position than that in which we find ourselves.

Whilst it is, no doubt, very desirable that we should produce as much oil as we can within our own borders, a word of warning is necessary as to its effect on the volume of employment, particularly in the production of the raw coal. Loose talk, such as "doubling the output of the mines", which one sees regularly in the Press, as the result, can only inspire false hopes, hopes doomed to disappointment.

The quantity of petrol imported into this country to-day is about 1,235 million gallons. If, at one stroke, the whole of it could be produced in Great Britain the mining of the additional coal required would give employment, at the present rate of production in the mines, to 50,000 miners. This is assuming it all to be produced by the hydrogenation process. If, on the other hand, part of the oil were produced by the low-temperature carbonization system, there would be a corresponding reduction in the amount of coal required for hydrogenation, but an increase in the total coal required, depending, in quantity, on the extent to which the smokeless fuel can displace raw coal for domestic use. This would increase slightly the number of men in the pits above the 50,000 already mentioned. The number, however, could not be great, and at first would be small unless, as is sometimes advocated, the use of raw coal should be prohibited in open grates in all our cities and big towns. If we assume that half the household coal used (36 million tons) would be replaced by smokeless fuel the result would be this: To produce this 18 million tons of smokeless fuel about 26 million tons of raw coal would be required, or an addition of about 8 million tons. A million tons gives employment to 3,500 miners so that this means work for just under 30,000. As, however, about 20 per cent of the total petrol would be produced in the process, a corresponding reduction must be made in the employment given to the miners supplying coal for the hydrogenation process. This would reduce the numbers from 50,000 to 40,000. The two together give a total of 68,000, or, allowing for a very wide margin of error, less than 80,000 if we produced the whole of our light hydrocarbon oils and some of the heavier oils from our own coal.

Anyone criticizing these figures on the ground that they are too low should remember that they are based on a week of 4·9 shifts only, not $5\frac{3}{4}$, and on an output of only 24 cwt. per person employed per shift.

Concentration on the best pits with full-time employment for all the workers engaged in the industry, with increased mechanization and reduced consumption due to more scientific utilization of the raw coal, would reduce the numbers by nearly twice this figure, so that if these two developments were to take place side by side there would be, in the end, a rationalized industry resting on a sound foundation, paying good wages to the workers, a fair return on its invested capital, and giving regular and full-time employment, but such employment to only about 700,000 workers.

To this, of course, must be added the very considerable volume of employment provided by the development of the new processes, and into which large numbers of miners who now have no prospect of ever getting back to the pits could be absorbed.

Along this line there is great hope for the industry, but no foundation for the exaggerated estimates of the additional employment which embarking on it would bring for the miners.

A rapid and extensive development in this direction is highly desirable, and this warning is not intended in any way to belittle the possibilities, but merely to put the raw-material basis of the new industry (coal) in its proper perspective. It does seem that we are lagging behind in this vitally important matter, for it is estimated that Germany is to-day producing 35 per cent of her requirements of petrol and oil from coal, and is aiming at complete self-sufficiency, whilst in Britain we are producing less than 5 per cent of what we use. An oil-from-coal plant on the Billingham scale in every district in which the quality of the coal is suitable for one or other of the processes would be a big step towards making up this leeway.

Of the type of organization likely to secure the best results, and to secure them quickly, this is not the occasion to speak at length. There are many schemes propounded. The miners demand that not only should the mines be nationalized, but that the whole of the new industries which use coal for the generating of power, light, and heat, or the production of the many derivatives obtainable from it, should be brought into complete State ownership and operated directly under State control and management.

Others advocate the setting up of a National Coal Board to control all the multifarious activities of the industry.

There are some who would have the new industries organized on a co-operative basis, some who prefer the idea of district organizations linked up with the mining industry itself, and others again who favour the formation of large-scale bodies separate entirely from the coal industry except in the utilization of its product. Many believe that as private enterprise has been so largely responsible for the remarkable results already achieved, the best course is to permit the new developments to expand naturally in the same way.

On whatever lines the development, it is highly improbable that either Parliament or the nation will agree to nationalization for reasons already stated in the chapter on State Control.

The most likely and possibly the wisest method would be to give the fullest and freest play to that right of private enterprise which has brought such fruitful results in other industries, notably the motor-car industry, whilst, in return for some measure of financial assistance, the Government could insist on some degree of national supervision, regulation, and control through the Ministry of Mines, as is now the case in the mining industry itself.

OTHER USES FOR COAL

The extraction of oil from coal is not the only direction in which new uses may be found for coal.

The use of pulverized coal is comparatively new but has shown a steady and progressive increase. In 1935 no less than 5 million tons were pulverized, an increase of 85 per cent since 1929, the principal undertakings which have adopted this method being the electricity generating concerns and the cement industry.

The manufacture and utilization of colloidal fuel (a mixture of pulverized coal and oil) is still in the experimental stage, but research work is continuing and there is no reason to doubt that sooner or later that work will be crowned with success and a satisfactory fuel evolved for both marine and land use.

From the tars recovered from the carbonization of coal many useful derivatives are obtained. Sulphur, creosote, ammonia, toluene, benzine, naphtha, are the raw materials of a whole range of diversified industries. The by-products of coal are used extensively in the dye industry, in the manufacture of explosives, anaesthetics, antiseptics, etc., whilst the use of the resins is continually extending in the plastic industries, and an ever-increasing number of articles in everyday use is now being made from coal derivatives, in the new radio industry particularly.

While none of these can add appreciably to the volume of employment in the actual mining of raw coal, they reveal the wonderful range of products obtainable from this great national asset of coal and provide employment in a host of diversified industries, an extremely valuable feature when employment is being steadily reduced in the main industry by the march of science which has created them.

The use of coal is extending in the agricultural and horticultural industries and in central heating. Research work is going on continuously with the object of finding a means of eliminating waste in the domestic grate and minimizing the smoke nuisance in our great cities.

There is scope for the further development of the steam motor vehicle and the heavy lorry running on coal gas. In all these directions the Coal Utilization Council is rendering great service as well as arresting the tendency in some quarters to turn from coal to oil.

All these movements should be encouraged as well as the "oil from coal" processes, not only in the interests of national prosperity, but of national defence, for oil has now become to this island nation at least as important as food in time of war.

CHAPTER XXXII

CONCLUSION

SENTIMENT has its part to play in the life of a nation as in the life of an individual. The feelings of the sentimentalists do them credit; the strength of their criticism may be a measure of the depth of their sentiment, but its value is too often discounted by lack of knowledge. The problems of the coal-mining industry are economic problems, and the social consequences of the adoption of any policy which will place it on a permanently sound basis are the concern of the nation as a whole and not of the industry alone. It is both foolish and paradoxical to demand increased efficiency, and then, when that efficiency reduces employment, to condemn those who have promoted it.

It is, then, because I put first things first, that I have, throughout, stressed the fact that the economics of the industry are by far the most important and refrained from playing at all on sentiment.

I have no need to defend myself against any charge of lack of sympathy with the low-paid workers. In speech after speech in the House of Commons I said their wages were too low. I have always differed with the Mineworkers' Federation on the policy of flat-rate increases for all workers, for while I have every sympathy with the mineworker who is only receiving 38s. or 40s. per week, I am not prepared to shed tears over the hard lot of the coal cutter who receives 70s. or 80s. or 90s. per week while a skilled engineer receives only 59s. I could not put my own view on this matter better than I put it in the House of Commons on June 1, 1932, in the first speech on the industry which I made in that chamber. I said:

"We who sit on these benches have lived all our lives under the shadow of the chimneys of the collieries. We do not appeal to sentiment. We could paint just as harrowing a picture of the hunger, poverty, hardship, and distress which exist in our constituencies as any hon. member opposite, and if we refrain from playing upon sentiment it is because we know that these hard-hit areas have already the sympathy of the House of Commons.

"All the sympathy and sentiment in the world will not open a single colliery, secure a single order, or put one man into employment" (Official Report, June 1, 1932).

If the nation is to insist on the mining industry putting its house in order in the economic sense, then the industry must have the freedom to do so in order that it may provide full-time employment at good wages to all whom it employs. But in so doing let the people recognize the social consequences of the policy, and insist also that the nation shall accept full responsibility for them without blaming those charged with the difficult task of adapting the industry to the new conditions of the changing world under the handicap of never-ending political agitation and control. State control cannot be extended much further if the industry is to continue to operate under the system of private enterprise.

So far as the employed miner is concerned the labourer is worthy of his hire. The justice of his case for some increase in wages for some of the workers has been generally acknowledged and the increase has already been granted in part. The "average earnings per man shift" are 10d. higher for the first quarter of 1936 than for the last quarter of 1935, or 4s. 2d. per week on a 55 shift per week basis. The selling agencies will lead to a further advance, on which the low-paid workers should have the first claim.

As for those who are unemployed in the mining areas, they have deserved well of the State. They include a large body of the older men, many of whom rendered such service to the nation as can never be adequately measured or too freely acknowledged in the hour of the nation's danger from 1914 to 1918. They include large numbers of young men who have either never worked at all or who have had only brief spells of employment in the pits. It cannot be too often repeated that this is a problem quite distinct from that of the industry itself, for the fact that they will never be re-employed in the mines has been known for years.

There is nothing to our credit in the fact that the rich and powerful nation which showed itself possessed in war time of such wonderful reserves of organizing ability should have so signally failed to deal adequately with this problem.

Bigger, bolder, and far more comprehensive measures are necessary than have as yet been attempted by any Government if we are to cut out this canker which is eating into the heart of the nation, and resulting in the physical deterioration and moral degradation of thousands of our own fellow-countrymen, whose only offence is that they happen to have been born and bred in parts of "this sceptred isle" which were devastated by the economic consequences of the war (and the peace) as much as the shell-torn battlegrounds of France and Flanders were devastated by the military operations of that stupendous struggle. What those measures should be it is not for me to say, or at all events not here. It is sufficient to say here once again that the task of finding a solution is one for the Government of the country and not for the industry, for while neither employers' nor workers' organizations have been always wise, the main cause of the unemployment is undoubtedly the decline in world trade and the change in world conditions over which they have had no control.

There are many other aspects of the coal and allied industries on which one would like to touch, but this volume has already grown to greater proportions than originally intended.

Some repetition has been unavoidable in dealing with such matters as wages and "average cash earnings", hours and output, etc., and for this I must apologize.

My task is ended, and while I realize that there is much I have written which will invite both criticism and controversy, I hope this may be compensated for in some measure by bringing to "the man in the street" some knowledge and understanding of the nature and complexity of the problems connected with the conduct of this great and important industry.

The relations between owners and men are one of the most important factors in the future prospects of the industry, and it is a good augury for the future that these have been greatly improved since the appointment of the present President and Secretary of the Mineworkers' Federation to their respective positions. There is now in evidence on both sides a more general recognition of community of interest, a greater readiness to negotiate amicably on matters in dispute, and a marked reluctance to use either the strike or the lock-out, except as a last resource.

The thorny question of wages and wages regulation is one which is always liable to lead to trouble and to cause stoppages which inflict serious injury on the industry. In the settlement of the 1935–1936 dispute recently concluded, however, both parties during the course of the negotiations showed a real willingness to see the other's point of view, something which has not always been evident in these discussions, and if this spirit continues to be evident, some measure of co-ordination established between the districts, and the selling agencies allowed time to fructify and bring the results expected, there should be no danger of any dispute of sufficient importance to justify any strike or lock-out, with the set-back to progress which must inevitably follow. Reorganized on the lines now being undertaken, and rationalized on the lines suggested, the mining industry will doubtless be able to pay higher wages and enable the miner to attain a higher standard of life and to share, as his hazardous occupation entitles him to share, in the benefits and amenities made available to all mankind by the march of science and civilization towards a better state of things for all.

King Coal is quite safe on the throne he has occupied for so long, but if he is to be supreme and securely established in the many years he has yet to reign he must adapt himself to the changes in the world around him, changes which threaten his supremacy, and changes which, in a world which is never at rest, will certainly challenge his position and power to an ever-increasing extent in the next few years. Let the challenge be accepted in that spirit and there need be no fear for the future of the coal industry in this country.

THE HALF YEAR, JANUARY–JUNE 1936

FIGURES for the first half of 1936 are available just in time to enable me to summarize them briefly.

They show that output is well maintained, being 110½ million tons (97 per cent of industry). As a result of the increases granted at the end of 1935, average cash earnings have risen from £2 5s. 6d. to £2 9s. 6d. Average earnings of adult workers are about 4s. more, or £2 13s. 6d. The average earnings of the workers underground and at the coal face are given in Mr. Lee's speech on page 118, £3 0s. 0d., and £3 5s. 0d. respectively (March quarter). All are exclusive of allowances in kind. None of the increase is due to the selling agencies, the benefit of which has not yet been felt.

Home consumption has risen slightly, but exports have again declined, being only 22 million tons (including bunkers) against 25 in the first half year of 1935, due mainly to loss of the Italian market.

The industry as a whole showed a credit balance in both quarters, 1s. 7¾d. in March and 4¾d. in June. The exporting districts continue to fare badly, South Wales in particular, where there was a debit balance of 6d. per ton over the whole period.

Short-time working continued to be a prominent feature of the industry, the average number of shifts worked being exactly five per week, a slight improvement on the 1935 figure.

Wages costs rose as a result of the higher wages. Other costs remained about the same, and there was a substantial and welcome increase in the proceeds, due to a general advance in selling prices.

APPENDICES

APPENDIX I

THE STATISTICS OF THE INDUSTRY

THE Mines Department has a special statistical branch for compiling records and dealing generally with the tremendous mass of figures associated with the conduct of this vast industry.

The results of each quarter's working as far as production, wages, costs, numbers employed, credits or debits, etc., are concerned, are set out in a quarterly summary giving the figures for nine districts covering the whole country. As soon as practicable after the year is ended, a similar summary is issued giving the same statistics for the year. In each, the figures for the districts are summarized for Great Britain (price 1d., H.M. Stationery Office).

In the Annual Report these figures are summarized for the four quarters for the whole country and tabulated in the same way as the other summaries, but leaving out the districts. The summaries and this table in the Annual Report deal with 96 to 97 per cent of the industry. The *totals* of output, etc., are given in other parts of the Report. The Annual Report covers a very wide field, embracing all the activities of the Mines Department and giving the fullest information with respect to every phase of the industry (price 3s. 6d., as above).

In such a complex industry the figures may be liable to some varying degree of interpretation if the methods of compilation are not clearly understood. The following notes will help the reader to grasp these, and to understand the reasons for any variations he may discover in the figures.

Production: In the summaries and the table referred to

above, the output figures cover 96 per cent or 97 per cent only, and the total output figure is given in another part of the Annual Report. Thus, in 1935 the two figures were 214,944,239 and 222,248,822. These totals are subdivided into four headings:

1. Tonnage of saleable coal raised (i.e. the above total).
2. Mine consumption.
3. Miners' coal.
4. Tonnage commercially disposable.

Items 2 and 3 account on average for about 15 million tons, and this subtracted from No. 1 gives No. 4.

Numbers Employed: The present method of compiling these figures dates from 1925. Prior to that date particulars are only available for persons "ordinarily employed". The workers engaged in the industry are now classified according to age and sex, and also whether employed above or below ground. The average numbers employed are arrived at by taking the numbers on the colliery books at four selected dates (March 16th, June 15th, September 14th, and December 14th in 1935) and dividing the total by four so as to arrive at an average figure for the whole country for the full year. The wage earners are divided into those under 16 years of age, those between 16 and 18, those over 18 and under 20, and those over 20 years of age. Clerks and salaried persons are in a separate category, and the average numbers employed arrived at in the same way. The total numbers include all persons employed "in and about coal mines". The ages are taken in December, and as tabulated are strictly accurate for that quarter only.

Exports: The total is made up of coal exported abroad, coal supplied to steamers engaged in the foreign trade, and the coal equivalent of exported coke and manufactured fuel. Coastwise shipments and coal used by steamers in the coasting trade are not exports.

Costs: Wages costs average 66 to 68 per cent of the total. Cost of stores and timber, royalties, and Miners'

Welfare Fund contribution are shown separately. The remaining costs are grouped together under the heading "other costs". They include salaries, management, repairs, insurances, office and general expenses, depreciation, etc. Interest on debentures or other loans, pensions, or charitable contributions, bank charges, amortisation, and taxation are not admissible as costs. For the purposes of the ascertainments, there are twenty-one districts, and for convenience these are grouped into nine in the Mines Department Statistical Summary.

Miners' Coal: This is supplied free in Northumberland and Durham. In the other districts a nominal charge is made for the coal, but in all cases the miners pay for delivery. The proceeds (in 1935 they were 0·89 of a penny per ton) are treated as a reduction of the costs of production of the coal "commercially disposable".

Wages: The method of showing the wages earned is crude, unscientific, and completely out of date. In the form in which it is given, the information serves only as a very rough guide to actual earnings. All the workers "in and about" the mines are added together, skilled mechanics, coal cutters, hewers, fillers, stonemen, electricians, masons, under-officials, joiners, deputies, etc., with boys of 14 to 16 and youths under 20. This figure is called the "number of wage earners employed". The total amount of the wages bill for the quarter, or the year, is then taken, and the number of man shifts worked in the period. Wages are then shown in two forms. The money paid as wages is divided by the number of man shifts worked, and the result given as the "average earnings per man shift worked". This is the figure shown in the quarterly and annual Statistical Summaries of the Mines Department. In the Annual Report, in addition to this, the total wages paid for the year are divided by the average number of wage earners for the year and the resultant figure given as the "Average Cash Earnings per person employed per annum", all wage earners included. There is one satisfactory feature, and that is that the number of boys and youths is given, but as their wages are not shown separately the value of this is lost. The foremen and under-officials are also included, and one result of their inclusion is the contention that it cancels out the effect of the young persons' wages being included in the figures showing the adult workers' earnings. This is, of course, a claim unworthy of serious consideration, but the method of compilation permits it to be made.

The whole system of showing the workers' earnings is obsolete. It should be replaced immediately by a new one in which the workers, in addition to being classified according to age and whether employed above or below ground, should be classified also according to occupation. No method of showing "average" wages can be regarded as satisfactory which lumps together the earnings of the boy getting 15s. per week with those of the coal cutter earning £5, the man on the subsistence level with the overmen, and the skilled mechanic with the labourer. The resultant figure is too general and far too wide in its scope to be of real value. A new and scientific method would mean some additional labour, but the results would more than justify the trouble involved.

Proceeds: The figures given by the Mines Department represent the amount received for the coal disposed of commercially after deducting selling and delivery expenses.

Royalties: This charge includes the rental value of freehold minerals where they are worked by the proprietor.

Credit Balances: "Credit balances" are not profits. An average of approximately 3d. per ton should be deducted from the credit balance for costs such as bank charges, etc., inadmissible under the wages ascertainments provisions of the agreements.

APPENDIX II

ANNUAL PRODUCTION

WITH QUANTITIES EXPORTED AND SUPPLIED AS BUNKERS FOR USE OF STEAMERS ENGAGED IN THE FOREIGN TRADE AND IGNORING EXPORTS OF COKE AND MANUFACTURED FUEL (ABOUT 4 MILLION TONS)

In Tons to the nearest million

Year	Production	Export	Bunkers
	Million tons	Million tons	Million tons
1913	287	73	21
1920	230	25	14
1921	163	25	11
1922	250	64	18
1923	276	79	18
1924	267	62	18
1925	243	51	16
1926	126	21	8
1927	251	51	17
1928	237	50	17
1929	258	60	16
1930	244	55	16
1931	219	43	15
1932	209	39	14
1933	207	39	13
1934	221	40	13
1935	222	38¾	12½

NOTES.—National stoppages in 1920, 1921, and 1926. Eight hours day in 1913. Seven hours day 1919–1926. Eight hours day 1926–1930. Seven and half hours day 1931–1935. State control ended March 31, 1921. Exports in 1923 artificially stimulated by French occupation of the Ruhr. 1929 was a good year in world trade and, in addition, British exports of coal were helped by the Baltic being frozen over, which prevented Polish supplies reaching the Scandinavian countries. Shipments to the Irish Free State are included in exports after April 1, 1923.

APPENDIX III

DISTRIBUTION OF OUTPUT

In the year 1935 the amount of coal produced by British mines was 222 million tons. Of this, 164·47 million tons was retained for home use. As nearly as can be ascertained this was divided as follows:

	Million tons
Domestic coal	36
Gas-works	16·73
Electricity works	12·24
Railway companies	12·29
Bunkers (coastwise trade)	1·25
Blast furnaces	10·79
Iron- and steel-works	7·47
Collieries (engine fuel)	11·61
General manufactures and all other purposes (including miners' coal)	56·09

NOTE.—The Ministry of Mines figure for "General manufactures," etc., includes domestic fuel at 92·09 millions. The latter is estimated at about 36 millions, exclusive of miners' coal. The home figures are subject to adjustment for the coal equivalent of coke and manufactured fuel exported and for shipments to Ireland. This is why the total for "home" use when added to the total for exports and bunkers does not agree exactly with the total production figures.

APPENDIX IV

AVERAGE YEARLY OUTPUT PER PERSON EMPLOYED AND WAGES COSTS PER TON PRODUCED, THE LATTER "COMMERCIALLY DISPOSABLE"

Year	Output per person employed	Wages cost per ton	
	Tons	s.	d.
1913	260	6	10½
1920	187	25	9½
1921	144	22	2½
1922	217	12	1¾
1923	229	12	4¼
1924	220	13	3
1925	221	12	9½
1926	Not available	12	4*
1927	245	10	7½
1928	253	9	5½
1929	270	9	2
1930	262	9	3¾
1931	253	9	2¾
1932	255	9	0¾
1933	262	8	9½
1934	280	8	7¼
1935	289	8	6½

* January to April.

NOTES.—National stoppages in 1920, 1921, and 1926. State control ended March 31, 1921. Eight hours day in 1913. Seven hours day 1919–1926. Eight hours day 1926–1930. Seven and a half hours day 1931–1935. The 1926 wages cost includes cost of subsidy.

APPENDIX V

NUMBER OF WORKPEOPLE EMPLOYED WITH AVERAGE OUTPUT AND EARNINGS PER MAN SHIFT WORKED

Year	All employees. To nearest thousand. Number employed	Wage earners. Average output per man shift	Wage earners. Average earnings per man shift	
		cwt.	s.	d.
1914	1,050,000	20·32	6	5¾
1920	1,226,000	14·54	16	10
1921 Jan.–Mar.	1,132,000	14·46	19	2
1921 Oct.–Dec.	1,132,000	17·73	12	8
1922	1,148,000	18·02	9	11¾
1923	1,203,000	17·83	10	1
1924	1,214,000	17·59	10	7¾
1925	1,102,000	18·02	10	6
1926 Jan.–April	1,116,000	18·46	10	5
1927	1,024,000	20·61	10	0¾
1928	939,000	21·29	9	3½
1929	957,000	21·69	9	2¾
1930	931,000	21·62	9	3½
1931	868,000	21·61	9	2¼
1932	819,000	21·99	9	2
1933	789,000	22·47	9	1½
1934	788,000	22·94	9	1¾
1935	769,000	23·35	9	3·15

NOTES.—National stoppages in 1920, 1921, and 1926. State control ended March 31, 1921. Eight hours day in 1914. Seven hours day in 1919–1926. Eight hours day 1926–1930. Seven and a half hours day 1931–1935. Output figures vary in districts from 28·07 cwt. to 19·67 cwt. per man shift (1935 figures).

Earnings are cash earnings. Allowances in kind average 4½d. per man per shift, and vary from 1s. 1d. to almost nil per man shift worked. Numbers employed are totals. Average number of clerks and salaried persons included in last three years is 15,000 to 15,500. For wage earners this should be deducted.

APPENDIX VI

AVERAGE WEEKLY CASH EARNINGS OF ALL WORKERS EMPLOYED

Year	£	s.	d.
1913	1	11	6
1920	4	6	11
1921	3	14	11
1922	2	8	1
1923	2	11	8
1924	2	13	2
1925	2	10	8
1926	2	13	9
1927	2	7	2
1928	2	3	9
1929	2	5	6
1930	2	3	10
1931	2	2	11
1932	2	2	1
1933	2	2	5
1934	2	4	5
1935	2	5	6

NOTE.—National stoppages in 1920, 1921, and 1926. These figures are the average cash payments received each week. They include the weekly cash earnings of youths and boys. See references to "average" wages (page 117), earnings per man shift worked (pages 117, 118, and Appendix V), and cost of living index figures (pages 12 and 118). The figures do not include allowances in kind (see Note on page 273 and at end of Appendices V and VIII).

APPENDIX VII

DISTRIBUTION OF LABOUR

THE following table gives the total number of persons employed in 1935, classified according to age and sex and whether employed above or below ground (at December 14, 1935). They should not be confused with the averages.

WAGE EARNERS BELOW GROUND	
Males—	
Under 16 years of age	19,187
16 and under 18 years of age	27,031
18 and under 20 years of age	30,964
20 years and over	521,918
	599,100
WAGE EARNERS ABOVE GROUND	
Males—	
Under 16 years of age	11,238
16 and under 18 years of age	9,358
18 and under 20 years of age	8,398
20 years and over	121,805
Females—	
Under 16 years of age	279
16 and under 18 years of age	385
18 and under 20 years of age	383
20 years and over	1,399
	153,245
TOTAL WAGE EARNERS	752,345
CLERKS AND SALARIED PERSONS	
Males	14,435
Females	721
TOTAL	15,156
TOTAL OF PERSONS EMPLOYED	
Wage earners	752,345
Clerks and salaried persons	15,156
GRAND TOTAL	767,501

APPENDIX VIII

DISTRICT VARIATIONS IN OUTPUT AND WAGES

THE following table shows the variations in output and wages caused by geological differences, proximity to markets, the demand abroad, etc. The principal exporting districts are South Wales, Scotland, Northumberland, and Durham. The table covers 96 per cent of the output.

The effect of full-time working on wages is seen in the Scottish figures. Corrected for the earnings of boys and youths, the average earnings for all adult workers is £2 16s. 6d., including allowances. The combined effect of low prices in the home market and reduced exports abroad is seen in the Northumberland figures where the pits worked nearly full time. The result of short time added to these is seen in the Durham figures. The more advantageous position of the inland districts is shown in Yorkshire and North Derbyshire, where the workers received more in money wages than those of Northumberland for a day's work less. Apart from Scotland, the highest average wages in 1935 were in South Wales and the grouped districts. The average earnings for adult workers in South Wales was £2 12s. 1d. per week, including allowances.

The average increase in the earnings of the adult workers, by making the proper deduction for the earnings of boys and youths, is somewhere between 2s. 6d. and 4s. 8d. In the figures here given it is arrived at by taking a figure of 3½ per cent for boys at 15s. per week and 10·5 per cent for youths at 25s. per week. The calculations are not affected by the fact that the lower-paid officials are included in the total wages bill. They are not highly paid, and their numbers are relatively small. In the South Wales coalfield alone, over 8,000 workers earn over £4 per week, so that the in-

1935 FIGURES. BASED ON THE MINES DEPARTMENT SUMMARY (96 PER CENT OF OUTPUT)

District	Average number of workers employed	Average number of shifts worked		Output per man shift worked	Average output per worker per annum	Average cash earnings per person employed, including all workers under 20, per week		
		Per annum	Per week					
				cwt.	tons	£	s.	d.
Scotland	77,650	305	5·86	25·21	385·7	2	11	8½
Northumberland	39,236	279	5·36	23·71	330·9	2	2	5
Durham	101,401	263	5·05	22·07	290·4	2	0	9
South Wales and Monmouth	121,582	264	5·07	20·40	269·4	2	7	4
Yorkshire	134,023	229	4·4	26·53	303·6	2	5	3
North Derbyshire and Nottinghamshire	82,267	219	4·21	28·07	307·2	2	4	2½
South Derbyshire, Leicestershire, Cannock Chase, and Warwickshire ..	49,802	237	4·55	22·93	271·3	2	4	6
Lancashire, Cheshire, and North Staffordshire	77,643	257	4·94	20·35	261·5	2	6	1
Cumberland, North Wales, South Staffordshire, Shropshire, Bristol, Forest of Dean, Kent, and Somerset ..	36,663	280	5·38	19·67	275·5	2	7	8
Great Britain	720,267	256	4·92	23·35	298·4	2	5	6

For explanation of any apparent discrepancy in these figures, see notes on "The Statistics of the Industry" (Appendix I). For example, they cover only 96 per cent of the industry, the output figures are for the wage earners, not "per person employed", and the cash earnings exclude allowances in kind.

clusion of the officials could not affect the average at all, or but very little indeed.

In Durham and Northumberland housing and coal are free, and the value of the allowances is estimated by the Mines Department at 5s. 6d. per week in Durham and 5s. in Northumberland. The average cash earnings for adults in Durham was £2 3s. 10d., and in Northumberland £2 5s. 8d. The adult workers' average wage may be calculated in the same way for the other districts and the allowance for the district added. The corrected figure for Great Britain is £2 9s. 3d. (adults' average exclusive of allowances in kind).

APPENDIX IX

DISTRICT VARIATIONS IN PRODUCTION, COSTS, PROCEEDS, AND BALANCES

The table on the page opposite gives the variations in the total output, costs of production, proceeds, and the credit or debit balances. It shows at a glance the unhappy position of the exporting districts.

1935 FIGURES, BASED ON THE MINES DEPARTMENT SUMMARY (96 PER CENT OF OUTPUT)

District, 1935	Coal disposable commercially	Net Costs: Amount	Net Costs: Per ton disposable commercially	Credits: Amount	Credits: Per ton disposable commercially
	tons	£	s. d.	£	£
Scotland	27,553,609	15,683,091	11 4·60	1,231,290	10·73
Northumberland	12,347,253	7,042,299	11 4·88	77,067	1·50
Durham	27,745,066	17,566,513	12 7·96	(414·670)*	(3·59)*
South Wales and Monmouth (February 1935 to January 1936)	30,500,275	23,148,955	15 2·16	(138·029)*	(1·09)*
Yorkshire	37,755,767	23,201,228	12 3·48	1,607,395	10·22
North Derbyshire and Nottinghamshire	23,456,295	13,883,692	11 10·06	1,345,927	13·77
South Derbyshire, Leicestershire, Cannock Chase, and Warwickshire ..	12,511,741	8,308,826	13 3·38	859,545	16·49
Lancashire, Cheshire, and North Staffordshire	18,479,568	13,937,006	15 1·00	590,981	7·68
Cumberland, North Wales, South Staffordshire, Salop, Bristol, Forest of Dean, Somerset, and Kent ..	9,280,724	6,722,136	14 5·84	44,074	1·14
Great Britain	199,630,298	129,493,746	12 11·68	5,203,580	6·26

* Debit.

APPENDIX X

EXTENT OF VOLUNTARY AMALGAMATIONS. STATEMENT ISSUED BY THE MINING ASSOCIATION (MAY 1936)

District	Number of large undertakings	Percentage of district output produced by large undertakings
Northumberland	11	90
Durham	21	94
South Yorkshire	29	96
West Yorkshire	16	87
Nottinghamshire and North Derbyshire	18	87
Lancashire and Cheshire ..	14	83
South Wales	15	82
Scotland	22	84
Total	146	88*

* Equivalent to 76 per cent of the total output of Great Britain.

APPENDIX XI

PROFIT AND LOSS ACCOUNT OF THE INDUSTRY 1913 TO 1935

Figures for the years 1913 to 1919 compiled from the evidence of Sir A. Lowes Dickinson before the Samuel Commission. For 1920 to 1935 from the Mines Department Summaries. Credit figures do not represent a true profit, 3d. per ton should be deducted for interest on loans, etc. See pages 348 and 349.

	Credit		Debit		
	s.	d.	s.	d.	Basis
1913*	1	5·88	—		On Coal Raised
1914	1	2·04	—		On Coal Raised
1915	1	8·28	—		On Coal Raised
1916	2	11·16	—		On Coal Raised
1917	2	2·76	—		On Coal Raised
1918	2	2·40	—		On Coal Raised
1919	2	8·04	—		On Coal Raised
1920	3	3¾	—		On Coal Commercially Disposable
1921	—		6	11¾	On Coal Commercially Disposable
1922		11½	—		On Coal Commercially Disposable
1923	2	2	—		On Coal Commercially Disposable
1924	1	2	—		On Coal Commercially Disposable
1925†	—			10¼	On Coal Commercially Disposable
1926†	—		1	6	On Coal Commercially Disposable
1927	—			5¾	On Coal Commercially Disposable
1928	—			11	On Coal Commercially Disposable
1929		4½	—		On Coal Commercially Disposable
1930		4¼	—		On Coal Commercially Disposable
1931		3½	—		On Coal Commercially Disposable
1932		2	—		On Coal Commercially Disposable
1933		2¾	—		On Coal Commercially Disposable
1934		5	—		On Coal Commercially Disposable
1935		6¼	—		On Coal Commercially Disposable

* 1913 figure for coal "commercially disposable" was 1s. 6½d.

† Exclusive of subsidy.

INDEX

Printed in Great Britain by
UNWIN BROTHERS LIMITED, LONDON AND WOKING